Advance Praise for
A Lucky Life

"Steve Simmons doesn't ever sit on the fence when it comes to his writing. He takes a position and tells it like he sees it. I will buy his book and I am quite certain I will throw it in the fire and burn it — but only *after* I've read it!"

> **— Brendan Shanahan, president, Toronto Maple Leafs**

"The highest calling of a sports columnist is not to be right, but to be read. Steve Simmons is right most of the time and must be read all of the time. There is no higher professional compliment I can think of."

> **— Cathal Kelly, sports columnist, (Toronto) *Globe and Mail***

"I check out every column Steve Simmons writes. I look to see if my name's in it. If my name's not in it, I read on. He's the best in the business."

> **— Paul Beeston, longtime president, Toronto Blue Jays**

"When I lived in Toronto I read all the papers daily. Six days a week I read the *Toronto Sun* starting from page 1 of the sports section. On Sundays I always read the *Sun* from back to front. I couldn't wait to read Steve's column. Now I'll log on some Saturday nights to read it. He covered our team fairly, honestly and accurately."

> **— Pat Gillick, former Blue Jays general manager**

"For more than 40 years Steve Simmons has enthralled, and sometimes enraged, readers with his thoughtful, beautifully crafted sports columns. Like many of his subjects, he stands among the greatest of all time."

> **— Roy MacGregor, best-selling author**

"Steve Simmons is the dean of Toronto columnists — the longest serving and the best of any sports columnists at the four Toronto newspapers. This is a book I am buying as Steve takes us to rinks, ballparks, stadia and Olympics around the world recalling memories from his 40-year career."

> **— Bob Elliott, Hall of Fame baseball writer**

"Living close to the border, I've had the privilege of reading Steve Simmons for three decades and have long considered him the best sports columnist in Canada. He was a must-read, and the same goes for this wonderful collection of his work."

> **— Jerry Sullivan, longtime sports columnist, *Buffalo News***

"For 40 years Steve Simmons has covered the waterfront of Canadian sports, although, thoughtlessly, the editor has omitted an Olympic yachting column from this compilation. There are Simmons slings and there are Simmons arrows. And in these pages, they hit their target."

— **Michael Farber, *Sports Illustrated* and TSN**

"Steve needn't use the well-worn line of 'sorry there isn't room or time to mention everyone,' because this compilation of his lifetime work pretty much does that. Thus, there is appreciation for the scope of the Canadian sports world and for Steve's ability to miss nothing of interest with his stimulating viewpoints."

— **Dave Hodge, legendary broadcaster**

"I have read Steve's work for many years — a tremendous storyteller who always paints a picture. His insight into the sporting world and his ability to portray it make his work a pleasure to enjoy. An advocate for Canadian athletes, he fills an important role as a journalist in our country."

— **Kelly McCrimmon, general manager, Vegas Golden Knights**

"I used to do a segment with Steve Simmons on TSN *Wednesday Night Hockey* called '2 for Instigating.' This book could be called *40 Years of Instigating*."

— **James Duthie, TSN**

"Steve Simmons is absolutely the finest sports columnist in Canada, and he would rank in the U.S. He cares at all times, and has fun when the time is available."

— **Dave Langford, former sports editor, *Globe and Mail* and Postmedia**

"Luckily for him, Steve Simmons had a front-row seat to most of the major sports events relevant to Canadians over the last 40 years. Luckily for us readers, he got that seat because of his insight, wit and skill with words. So sit back, read on and enjoy the ride."

— **David Shoalts, author and former *Globe and Mail* sports columnist**

"There is no one in the sports journalism business that I respect more than Steve Simmons. His 'Sunday Notes' column is a must-read every week. So is this book. You won't be able to put it down."

— **Ron Cook, sports columnist, *Pittsburgh Post-Gazette***

TRIUMPH
BOOKS

A Lucky Life

A Lucky Life

Gretzky, Crosby, Kawhi
and More from the
Best Seat in the House

Steve Simmons

TRIUMPH
B O O K S

This book is available in quantity at special discounts for your group or organization. For further information, contact:

Triumph Books LLC
814 North Franklin Street
Chicago, Illinois 60610
(312) 337-0747
www.triumphbooks.com

All columns and feature articles appearing in this collection first appeared in either the *Toronto Sun* or the *Calgary Herald* between the years 1986 and 2021 and are reissued with the permission of Postmedia Network Canada Corp.

Printed in U.S.A.
ISBN: 978-1-63727-108-7
Design by Patricia Frey

To Sheila and the boys, Michael and Jeffrey.
You make every day better.

"Writing turns you into somebody who's always wrong. The illusion that you might get it right someday is the perversity that draws you on."

— Philip Roth

"I wrote a sports column for 25 years and I learned something writing a sports column. I learned that losers were always more compelling than winners. I learned that tragedy is more important than triumph and I learned that heartbreak is the common denominator for a great column."

— Tony Kornheiser

Contents

Foreword

When you play as many NHL games as I did, 1,474 in total, a lot of the events blend together over time. I do remember this one, although I don't remember the year. It was a practice day and Steve Simmons and a bunch of other reporters walked into the Maple Leafs dressing room, as media were allowed in most days, and I do remember yelling rather loudly: "He's here." And then I started laughing, as did a bunch of the Leafs players.

Truth is, I was trying to get Tie Domi's attention. A few days earlier in the *Toronto Sun*, Simmons had run an item in his Sunday column that Domi wasn't happy about. In the column, Simmons took Domi's name after an on-ice incident of some kind and scrambled the letters in his name. He came up with "Me Idiot."

I suppose he thought it was funny. Domi, our tough guy and one of our team leaders, clearly didn't share his sentiment. He had been walking around for a couple of days complaining about the shot in the paper.

But what happened afterwards says a lot about Simmons and a lot about Domi. They were talking by his locker as most of us in the room were getting dressed. And they were still talking as most of us were leaving. I waited around, thinking there might be a confrontation of some kind, and they were still talking. I found out later that they had a helluva conversation, and out of that disagreement, a better relationship was born.

That whole thing gave me an appreciation for who Simmons was and how he conducted his business. He wasn't one of those hit-and-run guys. If he wrote something harsh about me, about Domi, about anybody else, he showed up the next day and faced the music.

I never had what you'd call a close relationship with Steve — and we've had our moments — but as time went on, and my career grew longer, I came to appreciate how he approached his work. And I came to realize how he always seemed to be around for so many moments of my career.

He was there, covering the Calgary Flames, in 1986 when I had my breakout playoff with the St. Louis Blues, leading the Stanley Cup playoffs in scoring.

From there, I got traded to Calgary. He left for Toronto. I got traded to Toronto. The first telephone interview I did after the trade was with him.

Even in 1990, the year after winning the Stanley Cup in Calgary, I got to play for Team Canada at the World Hockey Championship alongside Joe Nieuwendyk, Steve Yzerman and Paul Coffey, among others. I traveled to Switzerland for the event. One of the first people I saw outside our hotel upon arrival? Simmons.

A few years after that, playing for Pat Burns with the Leafs, I was injured in the playoffs and the talk of the city seemed to be whether I'd be able to play the next game. This was before the Internet and before social media. I came out of the doctor's office that morning, got clearance to play, and rather than have the radio speculate all day about it, I called the all-sports radio station the FAN in Toronto and went on the air live with Simmons and Mary Ormsby. I told them I was playing the next game. It was big news at the time.

I'm not sure something like that wouldn't happen today, but these are different times. I can't believe this, but my last game was 19 years ago. We'd all like to play forever, but I can't complain about a 20-year career, especially after starting out as a seventh-round draft pick who was a long shot. Steve Simmons was writing about hockey and other sports before I began playing professionally. And all these years later, he's still doing it.

He was there at the beginning of my career, and he was there waiting for me outside the Toronto bar from which I announced my retirement in 2003. I didn't always agree with what he wrote. I didn't always agree with how he wrote it. But I came to appreciate who he was and how he did his work.

He was always there. Still is.

— Doug Gilmour
Hockey Hall of Fame Class of 2011

Introduction

I was there.

When Wayne Gretzky won his first Stanley Cup and won his last, when he played his final NHL game, when he wasn't chosen for the shootout in Nagano at the 1998 Winter Olympics and when he was executive director of Team Canada that won gold in 2002.

I was there.

When Donovan Bailey won races on consecutive Saturday nights in Atlanta in 1996, a world record in the 100 metres, a trouncing of the great American team in the 4 x 100 metres relay one week later, maybe the greatest Olympic achievement of any Canadian athlete.

I was there.

When Sidney Crosby scored the Golden Goal in 2010. When Kawhi Leonard hit the shot that bounced and bounced and bounced some more. When Joe Carter hit the home run and when Jose Bautista flipped his bat.

I was there.

When Michael Jordan retired in Chicago in 1993 and when he came out of retirement to play his first game back in Indianapolis on a Sunday afternoon in 1995.

For the past 40 years, I have been fortunate to have the best seat in the house, documenting and being inspired by many of the greatest sporting moments of our country and those around the world. I am one of a very few Canadian journalists fortunate enough to have seen so much, including 17 Olympic Games, writing for three Canadian newspapers over my career. All told, I spent some 3,500 days on the road, packing and unpacking and packing again.

In person, I got to watch Pete Sampras win the U.S. Open and Roger Federer win Wimbledon and Tiger Woods hit the first drive of his professional career, at the Greater Milwaukee Open. I was at or near the finish line for all nine of Usain Bolt's spectacular Olympic victories in three consecutive Summer Games, something that will never be done again.

I saw Mike Tyson at his terrifying best, taking 91 seconds to beat Michael Spinks, and maybe at his horrifying worst, being dominated by Lennox Lewis and Evander Holyfield. And I was ringside, almost accidentally, for the greatest eight-minute fight in history: Marvin Hagler vs. Thomas Hearns.

I was there when the New York Rangers won their only Stanley Cup of the past 80 years and when the Raptors won their only NBA championship, in Oakland in 2019. I sat about 10 rows up when Ben Johnson beat Carl Lewis in Rome at the world championships in 1987, before beating him again one year later in Seoul, before the disqualification. And I was in the press box at Busch Stadium when Mark McGwire hit his 70th home run, before we really knew why.

I was there to watch Doug Flutie win too many Grey Cups and too many awards. Same for Damon Allen and Anthony Cavillo and Henry Burris and Ricky Ray and all the Canadian football legends. I was there — among the masses — to see Tom Brady and Joe Montana and John Elway and Peyton Manning and Aaron Rodgers and Steve Young all win Super Bowls, many of them more than once. That group is the greatest to ever play.

I was in Oakland for Roberto Alomar's franchise-changing home run for the Blue Jays in 1992 and in Atlanta when Ed Sprague made a World Series possible for the Jays with a pinch-hit home run just a few days later.

And I was there to see Mario Lemieux win both of his Stanley Cups, to witness the playoff magic of Patrick Roy and Martin Brodeur, and to see Dominik Hasek win gold in Nagano, almost by himself.

At its best, sport is so much about moments and memories, so many of them personal. What does it mean to you, that day, that night, that game, that ending? Where were you in '72 or in 2010 or for whatever grabs you and carries you from year to year, place to place and celebration to celebration?

What a professional life this has been, writing about sports from six of the world's seven continents.

My first Stanley Cup had Mike Bossy and Bryan Trottier's New York Islanders winning their second of four Cup championships, this one against the Minnesota North Stars, who now play in Dallas. I covered the first game the Calgary Flames ever played after moving from Atlanta. They played the Quebec Nordiques, who now play in Denver. I also covered the last game the Colorado Rockies played in Denver before moving to New Jersey and becoming the Devils.

Over the years, I've written more than 8,000 columns for the *Toronto Sun*, *Calgary Herald*, *Calgary Sun* and Postmedia papers, probably close to seven million words. Some of them were great. Some were good. Some I'd like to have back.

I've taken my share of shots and received just as many back. If you give them, you'd better be prepared to take some too. Some days I feel like my friend George Chuvalo, who just kept on standing, no matter how many times he was hit. Nobody could knock out George. He just kept on punching.

The assignment here was to pick some 90 columns for this book, which wasn't easy when you consider what a tiny percentage that is of my overall work. Here, I've tried to be topical, historical, analytical, varied and relevant. I hope you enjoy reading this as much as I've enjoyed bringing it to you.

The columns that appear in this book were primarily written as one-day assignments. That's a columnist's life; you write on Monday and move on to Tuesday, never knowing what the next day or the next story will bring.

Many of the pieces here were written on deadline, against a ticking clock: That's so much of the job. It's not novel writing. There is no time to rewrite.

And all the pieces here were originally edited, mostly by the desk of the Toronto Sun. *For purposes of clarity and accuracy, they have been edited once again for this collection.*

CHAPTER 1

Legends and Champions

The Great Goodbye

April 19, 1999

NEW YORK — They would travel to the rink together in the morning, the way they always had, before all the emotion and appreciation and honest sentiment had taken over the day.

Wayne and Walter Gretzky, together. Father and son.

One last game. One last time.

He had made the decision on Saturday, how he would get to Madison Square Garden, who he would go with, how it would all work. It had to be him and his dad. The way it used to be. The way it always was.

"Same as any kid," Wayne Gretzky said in the early evening, his astounding National Hockey League career over. "Same as you guys with your fathers. There's no relationship like father-son."

He still was wearing his uniform as he spoke long after the game, the way young kids do when they go to hockey, with everything on but their helmet and skates. He didn't want to take his equipment off. "Subconsciously I don't want to take it off. I'm not going to put it on again ...

"It's hard. Hard to take it off."

Before that he had spoken to his father only briefly this day. He had watched him ride on to the ice in the Mercedes-Benz the Rangers were presenting him with. And he saw his father for just an instant after the myriad post-game ovations in the whirlwind of emotion and congratulation that was the end of the Rangers season and the end of Gretzky's career. "My mom (Phyllis) just said she was happy for me," Gretzky said. "He (his dad) told me he was very, very proud of me. It was nice."

The words came 28 years after Walter Gretzky told his son about the future. After he told him he was different from all the other kids.

"You're a very special person," Walter told him. "Wherever you go, probably all your life, people are going to make a fuss over you. You've got to remember that and you've got to behave right. They're going to be watching for every mistake. Remember that you're very special and you're always on display."

Right to the end that message seemed prophetic, words from a father to a son, words that have defined a hockey generation. Wayne Gretzky's last week of hockey was an ovation that wouldn't end, a celebration of tears and accolades, emotions and storytelling.

Remember when? You couldn't help but look back and smile and shed tears of circumstance and joy. Walter Gretzky was standing in the rotunda area at Madison Square Garden, trying to remember when. Sometimes he could and sometimes he couldn't. The aneurysm he suffered in 1991 has stripped him of some of the memories of his son's most phenomenal accomplishments. "Some of the things I don't remember," Walter said. But still there is so much to hang on to, so much to be proud of, so much to revel in.

"There was the night he telephoned me," Walter Gretzky was telling the story proudly.

"I just called to let you know," Wayne said. "Let me know what?" Walter said. "That I scored 50 goals in 39 games."

And without hesitation Walter Gretzky said: "What took you so long?"

That's Walter, always expecting more, never wanting his son to feel too big or too important. Another Gretzky story was told yesterday by a close friend. It was during the time that his father was in the hospital in Hamilton. Wayne just had to get out for a night to ease his tensions. He and his friend went to a well-known Hamilton bar. There was a lineup of about 30 people outside.

When Gretzky arrived, the doorman instantly recognized him and waved him to the front of the line. Gretzky politely declined, saying he didn't want to go ahead of anyone waiting. So the doorman told everyone in line they could go in.

The humility comes from Walter Gretzky, the telephone company worker from Brantford who never took a day off. "I get all the accolades and the glory, but really he deserves it, not me," Wayne said about the best-known father in Canada. "He never made more than $35,000 a year, but everything he made he put into his family."

Wayne Gretzky came to the rink yesterday with his dad, hugged him on the ice, hugged him after the game; they cried together in happiness and sadness, a lifetime of dreams changing directions.

"I went and met my family (Saturday) night, left at 8:00. I said, 'I'm leaving.' My dad said, 'Where are you going?' I said, 'It used to be in the old days you told me to go to bed, now you're asking why I'm leaving.'"

And when Wayne Gretzky finally stood up to leave yesterday, still in full equipment, more than an hour after his professional hockey career had ended, he walked to the Rangers' dressing room one last time.

He had to get changed. He had to see his family.

He had to see his dad.

They had to talk about the game one last time.

The Old Man and the Kid

March 15, 2015

BARRIE — On the day they met, the old man and the kid, Sherry Bassin began talking to Connor McDavid about the book *The Two-Second Advantage*.

And talking and talking and talking some more. That's what he does.

The book is a scientific examination of greatness and the innate ability of the exceptional to anticipate events before they happen. It isn't a sporting book of any kind, but Wayne Gretzky figures prominently in it.

"One day," Bassin recalled telling the 15-year-old McDavid, "they'll be writing another chapter about you."

"I meant it then," he said the other day. "I mean it now."

That was the beginning of the relationship between McDavid, the hockey prodigy, and Bassin, the senior-citizen junior-hockey lifer.

Now they're just Mac and Bass. The arena travelling show. Best friends forever, as kids are apt to say, even with 57 years in age separating them.

"He's a great guy and I love listening to him," McDavid, NHL superstar in waiting, said of his general manager and pal.

"I think we'll be friends (for a long time). When he talks, people listen. He has that effect. He's a great speaker. Any time he gets in front of an audience, he gives a pretty good speech. It's always something you take away and remember for a while.

"I'm very lucky to have him around ... He's been through it all and he has no bias. He'll tell you straight how it is. It's one of the things I love about him."

When McDavid broke his hand in an ill-advised fight in November, the entire hockey world stopped to ponder what it all meant.

But no one thought about the mishap more than the kid himself, who saw his dream season, his world junior possibility, his matchup with Jack Eichel crumbling away in a hospital room.

It was a terrible time.

"When he got hurt," said Bassin, "I got hurt. When the doctor came in, and it didn't look good at first, he was sitting on the hospital bed, slumped over, and he was looking so sad that I just went over and put my arms around him and I hugged him and I said, 'I love you. You're going to be OK. This is going to be OK.'

"It was pretty emotional for all of us. His dad was sitting right there and everybody got choked up. I think that sealed the special bond we have."

When McDavid first showed up at the Erie Otters mini-camp after being chosen first in the OHL selection draft in 2012, he went out on the ice wearing his minor midget team colours.

Bassin was confused by this. He called McDavid over and asked about the colours.

"He said, 'Mr. Bassin, I haven't made that team yet.' And I'm thinking nobody calls me 'Mr. Bassin' and, sometimes in this business, you get calls from agents 24 hours after a kid gets drafted asking for their team stuff. It tells you a lot about Connor. He has a certain humility about him, a sensitivity to his environment. He wasn't big-timing anybody. He was academic player of the year and, until you read his grades, you wouldn't know he was doing that.

"This is a special person. He's grounded with an inner drive I can't even explain. I tell all my players: 'Do I like who I am when I'm around you?' And then I answer for them: 'Well, I love who I am when I'm around Connor McDavid.'"

They play this dressing-room game, Bassin and McDavid, although it started when Bass told Mac it wasn't his fault.

"It's not your fault," he said. "What's not my fault?"

"Don't worry," said Bassin, "it's not your fault."

"What's not?"

"It's not your fault you're ugly."

And a few seconds later, after the kid caught on and had a long laugh at the silliness of it, it became a part of the ongoing repartee around the Otters.

They go around the dressing room now and randomly say to a player, "It's not your fault," and then the other will say, "It's not his fault."

And they'll shake their heads, and it has become part of the mindless dressing-room dialogue that makes sport so different.

"It's like any good friendship, that's what it's like," said Mac, talking of Bass. "We poke fun at each other. We laugh a lot ... We've grown very close over the years. He's almost like a (second) dad to me."

Or maybe another grandfather.

They talk a lot together or, to be accurate, Bassin talks and McDavid listens. Bassin, the 75-year-old father of three uber-successful children, owner of law and pharmaceutical degrees and a longtime Durham College lecturer loves to talk life more than he loves to talk hockey — and he does love to talk hockey.

McDavid was on the last Canadian team to win the world junior. Bassin was general manager of the first to win gold, back in 1982.

"He's always telling me stuff with a message," said McDavid.

"It's not my job to teach hockey," said Bassin. "We've got good people here to do that. We talk about life, about values, about successful people and what makes them successful. About work habits. About all the things that go into success."

"I love listening to his stories," said McDavid. "He's been around, he knows everybody. It's different sometimes when you're around him all the time because you hear a lot of the same stories and stuff like that. But his messages are so great. He's taught me a lot."

Bassin gets particularly excited when someone becomes enamoured with McDavid's immense skill.

He sees it every day. He lives it. He knows what it's about.

But when word comes from a Hall of Fame player, such as Barrie Colts coach Dale Hawerchuk, he gets almost giddy.

"Did you hear what Hawerchuk said?" Bassin shouts, and then he tells you what Hawerchuk, who scored 102 points as an NHL rookie, said.

"He said (McDavid) skates like Bobby Orr did, where it looks like everybody else couldn't skate at the same level. He has vision like Gretz and hands like Mario (Lemieux). He's the real deal, that's for sure."

"Yep, that's what I said," said Hawerchuk. "And I stand by it. He's the full package."

Time is running out on this season for the old man and the full package.

Almost certainly, McDavid will be in the NHL next season. And, barring a change of mind, the 75-year-old Bassin will be back running the Otters, making the five-hour drive from his home in Oshawa to Erie.

He thought for a minute or two about retirement, with McDavid moving on — possibly the perfect ending.

But then there would be a game to scout in Detroit, and he'd be back in his car, highway driving again, doing what he's done his entire adult life.

"I've had a lot of good players over the years, but nothing on a three-year basis like this," said Bass.

"They don't make people better than this. I can't describe our relationship, it's so special. I always talk about our hockey family, and he's part of my family.

"I know he's leaving us at the end of the season, but I just don't want to think about it. I'm going to miss him as a person because we have this connection that's hard to explain.

"We really understand each other. He really understands me. When Canada won the world junior, all the press was around him and asking him how he felt. And he said — and I remember this clearly — 'You can't describe it unless you've lived it.'

"And I'm watching this and I'm thinking, 'That's exactly what I said when we won in 1982 and 1985.' It knocked me over when he said that. You realize the connection. It really is something special."

The Home Run That Changed Everything

October 17, 1992

His fists went up in the air.

Immediately. Defiantly.

"I knew," said Roberto Alomar. "All I'm thinking is: 'It's gone, it's gone, it's gone.'

"I threw my arms in the air. I was real happy. Yeah, real happy."

The picture will be one we will always remember. Robbie Alomar, bouncing like Carlton Fisk, arms raised like Kirk Gibson. Another post-season moment. Another piece of baseball history. Another TV clip to keep on file forever.

This time, a Blue Jays moment.

Perhaps the greatest in a 15-year history.

The Blue Jays are a win away from going to the World Series for the first time and Alomar beat the flu, the sun, Dennis Eckersley and the Oakland A's to carry the Jays on his slight but rounded shoulders to this franchise's most significant victory.

"I don't have big muscles," Alomar joked later, surrounded in the crush of energy that was the Blue Jays clubhouse. "Sometimes the little guy can make the big play in the big game."

Alomar didn't just make the big play in the big game — taking Eckersley downtown in the ninth inning to bring the Blue Jays back — he made almost all the big plays.

Bob Welch was cruising nicely into the eighth inning, leading 6-1, when Alomar's double to right-centre ended his day. Welch left and trouble began for the A's.

In the ninth, with Devon White on third base, the Jays trailing by two, Alomar's home run off Eckersley tied the game.

In the bottom of the ninth, with pinch-runner Eric Fox on third base, Terry Steinbach hit a chopper to Alomar, who threw out Fox at home.

"The game of my life," Alomar called it afterwards, the smile never leaving his face, the black beneath his eyes now smudged from the celebration. "That was the biggest hit, the biggest game. I wasn't trying for a home run. It just happened."

He is 24 years old, born to a baseball family, a Puerto Rican playing for a Canadian team, and this is the first "game of his life." There will be others. Many others. With Roberto Alomar, brilliance happens. He doesn't think about it. He just does it.

"I don't like to talk about myself," he said. "That's not me. I can't tell you I did this incredible thing. I just play."

So others talk about him.

Like Tony La Russa.

"Robbie Alomar is the best player in the American League." He said that before the series began. When asked about the quote yesterday, he only rolled his eyes and said "Next question." He didn't want to consider his words. He did not want to consider this crippling defeat.

Roberto Alomar wasn't sure what to think. He wanted to talk to his father, Sandy, who was in the Coliseum stands yesterday. But because the game went on so long, his dad had to leave to catch a plane.

He wanted to do something about the headache he had, and the fever that was burning inside, but that would have to wait. There were too many people to talk to, too many questions to answer.

"I'm going to be there tomorrow," said Alomar. "I don't care how I feel, I don't care. I gotta play."

And he wanted to spend some time with his teammates. That was impossible in this wild scene. That, too, would have to wait.

There was little time to consider the moment. The game ended yesterday. There is another game today.

But this one is worth savouring. This isn't just a comeback story. The Blue Jays did the impossible. They beat Dennis Eckersley, the fist-waving, mocking, emery board–carrying reliever. And when he did, Alomar, in defiance, waved his fists back.

"When you beat Eckersley it's the best feeling in baseball," said Alomar. "The guys were kind of mad about (him waving his fists). It didn't bother me. But some guys don't like it.

"But we're not trying to beat Eckersley. We're trying to beat Oakland."

The boyish smile came to Alomar's face as he was asked for the millionth time about his day, about his home run. "Today, I did the most I can," he said. "I put dinner on the table for us."

Next up for the Blue Jays: just dessert.

The Great Chase for Vladimir Guerrero Jr.

May 24, 2018

It took the trading of two prospects, a trip to Home Hardware for mosquito wear, a three-hour drive on bumpy Dominican roads, a New Year's Day flight, a Canadian birth certificate, a conversation in French and a one-time, break-the-budget investment for the Blue Jays to secure the services of teenaged phenom Vladimir Guerrero Jr.

It was that complicated a chase for then–general manager Alex Anthopoulos, then–Latin scouting director Ismael Cruz, then–club president Paul Beeston and the rest of the Blue Jays staff involved, so many of whom are no longer with the American League club.

And that's just the beginning of a story with connections to Montreal, Toronto, two cities in the Dominican Republic, former Jays slugger Edwin Encarnacion and the tremendous background work done by Cruz, who is considered the architect of the $7.3 million (all figures Canadian) signing — $4.7 million for Guerrero, $2.6 million in Major League tax money — all finalized on July 2, 2015, the day after Guerrero was eligible to sign with a big-league club.

"It was the first time that I know of that a team threw the whole international bonus at one guy," said Cruz, now with the Los Angeles Dodgers. "We thought we had a good chance to get him. Then I was hearing the White Sox and maybe Texas were getting close to him and I was thinking, 'Oh f— , this isn't going to happen.'

"You think you've done all your work, but by the end of it, you're never sure anyone is going to sign until they do. I think we had a good connection with his uncle (Wilton, the agent) and with his dad (Vladimir Guerrero Sr.). And Alex clicked with the family right from the beginning. And Wilton remembered (Paul)

Beeston from other things. There were all these Canadian connections with those guys."

It was the rare time — maybe the only time in Blue Jays history — in which the club made a major signing because of its geography.

This is how much the Blue Jays wanted Guerrero: Anthopoulos was willing to risk a mosquito-borne virus called Chikungunya that was causing much distress in the Dominican Republic and had hospitalized Cruz's father. He was willing to take it on, but not without precautions.

"I was going to the Dominican, and nobody on our staff wanted to go," said Anthopoulos. "I thought, 'I have to go but I can't get sick.' (Scouting director) Andrew Tinnish volunteered to come with. So I went to Home Hardware near my house ... I bought these belts, repellents, all kinds of protective equipment. Everything they had, I bought."

Recalled Cruz: "When they got off the plane and Andrew was carrying around this kind of fan, with mesh over his head, and they're wearing that camouflage stuff, I'm thinking, 'Dude, come on, this isn't Africa.' They were all freaked out about the virus. We couldn't stop laughing, looking at them."

It was January 1, 2015 — seven months to signing day. There was much work to be done.

The day began with an airport pickup, a meeting with the soon-to-be Hall of Fame father, then a drive cross-country to meet with Vladimir Jr.'s mother and step-father.

During the drive, Anthopoulos, Tinnish, Cruz and Vladimir Jr. were all in the vehicle. Most of the time along the road, Guerrero, like a lot of teenagers, was affixed to his cellphone.

"It's hard to get to know a kid that young at any time, but we were trying. I wondered what he was watching or listening to," said Anthopoulos.

"Mostly, he was watching his dad's at-bats. We had the drive together, we had lunch at his mom's place. The more time we spent around him, the more we liked him, the more he opened up to us. It took a while."

"Vladdy's not like his dad," said Cruz. "His dad is very shy, very quiet. Vladdy's the opposite. He's outspoken. He doesn't mind telling you what he thinks. He's confident for a young man."

The rules of baseball had changed in 2015.

The Jays wanted to work out Guerrero privately, but Major League Baseball had forbidden teams from working out unsigned players at their own facilities. Anthopoulos needed to find an independent park for Guerrero to show his stuff.

Cruz had seen lots of him.

Anthopoulos had made two previous trips to the Dominican to see Guerrero. He had also seen at least 100 at-bats on video. Still, he wanted — needed — to see more.

In search of a field, Anthopoulos touched base with Edwin Encarnacion, then the Jays' first baseman, who lives in the Dominican in the off-season.

"I called Edwin and asked if he could help," said Anthopoulos. "He called a buddy who owned a team in the Dominican League. He got us a ballpark. Edwin came along for the workout.

"Vladdy Jr. was there.

"(Richard) Urena was there. This Cuban kid the Dodgers signed (Yadier Alvarez) was there. Edwin saw Vladdy for the first time.

"I asked him: 'Any risk in signing him?'" The quiet Encarnacion turned to Anthopoulos and said: "Nope."

"It's good knowing someone else is seeing what you're seeing," said Anthopoulos. Anthopoulos credits Cruz and Beeston for getting the Guerrero deal done.

Beeston credits Anthopoulos and Cruz.

Cruz credits Anthopoulos and Beeston.

Any way you consider it, it was a team effort by the Blue Jays front office and scouting staff.

"In all, I went to the Dominican four times to see him," said Anthopoulos. "Ismael Cruz saw him all the time. He was the point man for us in all this. This doesn't happen if he doesn't do all the legwork he did. He was running the show for us on this. He did an amazing job on this.

"I give Paul Beeston a lot of credit for allowing us to do this. He could have said no. It was expensive and it cost in many different ways. We were going all in on this. We had to make a trade with the Dodgers for international money. We gave up two players for that. We had to pay a tax for this. We had to lose a year in the international market for this. Paul had to sign off on everything we did. We don't get this deal done without his support."

Beeston doesn't see it that way: "The only thing I did was approve the dollars. We didn't go over budget on this. Alex was working with Ismael and with the family, I can take no credit for that.

"I've never seen two guys more convinced about a player than Alex and Ismael were. If you don't believe in your GM and in your Latin American scouting director, you have the wrong GM and the wrong scouting director. They weren't just enthusiastic about this. They were effusive.

"Alex started watching him when he was 14. Ismael saw him earlier than that. It's probably what they (scouts) saw when they saw Bobby Orr for the first time. It's that 'I can't believe I'm seeing this' feeling. Only thing is we had to wait until July 1 to sign him. We had the money in our budget, we just had to move it around. We didn't have to go to Rogers for approval on this."

Said Cruz: "This doesn't happen without Alex. You know how Alex is when he wants something. He just goes and goes and goes. And we had an advantage other teams didn't have. We were Canadian."

LUNCH AT THE HOME of Riquelma Ramos, Vladimir Jr.'s mom, may have been a turning point in the wooing of the young hitting prospect. There was Anthopoulos, Tinnish and Cruz representing the Blue Jays, Guerrero, his mom, his step-dad, his uncle Wilton sitting together, eating and talking baseball and life.

Somewhere in the conversation, Ramos and Anthopoulos began speaking in French.

"It's not something you hear often," said Cruz. "It was funny sitting in a Dominican house and hearing two people speaking French. His mom lived in Canada for a while.

"Vladdy had always identified himself with Canada. He has very good memories about it. Every time you speak with him about Canada, you can see his eyes light up."

Watching his mother in conversation with Anthopoulos in French may have been a turning point in striking a deal.

"She speaks fluent French and she was very proud that her son had a Canadian and Quebec birth certificate," said Anthopoulos.

"She said a lot of good things happened in Canada in their lives. I think Vladdy showed the most interest in us because of the amount of time we spent with him and because his mom liked us. I think it impressed him that we were there with his family. Ismael arranged a lot of those meetings.

"His mom said, 'We still have family (in Quebec) and ties there.' I don't know in the end how much that moved the needle, but I think playing for a Canadian team, his mother speaking fluent French, that his father played in Montreal, all those things mattered to him and his family and it was important to all of them."

On July 2, 2015, the Blue Jays announced the signing of Vladimir Guerrero Jr.

Less than two months after that, Mark Shapiro was hired as president of the Jays, thus ending Beeston's term as club president. In October, almost four months after the signing, Anthopoulos resigned as general manager. The following month, Cruz left the Jays for a position with the Los Angeles Dodgers.

The three people most responsible for bringing Guerrero to Toronto no longer factor with the Jays. But they are watching, even from afar.

As of Wednesday, Guerrero was hitting .423 with eight home runs and 45 RBI for the Double-A New Hampshire Fisher Cats, the No. 1 hitting prospect outside of the major leagues.

"It's exciting to see what he's doing, but let's wait for the big leagues and wait for him to become an All-Star before we say much more," said Cruz. "But right now, everything he is doing is off the charts."

"It's great to see what Vladdy is doing already," said Anthopoulos. "We tried to low-key his signing. We didn't have a press conference or anything. We didn't want to put any pressure on him. The family came up to Toronto and he took batting practice, had a small availability and that was it.

"The way things are going right now, I'm thrilled for him, I'm thrilled for the organization, and I know he's not there yet, but with the strides he's made and how well he's doing, a lot of people had a hand in it. It's exciting. So far, it looks like everything has gone well."

As for Beeston, who remains in an honorary position without a portfolio with the Jays, the Guerrero signing ranks among his favourite Blue Jays achievements.

"If he can be generational," said Beeston, "what a signing this will be."

(*Toronto Sun* baseball writer Rob Longley contributed to this piece.)

Bye-Bye, Kawhi

July 7, 2019

It almost seems like a blur on this Saturday morning of anger, pride, celebration and confusion: the 352 days of Kawhi Leonard as a member of the Toronto Raptors.

So much happened so fast — culminating in the rarest of the rare, a Toronto big-league championship — and now that we've taken part in all of that and the possibilities are over, and the future again seems so uncertain, there are these odd, almost detached, feelings of contradiction, of elation and depression, of revelry and sadness.

All because we've never danced this dance before. All because, in some small way, our lives changed these past 12 months, our appreciation of basketball brilliance changed.

We saw it up close and in our neighbourhoods and across the land, and now we wake to the overnight news that Kawhi Leonard has gone to the Los Angeles Clippers and midnight has passed and Cinderella is gone.

Who knew last July that any of this would be possible when Masai Ujiri rolled the dice and came up a champion? He traded the very popular DeMar DeRozan for the highly questionable Leonard. He traded away Mr. Toronto, Kyle Lowry's best friend, for someone who had mysteriously walked out on the San Antonio Spurs.

It took months for Lowry to forgive Ujiri for trading away his pal, if he ever actually did forgive him.

And it took months for us to see what Leonard was, in totality, what he could be, the man of silence being true to himself, playing hard, playing great, leading the Raptors to the second-best record in the NBA and revealing almost nothing about himself along the way.

This isn't how professional sports work. The stars answer the questions. They make the commercials. They appear all over ESPN.

Leonard was like no one we'd seen or heard from before. He was more than a curiosity. He performed unlike anyone in this market has ever performed.

Toronto has had no shortage of stars over the years. We saw Doug Gilmour and almost a Stanley Cup appearance for the Maple Leafs. That was 26 years ago.

We saw the best of Roy Halladay and Roger Clemens and Carlos Delgado, and none of it meant anything in October.

We watched most of Mats Sundin's career and a fine run by Chris Bosh and an MVP season by Josh Donaldson and the famous bat flip of Jose Bautista but nothing that took us to the World Series.

Kawhi Leonard took us on a ride, and then took the Raptors for a ride. First by coming here, then by playing here, then by working with the sports science master, Alex McKechnie, and with the rookie coach, Nick Nurse, and somehow everything worked out. Everything centred around Leonard.

He hit the bounce-bounce-bounce-bounce series-winning shot against Philadelphia in Game 7 at the Scotiabank Arena. He played 52 minutes, some of it on bad limbs, in Game 3 against Milwaukee, with the Raptors trailing the East final 2-0 in overtime. They were that close to losing to the Bucks.

But Leonard, in that series, looked more like the league MVP than did the actual MVP, Giannis Antetokounmpo. This is how you define sporting greatness. What happens on the biggest night and the biggest moment in the biggest game? He had won before in San Antonio on a team that won regularly.

But these were the Raptors — known for their playoff emptiness. Known for letting us down. Known for people leaving, not arriving.

We got one season of Leonard in Toronto. A gift really. An unforgettable run. A championship that virtually no one predicted. His time in Toronto: Won and done.

What we didn't know, couldn't know, was this man of few words, huge hands and spectacular ability to play offence and defence in a league where the latter has become passé wasn't only a basketball player.

He was steely eyed cool and in the background, quiet as ever, trying to change the NBA, his NBA, and become one of the kingmakers of the sport.

He could have stayed in Toronto, made more money, given it another shot or five and tried to see how many titles he could win.

He could have done that, but instead he played his hand the way NBA super-stars do more often than stars of any other sport.

He essentially orchestrated the trade of Paul George (with his involvement) to the Clippers so that he could team up with him on a contender of note.

He even tried to push Masai Ujiri to see if he could deal for George.

In the end, this wasn't about going home as much as it was about teaming Kawhi with George and adding another superpower to the list of NBA super-power teams, the way Kevin Durant and Kyrie Irving managed in Brooklyn in previous days.

And now he's gone to Los Angeles after one special season here, and there's this odd feeling that goes along with his departure.

Did this really happen? Was it all just a dream? We may never have another season like this one. Kawhi Leonard made it possible. Masai Ujiri made it possible.

Won and done. And damn, we wanted more.

Donovan Bailey's Golden Run

July 28, 1996

ATLANTA — The title is unlike any other in sport, transcending the games and leaving its onlookers breathless.

The world's fastest human.

That's what Donovan Bailey is now.

Not just the Olympic champion. Not just the gold medallist from Canada. Not just the winner of the marquee event at the Summer Olympics.

The world's fastest human.

The fastest man ever, with an asterisk.

Donovan Bailey stood by the starting blocks expressionless, slowly loosening up, minus his usual smile. He walked around easily while Dennis Mitchell strutted boldly, while Ato Boldon flexed his muscles, while Linford Christie stared at anyone who would stare back and while Frankie Fredericks seemed so calm, so certain of victory.

Bailey stood by the starting blocks and then the world and the track unfolded in his favor. There was one false start. And another false start. And a third false start.

And then Christie, the defending Olympic champ, was asked to leave the race. He was asked, but he refused. Only after the referee, John Chaplin, walked on to the track did an angry Christie depart.

By then, Boldon was twitching. By then, Mitchell looked beat. By then, it was a two-man race between Bailey and Fredericks.

"All those false starts played right into Donovan's hands," said his coach, Dan Pfaff. "Good starters struggle when there's a lot of false starts. They become unnerved, and it was perfect for Donovan. We didn't have enough time to give him a full warm-up run. This gave him the kind of time he needed."

There is something almost inexplicable about Donovan Bailey. How he runs so fast and starts so slow. Maybe it's because, as a sprinting nation, we've been honed on Ben Johnson, who burst like a race car out of the blocks. Bailey comes out of the blocks like a child learning to walk for the very first time, his arms and legs flailing, not necessarily in the same direction.

But once it happens, once he reaches stride, it's over. That's how it went last night at the Olympic Stadium in a race that was supposed to begin at 9:00 PM. sharp and was almost 20 minutes — and three false starts — late.

"If you watched him, after every false start he got better," said Andy McInnis, the national track team coach. "With Donovan, it's not how quick he gets out of the blocks. It's how it sets up the rest of his race.

"You know he has the acceleration. A lot of people think if you get a good start you win. It doesn't always work that way."

Boldon of Trinidad, Tobago, New York and UCLA started first and fastest. But he left the track in tears, unable to control himself emotionally.

"I put everything into that race," said Boldon, who ran third in a time of 9.90. Fredericks was second in 9.89. The world record, which belonged by default to American Leroy Burrell, disappeared when Bailey was clocked in 9.84.

The fastest any human has run it is 9.79. That was Ben Johnson. The record was taken away after Johnson's disqualification in Seoul. It is still, as Johnson is apt to say, the fastest anyone has ever been.

But none of that matters to Bailey today, because the record book says no one has run faster.

He accomplished it when it mattered most, just as Johnson did on two occasions. Before all the turmoil, that's what made Johnson so special. It now is what distinguishes Bailey from the rest of the great sprinters of the world.

He won last night on the track of the Olympic Stadium, on a cool night, when finally there was something to take some attention away from the bombing in Atlanta earlier that morning.

He won, as he did last year in Goteborg, when almost out of nowhere he became the world champion.

As he walked to the medal podium last night, after exchanging a small Canadian flag for a larger version, Bailey closed his eyes and took in this moment. His first real international, fastest-on-the-planet, national hero moment.

He closed his eyes and seemed at peace. And as the national anthem played, the anthem of one of the two countries he calls home, his lips moved slowly. He stood on guard for thee.

Donovan Bailey then closed his eyes again, raised his right arm in the air and held his gold medal close to his lips.

It is his Olympic gold medal, with a subtitle: The world's fastest human.

The Amazing Usain Bolt

August 17, 2008

BEIJING — Twelve years after that steamy Atlanta Saturday night, Donovan Bailey stood with his mouth open wide. Only this time it wasn't in victory or celebration.

This time, it was astonishment.

"If it had to be anyone, I'm glad it's Usain," Bailey said after watching another stunning and spectacular 100-metre race at the Olympic Games, watching the Olympic record he owned for three Games obliterated with seeming ease by the dazzling Usain Bolt of Jamaica.

Not since Ben Johnson's famed and infamous run in 1988 has any Olympic sprinter rendered the rest of the field and the world so irrelevant.

It was a one-man show. That complete. That definitive. That breathtaking. Bolt burst awkwardly out of the blocks last night, and it may have been the only time he didn't look the part of champion. He then sprinted his way to a world and Olympic record, letting up with his long strides over the final 20 metres, putting his arms out to celebrate and pounding his chest while still running the 100 metres in an astonishing time of 9.69.

Who knows what he might have run had he not begun his celebration just past the 70-metre mark?

"I wasn't ever worried about the world record," said Bolt, who crossed the finish line with his left shoe untied. "My aim was to be Olympic champion. I was happy with myself."

Now he has both. The gold medal and the world record, and it seems inconceivable that anyone will challenge him in the immediate future.

And more than anyone, Bailey understands what that means. He was world champion and Olympic champion but never considered unbeatable. Not that long ago, American Tyson Gay and fellow Jamaican Asafa Powell were also world record holders. Gay didn't even manage to qualify for the final and Powell ended up as an also-ran, fifth place and .26 seconds behind Bolt. In sprinting, that's almost a lifetime.

"It seems like I'm handing it off (Olympic record) to a countryman," said Bailey, the double gold medal–winning Canadian. "He's from Jamaica. I'm born in Jamaica. I'm not one of these guys who wanted to hold the record forever. But if you're handing off your record to the greatest thing that ever happened to track and field, I'm OK with that."

The 6-foot-5 Bolt ran the 100 metres, then continued to run and sidestep around the track, posing with the flag, flexing his chest muscles, smiling, hugging, dancing, taking his bows at the packed stadium they call the Bird's Nest.

To those who were in Rome in 1987 or in Seoul in 1988, the victory was reminiscent of the manner in which Johnson turned the 100 into a one-man tour de force. All that seems lost over time and drug testing.

But the race by Bolt was current and magical and impossible not to want to view over and over again. That's the charm of the 100 metres: In spite of all the controversies, the failed tests, the lives altered, it remains the most compelling 10 seconds in all of sport.

Only Bolt is getting closer to changing the parameters. It may soon become the most compelling nine-second race.

"I don't know how fast I could have run because I didn't see the replay," Bolt said. But the silver medal winner, Richard Thompson of Trinidad and Tobago, seemed to understand.

"I could see him slowing down," Thompson said. "And I'm still pumping to the line. And I'm not getting any closer to him."

Officially, the victory by Bolt was the first 100-metre win by a Jamaican. Unofficially, Jamaican-born sprinters Johnson and Bailey won the 100 on the track in 1988 and 1996. Johnson, however, lost his to disqualification.

Jamaica is an island of only 2.8 million people, 298 million fewer than live in the United States, a country that has given birth to Johnson, Bailey, Linford Christie of Britain, Powell and now Bolt — five of the greatest sprinters in history.

And there is enough of a fraternity within the sport that Bolt recently asked Powell and Bailey, one of his idols, to pose for a photograph.

"He got excited when he saw me, the same way I felt when I first saw Donald Quarrie or when I met Carl Lewis," Bailey said. "Sprinters are like that. You look up to the people who set the standards. And it's totally cool.

"You win the 100 metres, you're the king of the Games. You smash the world record, even better ... When I took the photo with Usain in Jamaica, I'm thinking, 'Holy crap, this is beautiful.' This guy is running 9.7."

Then he ran the Olympics and won in 9.69. And it could have been faster.

"I was just having fun," Bolt said.

The Don Cherry Nobody Knows

May 31, 2018

LAS VEGAS — The Don Cherry almost nobody knows is sitting in the last row of seats in the lower bowl at T-Mobile Arena. Always the last row, so easy to notice, so far removed from the mainstream crowd.

This is Cherry in Las Vegas, in the entertainment capital of the world, the newest of hockey's new party cities, where there is noise and celebration almost everywhere and the loudest-speaking, loudest-dressing Canadian couldn't be any more the opposite of his loquacious television persona.

"I don't go anywhere," Cherry said. "I don't do exciting things. I'm kind of boring."

You won't see him in a restaurant, in a casino, in a hotel lobby, at a craps table, almost anywhere. Cherry doesn't go out. He rarely leaves his hotel room.

"He is almost a recluse," said Ron MacLean, his close friend and professional sidekick. Not a recluse completely, but an 84-year-old icon in his 37th year on television who sticks to a routine, a most unusual routine, rarely changing anything.

This is his second trip to Las Vegas. The first time was 62 years ago for his marriage to the lovely and late Rose Martini. How much has Vegas changed since 1956? "I don't know," Cherry said. "I couldn't tell you. I really don't go out much."

He has his way of doing things. When he first checks into his hotel room on the road, the first thing he does is pull the curtains shut. No sunlight for him. "I don't know why I do it, I just do it," Cherry said.

He goes into his room alone, puts the Do Not Disturb sign on his door, does not allow housekeeping to enter any day. "I never have the maid come in," he said. "I don't like anybody in my room. All the maids love me."

"I'm the same everywhere," Cherry added. "It doesn't matter that this is Las Vegas. I don't go anywhere. My son tells me I have to see the *Titanic* (artifact exhibit)." Cherry doesn't know if he will get there.

Every day on the road is seemingly the same. It doesn't matter what the city is or what is around him. He has breakfast in his room. Oatmeal and All-Bran in a glass, put together by his wife, Luba. Before practice or a morning skate, his longtime associate Kathy Broderick brings a muffin. Lunch, in his hotel room, consists of salmon sandwiches made by his wife.

"It's the greatest thing in the world," said Cherry, the eccentric. "Salmon, cheese, mayo. After a couple of days the salmon soaks into the bread."

"It's more like a pudding than a sandwich," MacLean said. "But it is delicious."

Cherry, who used to have restaurants in his name, said he's not a "restaurant guy. I've never gone out for dinner (on the road). Ever. I get invited a lot. I just don't go. I'm a construction worker. I'm a construction worker, minor-league hockey player. This is the food for me, this is what I've always eaten."

Dinner will come from room service on nights when there are no games and, routine being routine, at 9:30 every night, he will join MacLean in his room for a beer. Always at 9:30. Never earlier, never later. MacLean is a neat freak. It doesn't look like anyone occupies his room. It's all part of the routine, the back-and-forth that defines their television life and much more than that.

Cherry is a man so noisy on television, so full of bark and so defined by the crazy, outlandish clothing that identifies him, yet he is so happy to be in a dark hotel room "with his clicker," watching baseball. "I watch a lot of baseball," he said.

And one other thing about the hotels he stays in: "They have to have a good steam sauna. Ron and I have checked in to hotels and they didn't have the sauna, or it wasn't working, and we checked right out and left. We've gone hotel to hotel until we've found the right one.

"I'd like to say I do exciting things. To me, I don't see nothing. I'm in my room. I go to the sauna. I come to the morning skates. I'm disappointed in this series that other team (Las Vegas) doesn't skate at the big rink. They're at their practice rink. I'm disappointed in that. I think that's wrong. At the Stanley Cup, they should be skating at the same rink in the morning."

"My favourite time is coming to the morning skates. We sit up high, away from everybody else," he added. "This feels so good. It feels like I'm in the game. I always like being in rinks like this, wearing a shirt and tie, always looking good. This is what we do."

Cherry doesn't talk to the players he talks about. He doesn't want to get to know them personally.

"If you get to know them, you might like them," he said. "If you like them, you can't say anything bad about them. I don't talk to anyone. We sit up high. We don't talk to anyone.

"A few years ago, I had this thing with Matt Cooke. He was waiting for me in Carolina. He had hit (Marc) Savard. He hit Vinny (Lecavalier). And I said a lot about him on 'Coach's Corner.' He came up to me and said, 'I want to know if you have the nerve to say what you said about me to my face.'

"We went face to face. I was so close to his face, I could look inside his mouth and see his teeth were chipped. We went at it for at least 10 minutes. I didn't back down. They (the players) know. They know I'm right."

There haven't been any confrontations since then.

This is a remarkable year for hockey and the National Hockey League with first-year Las Vegas playing for the Stanley Cup and this party city abuzz with so much hockey excitement. It's a story beyond comprehension. The Final, a year after being exposed to the frenzy that is Nashville, has gone from one long party to another. But Cherry, he would rather be in Winnipeg.

"That was a disappointment to me," he said of the Jets losing to Vegas. "I still think Winnipeg is the best team. (Marc-Andre) Fleury stole three games. He broke their hearts. Winnipeg should be here. I love everything in Winnipeg. Winnipeg is great."

The rest of the hockey world is soaking up the sun, indulging in the casinos, staying out too late, eating steak that's overpriced, investing time in all the different music outside T-Mobile Arena and being exposed to so many of wonders that plastic surgery can produce. This is all new, all amazing.

Don Cherry, still working, still the must-listen voice between periods, prefers Winnipeg. In his hotel. With the curtains drawn. Where hockey is hockey and morning skates are morning skates.

"I picture him as our Howard Hughes at the Bayshore," MacLean said of Cherry, with a smile of admiration. "He's sort of a hermit. But he's our hermit."

The End for Don Cherry Comes without Apology

November 13, 2019

Don Cherry knew it would end this way. He didn't know when. He didn't know how.

He just knew that, one day, saying the wrong thing — or, in his stubborn mind, what others thought to be the wrong thing — would catch up to him and end his time with *Hockey Night in Canada*.

He told me that years ago.

He said he would never step down, as the Sportsnet news release indicated he did. He would never quit. They would have to push him out. And that's what happened on Monday afternoon.

He knew how many times he had walked the tightrope while working for CBC. He understood, for the most part, how far he could push the envelope — and, every once in a while, he pushed it too far. Internally, the CBC, where he spent the majority of his broadcast career, would go apoplectic looking uncomfortably away while figuring out how to balance profit, ratings and Cherry's bombast and butchering of the English language with its own rather stringent broadcast values.

More than once, maybe more than 10 times, he was on the verge of being fired. But the CBC held its breath, ignored its best instincts and hoped whatever controversy of the day would go away. Don Cherry was good business for *Hockey Night in Canada*, and *Hockey Night in Canada* was big business for the CBC.

Cherry could be old school.

He could be anti-French or anti-Russian or anti-Swede. Or anti-anything for that matter. He would intentionally mispronounce names and then those names became part of his act, the way the loud clothing was, the big collars and the ostentatious suits. As time went on, there were more shout-outs to the police and the men and women who served and sometimes, unfortunately, not enough hockey. Times changed, and in many ways, he didn't. That was part of his charm, but also part of his downfall.

When he crossed the line with his offensive comments this past Saturday night, this time it was different. This time, there was no Ralph Mellanby to fight for his survival. The National Hockey League issued a statement distancing itself from Cherry. Hockey Canada issued a statement. Even the Canadian Legion — and that must have hurt — issued a statement. There were never these kinds of responses before to his "you people" rant. Rogers Media had no choice, really, but to say goodbye, with the blessing of its chief advertisers.

It was time. It was probably past time. And I believe had he chosen to apologize the way his co-host Ron MacLean did, had he swallowed his pride for just a moment, he'd probably be back on the air this Saturday.

But Cherry won't — or can't — apologize. That's not who he is or what he's ever been about.

I first met Don when he was on a book tour in the early 1980s. He had just been fired by the Colorado Rockies after one season in Denver. He was looking for a job in hockey. We met at a bar, not surprisingly, and had a few cold ones, and from there a relationship was built. "Coach's Corner" had not yet been invented. But it was easy to see back then why he was such a television prospect.

He was impossible to dislike. He had an enormous personality. He had thoughts on just about every subject, some hockey, some not, and he could tell a story with a vigour few could match. That led to one show, then another show, then more than three decades of "Coach's Corner."

In the early years, we watched because you never knew what he was going to say about anything, and you sure didn't want to miss it. In the later years, it was more about shock value and on occasion an old man struggling to find words, but the gathering around the television, that never changed. It was still the place to be at the end of the first period.

In the press box in Toronto on Saturday night, there was always a large gathering of media around the television at the end of the first period. What was Cherry going to say this time? It was the same in the bars across Canada. So often, the hockey games are shown on several different screens, and usually without sound. But then the period would end and the best bar operators knew the sound should come on at the end of the first period.

Like him, hate him, believe in him, be disgusted by him, the one thing we never did was ignore Don Cherry. We always listened. Mostly, we always tuned in. Right to the last Saturday night. The show that ended his career. And hopefully, the show he won't be best remembered for.

I got to know Don reasonably well after his book tour and, over the phone, I got to know his first wife, Rose, a wonderful, gracious woman who passed away in 1997. In some ways, back then, she was the conscience of the family. She kept Don on the up-and-up as much as that was possible.

After a Saturday night on which Cherry said something particularly galling or controversial or outrageous, I would often call the home on Monday for a debrief. What did he say? What did he mean? Was his job in jeopardy? Rose would always answer the phone — Don rarely does, even to this day — and after the usual hellos and how-are-yous, she would ask the same question: "What did he do this time?" We would talk about it for a few minutes, analyze it, then talk about their lives or my life or whatever happened to be going on in the world that day. And she would promise that Don would call when he came home. Most of the time, he did.

Over the years, Don got bigger, more popular, louder, and that became so much of his act that you had trouble distinguishing the character he played on "Coach's Corner" from the man he happened to be. A living, breathing caricature of himself. On television, he was colourful and the proudest of Canadians, wearing outfits that defied description, but privately, he was something of an introvert, advocating roughhouse hockey, a creature of habit who would go on the road and stay in his hotel room and hope never to be noticed.

He didn't go to restaurants.

He didn't wear those costumes when he was sitting in the corner with his son watching GTHL minor midget games, which is one of his passions. He would bring his second wife Luba's salmon sandwiches on the road with him in the playoffs: That's what he ate. He had restaurants in his name, he just didn't eat in them. The old salmon sandwiches worked for as long as they lasted.

He knew how to behave when the lights came on every Saturday night and he knew how to properly disappear when it wasn't his time. That's the Don I've known: bighearted, bigmouthed, charitable, forever stubborn. He was a miracle of modern media, lasting as long as he did, against all odds, with so many out to get him until he got himself fired.

Fired without an apology.

Just the way he figured it would end.

George Chuvalo's Tragic Homecoming

August 20, 1996

He celebrated inside an Albuquerque ring on Saturday night, George Chuvalo did.

He was there with his new fighter, Johnny Tapia, a former addict and former wife abuser, and current junior bantamweight champion.

Chuvalo was there, where he most belongs, back in boxing, back in the middle of all the action, back in the ring.

And then he flew home and was stunned to find that tragedy once again had entered his life.

"I saw (my wife) Joanne at the airport. I didn't expect her to be there. And she looked at me, this crazy, crazy look," Chuvalo said yesterday with his voice quavering.

"Then she held my hand, tight. I know she wanted to say something. But I said it first.

"Steven's dead, isn't he?"

Steven Chuvalo was discovered by police, dead of a drug overdose in the home of his sister, Vanessa, on Sunday afternoon. Vanessa, like her father, had been out of town. Steven, out of prison and distraught by divorce proceedings brought against him, was staying with her.

She came home and found the door locked, and Steven had the key. She called a friend. A friend called the police. The police opened the door.

Steven Chuvalo, son of the longtime Canadian heavyweight champion, was 35, a onetime eaves-trough worker, a small-time criminal and a loser in a lifelong bout against a bastard of an opponent called heroin.

"It all sounds so ridiculous," George Chuvalo said.

"Three kids dead. How do you explain that? How do you make sense of that?

"I got to keep on going. I got to keep on going somehow. I have to keep it together. My daughter's lost three brothers and her mother. I got to be there for her. My four grandsons don't know what the hell is going on. How do I explain this?

"How the hell do you explain this to anyone?"

Boxers live by the scorecard, but the scorecard of George Chuvalo's life is all about death and agony and hurt so deep none of us can begin to comprehend his pain and the pain of his family.

Jesse Chuvalo, dead at age 20, in 1985.

George Lee Chuvalo, dead at age 30, in 1993.

Lynne Chuvalo, wife and mother of five children, dead at age 50, two days after George Lee's drug overdose.

And now Steven.

"He had problems but he was a real nice kid, a sweet, shy kid," said Chuck "Spider" Jones, one of Chuvalo's closest friends. "He was a handsome boy who loved his kids. But the drugs got him. They always do."

Johnny Tapia decided he needed George Chuvalo in his corner when he read an article about the former heavyweight contender. He read about the deaths, the suicides, the drug addicts and how Chuvalo had somehow remained on his feet. He wanted that kind of strength with him. He needed someone who knew his kind of tragedy.

So Tapia's manager got in touch with actor Mickey Rooney, who was in the Toronto production of *Crazy for You*. Rooney, an old friend, contacted Chuvalo. The deal was done. Chuvalo was in Tapia's corner for his impressive 12-round decision over Hugo Soto on Saturday night. It was supposed to represent the beginning of something big.

But tomorrow the Toronto boxing community will gather, as it has far too often in recent times. To cry, to hug, to console old friends and to bury another Chuvalo.

The family once numbered seven. Four are gone and the scars are many.

The grief of burying one's child has to be excruciating. But the grief of burying most of your family cannot be measured on any human scale. It is beyond our comprehension.

George Chuvalo searches for reasons, and asks why, and comes away mostly shaking in tears. He is a large man with huge hands and a huge heart. Once he was the toughest man in Canada. Now he has to be. He has no choice.

There are no answers to the questions he asks aloud and mumbles so quickly. How can there be? No man, not the worst and certainly not the best, is deserving of this kind of life and this amount of pain.

So he goes on, because it's all he knows, because there is still a reason when he searches for one.

There is still Joanne, his wife of more than a year. There is still son Mitchell and daughter Vanessa. There are still four grandchildren. There is a reason to continue.

He has to know there is a reason.

"I can't give up," George Chuvalo said. "I'm gonna have to find a way to go on. I'm gonna have to find a way ... "

Of Brady and Gretzky

February 9, 2021

When you saw Wayne Gretzky for the first time standing without a shirt on, you had to do a double take.

How could the greatest scorer, maybe the greatest player in hockey history, have a body like his? There was really nothing to see there. His arms were thin and not particularly muscular. His shoulders seemed rather small, even for someone as tall and lanky as Gretzky was.

Then the game would begin, and skating in a rather awkward pose, bent totally in half from the waist down, his body in equipment looking something like a sideways *L*, there he was, a player unlike any we've witnessed before.

You can't see vision the way Gretzky could. You can only imagine. At first, you couldn't understand how he saw what he did. You couldn't make sense of the angles, the baffling geometry, the subtlety of the way in which he made everyone around him better.

Michael Jordan was more like a dashing comet, never understated in the way Gretzky was. LeBron James looks like a statue, his body thick and chiseled, the way Mark Messier's was in the Gretzky years in Edmonton. Those guys look like they were born to play, to star. Gretzky looked like the skinny kid who might have been a high school target.

If you took Tom Brady to any football field and asked him to throw and run and catch and block and tackle, there would be nothing spectacular about what you would see. Other quarterbacks have had better arms. Others, certainly, could run better.

But like Brady, what made Gretzky better and different and more accomplished than anyone else were his subtle instincts — never easily defined, not put together on highlight tapes.

Years ago, coach Glen Sather said that if you turned out all the lights in the arena while the game was going on, Gretzky was the only one who would know where every player was. He had a sense unlike any other. He wasn't skilled and spectacular the way Mario Lemieux was. He wasn't smooth and elegant the way Jean Beliveau was, or strong and powerful like his idol, Gordie Howe.

He just obliterated all of them on the scoresheet. Anyone who has ever played. And you can't completely describe or explain how he did what he did. He just did it, year after team, season after season.

In his final year he had 53 assists. That wasn't good enough for Gretzky. He needed more. It was time to say goodbye, with him 1,007 points ahead of Howe, who played 280 more games than Gretzky.

No one can catch his point total now. Joe Thornton is the closest among active players, only 1,346 points behind the Great One. How many Stanley Cups would Gretzky have won had he stayed in Edmonton rather than getting sold off to the Los Angeles Kings? It's impossible to know, but the answer is certainly more than the four he won with the Oilers.

Now Brady has seven Super Bowl championships, a number impossible to quantify in any real way. The legendary Green Bay Packers have won only four Super Bowls as a franchise. The Cleveland Browns and Buffalo Bills are among those legendary teams never to have won.

Brady has seven, six with a varying degree of New England Patriots rosters, different receivers, different running backs, and now one, maybe the most miraculous, with the forever-downtrodden Tampa Bay Buccaneers and without coach Bill Belichick.

They brought in 43-year-old Brady to play quarterback in Tampa, brought in a waived Leonard Fournette to run the football, brought Rob Gronkowski out of retirement to play tight end, brought in Antonio Brown from self-inflicted football hell. In the Super Bowl, Brady threw two touchdown passes to Gronkowski and one to Brown, while Fournette ran for one. And in the one sport where free agency doesn't often change teams, a Super Bowl champion was born.

It was a champion born through Brady's eyes and vision and his ability to see possibility where there is none. That's where he and Gretzky are alike, and in similar ways so were Michael Jordan and Tiger Woods. You can't make someone competitive at a global level. They either are or they aren't. Jordan was possessed to win as Tiger has been. If Gretzky had two scoring points on a night, he wanted three. If he had three, he wanted four. It was never enough.

Up 24 points in the fourth quarter of Sunday's Super Bowl, Brady threw long. He tried for another touchdown. That's how his motor works. The win was already there and you could see in the post-game celebration how much it meant to him. He had convinced the Bucs they could do this. He wasn't just the quarterback, he was the spiritual leader. He played and he coached and when he needed to, he coached some more.

He has seven Super Bowls now, five Super Bowl MVPs. Gretzky won four Stanley Cups, eight league MVPs, and eight scoring titles with Edmonton.

Brady was born with the matinee idol looks, the right hair, the right look for quarterbacking stardom. He was born to win and, like Gretzky, has never been so easily defined. He's done what no one else has accomplished in a manner no one else has equalled.

The greatest always seem to do that, always in their own way, their own distinct style. There are more similarities between Brady and Gretzky than anyone could possibly imagine, in sports so very different.

CHAPTER 2

Of Ice
and Men

The Wild Life of Derek Sanderson

March 29, 2005

Derek Sanderson is saving his best stories for a book he may one day write or for a script that he hopes one day will find its way to film.

This is about as close as he will come to telling all now. It's his way of holding something back, for his own protection as he gets closer to the age of 60, as he marvels at what he has done and where he has been and how many stunning turns his life has taken.

"I never understood it all," said Sanderson, who has been hockey star, celebrity, millionaire, trendsetter, alcoholic, drug addict, homeless, born-again, rich-again, all in the span of one extraordinary life.

"I never understood what it was about me. Why a penalty killer was getting all that attention. I was never a star, never. I was never a great player, never. But people would say 'You've got charisma,' and I was a kid and didn't even know what charisma was. And I just went along with it all.

"I had no ambition to be a millionaire. I had no ambition to be a star. I never strived to be rich and famous. I strived to have a good time. I had no plans. Maybe that's why I floundered. I just lived one day to the next. Total ad lib."

Derek Sanderson is talking on a telephone from Boston 27 years after he played his last game. For some reason, it doesn't seem that long ago. For some reason the numbers — 598 National Hockey League games played, eight in the World Hockey Association, no more than 29 goals in any season, never more than 67 points — all seem less than the reputation. But he was better known in his day — the late '60s, the '70s — and more recognizable than anyone who plays today. He was the hockey face of his generation, with loud clothes, slick cars and long sideburns: the Joe Namath of the NHL. And while Namath just came clean about his most recent bout with alcoholism, his life has been near fairy tale when compared with that of his former business partner in failed nightclub ventures.

The low point Sanderson is asked to define can't necessarily be pinpointed. Where do you begin? Was it sleeping in New York's Central Park when he had no place else to go? Was it the days he can't even remember, the many months misplaced in a haze of booze and drugs? Was it falling on his knees in Niagara Falls or was it St. Catharines, somewhere near home, yet completely lost?

"Nobody goes into the guidance counsellor's office in high school and says, 'I want to be a drunk,'" Sanderson said. "Nobody puts a gun to your head and says ,'Start drinking.' But then you get into the cycle. It's poor me. It's nobody cares. It's my boss, my brother, my mother, my wife — everybody is a pain in the ass. You get in that mindset, you can't get out. I couldn't stop drinking. It was always in my brain. And then you say to yourself, 'Today is good, I'll stop tonight.' Then you have a drink and you say you'll stop tomorrow. It gets in your brain and you just keep going back to it. And sometimes you just don't want to get better."

Derek Sanderson left the Boston Bruins in 1972 to sign a record-breaking 10-year, $2.6 million U.S. contract with the Philadelphia Blazers of the World Hockey Association, with a significant amount of money paid up front. At the time, the money was beyond anyone's wildest imagination. It was the first million he would make, the first million he would blow.

"The important thing of that deal, it wasn't the money, although that kind of wrecked me," Sanderson said. "The important thing is what happened in court. This was the first time anybody really tested free agency without compensation in sport. Curt Flood tried it and Major League Baseball buried him. He went from being an MVP to hiding out as a bartender in Spain.

"Philadelphia came to me and said 'Will you take on free agency in court?' I said, 'They'll bury me.' But it was over in a short period of time. The whole thing was settled in an hour and a half. It was basically the birth of free agency in all of sport, although people today point to other things. But I know this is used in law schools today as a cite case. When they found for the WHA in court, they found for all of sport at that time, creating free agency. Everybody today should pay me 1% of their contracts for what I did for them."

The money, though, created a life Sanderson himself couldn't control. He lasted a little while in the WHA, hating the game, the league, the sudden star status, and writing cheques on the slightest whim. The money disappeared and Sanderson played out his career in his five different cities over parts of five seasons. By the age of 32, he was done.

This is normally when the story ends, the typical tale of the down-and-out athlete hitting rock bottom: Sanderson bottomed out and with it found a new beginning.

He had lost his job, his money, and, over time, his health. He has had 10 hip operations, with both hips being replaced. His knees have been repaired. There isn't a day when something doesn't hurt.

"I ran into a counsellor in St. Catharines and said I was sick and tired of being sick and tired," Sanderson said. "It's difficult to explain what happened after that. That's why I have to write a book because it's not something you can say in a few words. It's that powerful.

"Certain things happened that were monumental. I got clean, and you white-knuckle it for a while. I live every day by the things AA taught me. And it's spiritual too. I don't know anybody that can get through this without it being a life-altering experience."

Getting through clean and sober was victory enough. Making the climb back was just as miraculous.

He went home to St. Catharines, where his father told him General Motors was hiring in 1981, but somehow the idea of factory work wasn't for him. Instead, he went back to Boston, called a friend who ran a golf club, asked if he could find him some work.

Sanderson worked cleaning golf clubs, slept above the pro shop, pumped gas at a local service station, hustled the occasional game. Anything to get by.

"I let humility run my life," he said. "And you measure success by whether you stay clean another day."

While working at the Andover Country Club, he met a man who thought he should be telling his story to students in the Boston area. Suddenly he was a motivational speaker. And it was through those public speaking engagements that a female reporter from a local cable station came to interview him.

"She said, 'Why don't we do this interview?' I said, 'Why don't we go to dinner?'" Two years later, they were married.

From there, another golf club contact paid off. The chairman of a major Massachusetts brokerage firm lost his job and a golf friend took over. At first, he wanted Sanderson as a spokesman for the company. Sanderson took it one step further.

He went back to school, took a brokerage course, began working at a firm called Tucker Anthony, building a client base and working with those he knew best: professional athletes.

"I used myself as an example," Sanderson said. "How you can have every-thing and then have nothing. It was my job to protect athletes from themselves."

At its height, Sanderson directed the investments of more than 200 profes-sional athletes. He has since begun to slow down, spending more time with his teenaged boys, Michael and Ryan, more time with Nancy, his wife of 18 years. He can afford the leisure life.

"There has been a lot of silly stuff in my life, a lot of trouble" Sanderson said. "I tell athletes that I don't want what happened to me to happen to you. Some guys listen ... some guys never get it."

The Uncomfortable Firing of Brian Burke

January 10, 2013

It was late in the Stanley Cup playoffs when the word began drifting out about Brian Burke.

How he was acting erratically.

How his life was spiralling in dubious ways.

How the new owners of the Maple Leafs, still not officially in place, were not happy with what they saw, what they regularly were hearing, what they believed about their prized hockey team.

It was late in the playoffs and the question was asked almost everywhere I travelled, with too many stories — some false, some true — being spread around late at night. He had become the topic almost every day. The questions being asked: What's going on with Brian Burke? And how long before the Maple Leafs fire him?

One source told me in June that Burke would not manage one more game with the Leafs. That source proved to be correct.

Another told me he would be promoted to president, with Dave Nonis taking over as general manager. That turned out to be half true. Nonis is now general manager, Burke has a consultant's role for the moment — until he gets his next television or hockey job.

The question, floating around in June and repeated throughout the summer, was answered not necessarily directly Wednesday by Tom Anselmi, the chief operating officer of Maple Leafs Sports and Entertainment Ltd., when he said: "This was about a change in leadership, a change in voice, a change of direction."

Then he contradicted himself just slightly, or at least did his best at damage control when he first said: "I don't want to get into specifics" and followed that up with "This has nothing to do with Brian's personal life."

Maybe it doesn't. But it does come back to image as much as it comes back to hockey. An image that Leafs ownership was uncomfortable with. If this decision was only about hockey and nothing else, it is unlikely Nonis would be the Leafs' new general manager. He was part of every decision Burke made. He made some of them himself. In some ways, depending on whom you ask, he was already the de facto general manager.

Now he has the title to go along with it. And he no longer has to answer for what Burke might have said, how Burke might have reacted.

Whatever it was through his four up-and-down seasons in Toronto, Burke was many things, but dull was never one of them.

That's why this marriage should have worked. Burke was made for this town, this job. He should have had it for life. As the loudest, seemingly sharpest, most bombastic general manager in sports here in the centre of the sport's hottest market. This was a marriage made in hockey heaven but Burke never delivered as advertised — and I admit, I was one of his largest advocates at first, but he lost me as he became more about being Brian Burke than he was about running a hockey team.

The team was never what he said it would be. His personal contradictions — extending Ron Wilson then firing him, pronouncing Francois Allaire the best goalie coach in the world then calling him a dinosaur — were no more successful than a hockey team forever spinning its wheels. He did make some nice trades — primarily the deals for Dion Phaneuf and the combo trade that brought in Jake Gardiner and Joffrey Lupul — but for every move of consequence, there was a move or more to question. And he never got them to the playoffs. That will haunt him as he walks out the door.

He didn't win on the hockey side. But the new owners of the Maple Leafs — the media rivals Bell and Rogers — wouldn't have fired him necessarily for that. Not this soon, anyhow. They fired him because he feuded with anyone in the media who had an opinion. They fired him because they were tired of going to receptions and hearing: Did you hear where Brian was last night, or how he acted, or that, apparently, he was in places he didn't need to be?

You hear that once and you think nothing of it. You hear it twice, and maybe you turn a deaf ear. You hear it over and over again and you make a decision like this one: They wanted new leadership to go along with new ownership.

"It's not a product of any one incident or any one thing," said Anselmi. "It's about a whole bunch of things ... I don't want to get into specifics."

Then he danced around the complex, multifaceted relationship between a GM and an owner. Or in this case, three owners if you include the ever-patient chairman Larry Tanenbaum.

"It's symbiotic," said Anselmi. "It works or it doesn't work."

And in the end, the owners of the Maple Leafs, none of them present to account for themselves Wednesday, didn't want Brian Burke as the face or the voice of their franchise anymore. As strange as the timing may seen, it was time. Their time.

On the day Brian Burke was fired by the Toronto Maple Leafs, he held a news conference to discuss his dismissal. Upon my asking a question that day, Burke glared at me and responded: "That's the best part about today, Steve, is that I probably don't ever have to talk to you again." And we haven't spoken since.

Hometown Kid
Heading to Hall of Fame

November 7, 2013

This is where a Hall of Famer comes from.

Brendan Shanahan is driving west on Lake Shore Blvd., talking of his upbringing, his family, his lifelong friends, pointing out the sights that mattered most then and now.

Then he stops in Mimico, a place that looks like time has stopped.

He points to the swimming pool at Ourland Park, the field named for Angelo Sacco, shows me where his name remains in chalk on certain buildings. And he stops at the almost hidden piece of land alongside St. Leo's Catholic School, where Shanahan first learned to fight.

"I used to think it was so much bigger than this," Shanahan says, stopping the car and parking at the side of the road.

"This was a scrappy neighbourhood. When you wanted to fight, you wouldn't say, 'You wanna go?' You would just say two words: 'Gym wall.' And after school, someone would meet you there. That's how it worked."

Shanahan understood battling almost from birth as the youngest of four brothers born to Donal and Rosaleen. At the age of five, he shared a room with his 16-year-old brother.

The house was a game waiting to be played — a wrestling match, road hockey, hide-and-seek, kick the can, lacrosse, football. Whatever it was, Shanahan wanted to play, needed to compete.

This is where a Hall of Famer comes from. This is how a kid who believes he was "never the best player on any team [he's] ever played on — pro, junior or minor hockey," receives the highest recognition in his sport come Monday night.

He will be at the Hockey Hall of Fame with his 80-year-old hero — his mother — along with his wife and children, his brothers, their families and his oldest

48

friends. Everyone but his father, a victim of early Alzheimer's, gone now for more than half of his life. He will be missed and certainly mentioned.

They used to get up together for the early-morning practices, Don the firefighter and his youngest son. The other three kids, they all travelled to hockey together.

But by the time Brendan played, it was mostly him and his dad.

"I never saw my father skate, never knew if he had a pair of skates," says Shanahan.

"He was an Irish immigrant, came to Canada at 18. He came to love hockey. When I was little, I'd go to the rink with my brothers and hang around. At that time, organized hockey started at about age seven. I think I was four years old when the organizers of the Long Branch House League said to my father: 'Why doesn't he play?'

"My dad said I was too young. They said I was big enough, so they put me in a few years early.

"I was so bad that first year that when the buzzers went to change lines, the referees would pick me up and carry me to the bench. It sped up the game. The next year I got better ... "

Shanahan progressed from house league to the Etobicoke Hockey Association and then to the Mississauga Reps of what was then the MTHL. There was even a short stint with the Toronto Young Nats, a confusing year for a young man uncertain of what was happening to his father.

They would drive to the rink and sometimes his dad would get confused, nervous and anxious. Occasionally, they got lost. They had to return to Mississauga.

"I knew my father was going through something, but I didn't really understand what it was," he says.

"When I went to play junior in London, every time I came home he was a little different, a little more gone."

Donal was well enough physically to accompany Shanahan to the 1987 NHL draft, where his son was selected second overall.

"If you saw him, you wouldn't think there was anything wrong with him," Shanahan says. "But if you talked to him, you would know."

Three years later, after Shanahan's third season in New Jersey, Donal Shanahan was gone.

His funeral was at the church where Brendan had his first communion, just a few blocks from their home.

Everything was and is neighbourhood with Shanahan. His mom still lives in the same Mimico home. His name remains high on the bricks in chalk. His oldest brother lives just a few blocks away.

"If there's a time (in my speech) that I might get emotional, it may be this," Shanahan says. "My whole career happened without him, really. Even when he was still alive, he wasn't really there."

He wasn't there for the 50-goal seasons in St. Louis, the trades for Chris Pronger and Paul Coffey and the compensation for Scott Stevens, the Stanley Cups in Detroit. In 21 years in the NHL, Shanahan scored more than 50 twice, 40 four times, 30 six times, 20 seven times. In 17 of those years, he had 100 or more penalty minutes.

And still he's never really thought of himself as a goal scorer.

"We won the Quebec peewee tournament with a really strong team and three guys from that team — me, Jason Woolley and Bryan Marchment — all played in the NHL. And if you picked the top five players on that team, none of us would have been mentioned.

"I would have thought Steve Glugosh or David D'Amico or David Humphries, our goalie, would have been the guys going to the NHL. To be honest, I never thought about being a pro hockey player. It was never on my radar.

"I just assumed I was going to play hockey like my brothers. I'd go to college somewhere. I didn't even think I'd play college hockey. I figured I'd end up playing for the Irish Canadians in some rec league."

The times were so different then. Shanahan played high school football at Michael Power, ran track, was never considered among the jocks in school and didn't live anything of the consumed hockey life that young prospects lead today.

"My high school friends — and they're still my closest friends today — were as shocked and surprised by my career as I was. I know they've enjoyed the things I've been able to share with them. I also know if I hadn't played one day in the NHL, they'd still be my friends. We used to be called the Mod Squad. Not one of us had a parent who was born in Canada. We would call each other on the phone and wind up speaking to a parent who either didn't speak English or spoke English, but you couldn't understand them.

"Looking back, I was just one of the guys. I didn't think about pro hockey. I just assumed there was a whole class of players somewhere that looked like Darryl Sittler and Gilbert Perreault and Guy Lafleur that were 16 years old. And I wasn't one of them."

Shanahan began to think differently when he got to the London Knights.

For some reason, each time he moved up a level, his quality of play got better, his game more developed.

"I was more suited for bantam than minor bantam, more suited for midget than minor midget, more suited for the NHL than I was for junior. It's something I've not always been able to explain."

In London, though, he was terribly homesick.

"Most homesick guy they've ever seen," he says.

It didn't help when he was pulled out of school one day and informed that Randy Giesecke, who pushed him harder than any minor hockey coach he had played for, and left a lasting influence, had been murdered.

If ever he wanted to go home and be around family, that was the time. But one trait evident throughout Shanahan's career: He learned to battle, to never stop competing.

He credits Giesecke and former teammates Doug Sulliman and Brett Hull with helping him advance his game and his ability to score goals.

"I think it's a complete cop-out that you can't learn or be taught how to score at the NHL level," Shanahan says. "I hear coaches say all the time that you can teach defence, but you can't teach offence. I don't buy that. I'm an example of the opposite. I worked on my shot. I was a student of the game. I watched what Hull did and learned from that."

He was a rookie in New Jersey in Lou Lamoriello's first year as GM with the Devils. He wound up in St. Louis with Mike Keenan, in Detroit with Scotty Bowman.

But maybe even then he knew management was in his future.

"I played for some great GMs. To start out with Lou, have Ron Caron, Jimmy Rutherford, Glen Sather and Kenny Holland, I used to study them, watch what they did. I almost learned more from my general managers than I did from my coaches."

Only 12 players in NHL history have scored more goals. Shanahan is the 10th from that list to get the call.

The other two — Teemu Selanne and Jaromir Jagr — will join him in the future. He has more NHL goals than Joe Sakic or Bobby Hull, Mike Bossy or Lafleur, Rocket Richard or Stan Mikita.

You mention that and in the car, driving away from Mimico, Shanahan blushes.

He says, "The career I was able to have outdistances my ability. I know that."

He smiles driving east on Lake Shore Blvd.

This is where a Hall of Famer came from.

The Heartbroken
Wendel Clark

July 2, 1994

For the first time and maybe the only time in public, there sat Wendel Clark, all red-eyed and quivering.

He held a crumpled Kleenex in his right hand while his left hand fidgeted uncomfortably. His eyes looked up and then they couldn't look up anymore.

It's never easy to say goodbye.

Almost three days had passed since the stoic captain of the Maple Leafs had been traded to the Quebec Nordiques. Three days to think. Three days to wonder. Three days to try to compose himself.

And there he was, sitting behind a table at Don Cherry's Grapevine restaurant in Mississauga, trying to speak, trying to say the right things, trying to stop himself from crying.

He wasn't alone. Beside him sat Don Meehan, his lawyer, his agent, his close friend. Meehan was asked how he felt. His voice cracked also when he answered. On the floor stood Cherry, the loud one. "I feel like crying," Grapes said. "I got a thrill watching him play. If I were a hockey player again, I would want to be just like Wendel Clark."

This is how Clark said goodbye after nine seasons of triumph and pain. He said it with cameras clicking and videotape recording and with almost none of the "I'm just a Saskatchewan farm boy" attitude we have come to know from Toronto's most beloved athlete.

The introduction was simple. "My friend," said Meehan, "doesn't need any introduction."

And Wendel Clark's hands shook as he unfolded the white papers, his personal departure notes. He thanked everybody. Harold Ballard. Ballard's family. The Leafs trainers. Coaches, management, media, Steve Stavro, Cliff Fletcher. And then he almost lost it.

"Everybody knows how I feel about my teammates," said Clark, struggling for his composure, hoping the words would keep coming. "They feel the same way about me."

He hadn't answered his telephone for three days. Like everything else yesterday, he apologized for that. Three days and almost a thousand messages were left on his answering machine. "In a situation like this, you find out who your friends are," said Clark. And he found out how many he indeed had.

The conversation between Fletcher and Clark on the telephone was described as uneasy. Fletcher was almost as uncomfortable breaking the news to Clark as the captain was receiving it. Clark tried hard to put on his bravest front yesterday morning, to say nothing was wrong. But the hurt was evident.

He didn't want this to happen. He wanted to be the Maple Leafs' captain for life. "People can say there were ups and downs (for me in Toronto)," said Clark, "but I don't think there have been any downs."

On Monday, he will fly to Quebec and try to put on a happy face during a news conference there. Because he is Wendel Clark, he will say all the right things. He will say hockey is hockey, a city is a city, he'll learn French by osmosis, and that a contract is a contract. But quietly he'll be left to wonder.

What if he hadn't scored 46 goals last season? What if the Leafs had gone one more round in the playoffs? What if he had scored less against San Jose, more against Vancouver?

A trade isn't only about changing teams. It's about changing your life. Wendel Clark came to Toronto in the worst of times, in 1985, and made this city his home. He grew comfortable with us and we with him. In him we saw something we've seen in far too few professional athletes. He was never the greatest player, just the one we talked the most about. He became, over time, the rarest of sporting bodies: He became a Toronto icon.

"I don't think I'm a Toronto icon," said Clark. "Popularity came not because of who I am, but the team I played for. Toronto is Canada's team."

He stayed around answering questions for as long as there were questions to answer. And when it ended, Wendel Clark stood and looked around, almost lost. His eyes were glazed and his face was red and he was hoping for another question, another autograph request, something — hoping to find another reason not to say goodbye.

David Frost Not Guilty —
and Certainly Not Innocent

November 29, 2008

NAPANEE, ONTARIO — Just after the verdict was read, the sister of one of the star witnesses burst into tears, looked over to David Frost and called him a "scumball."

In his first words after being found not guilty on four counts of sexual exploitation, Frost turned his head slightly to the crying woman and said: "Go f— yourself."

There was anger and there was emotion in an Ontario courtroom yesterday as the not guilty verdict was announced by Justice Geoffrey Griffin in the murky case against the former coach and player agent.

With tears in her eyes, Sue Jefferson, mother of the jailed Mike Danton, bolted down the stairs and disappeared into the parking lot immediately after the case concluded. She needed to be alone. The mother of Jennifer Hicks, the most explicit defence witness in the case, just looked angry on her way out. Steve Jefferson, Sue's husband and Danton's estranged father, stood in the parking lot afterwards, as if wanting to pick a fight, but had nobody to fight with.

"The Crown let us down," said Jefferson. "I can't f—ing believe this. I guess what this proves is that money can buy you a ticket out of jail. This is a disgrace. The Crown was pathetic. They screwed it up. I don't know how the judge can sleep at night."

Frost was found not guilty on all four charges. But does that mean he's innocent? That is where the hair-splitting of this case comes into play. In making his ruling, Justice Griffin determined he had credibility issues with the four main witnesses in the case — the two girls (now women) testifying for the Crown; their former boyfriends (now 28-year-old men) listed as victims but testifying instead for the defence.

Griffin found holes in all of their testimonies, accusing the girls' evidence of being tainted by collusion, maintaining the boys would go to any lengths to protect their former coach but, in the end, he concluded that even if both sides were stretching the truth, the Crown did not fulfil its burden of proof. With the inconsistencies in so much of the testimony and the contradictions of previous police reports, Griffin said he had no choice but to find Frost not guilty.

In that, Frost benefitted from a case poorly executed by the prosecution. If anything, the Crown attorney's office should look into how it mishandled this case from day one, treating it as though it was a hot potato, passing it from prosecutor to prosecutor, with the inevitable conclusion coming yesterday. This was a legal mismatch of sorts: Defence attorney Marie Henein basically obliterated Crown attorney Sandy Tse.

And that, too, was evident in the judge's ruling. He called out the Crown for not making the case as complete as it could have been. He wondered why Frost's infamous control was never properly illustrated in court. Where were the parents of the hockey players? Why weren't they on the witness stand, especially the parents of one victim who were held over by the judge himself?

He asked more questions. Why were no coaches called to the stand? Why no expert witnesses? Where were the sports psychologists? Why no telephone records and cellphone records to illustrate how often Frost communicated with his boys?

All of those questions were legitimate. None of them were asked or answered before yesterday. Tse had no comment following the verdict.

From the beginning, Frost maintained the truth would come out, but yesterday, other than charming court with his first words in weeks, he said nothing as the trial ended, rushing into an SUV in the parking lot without uttering anything. He never did take the stand on his own behalf. The truth, after so many contradictory witnesses, remains open to interpretation.

Frost may have been "loud, vulgar, offensive, very aggressive, abusive and intimidating," said Justice Griffin. "But I am not prepared to conclude the level of control was as extreme and pervasive as the Crown would have me believe."

Griffin went on to say this case had nothing to do with the Danton murder-for-hire story, even though he brought that fact up at the beginning and near the end of his more-than-two-hour verdict and review of evidence. Griffin said this case "exposed a dark and very unhealthy side of hockey ... It's extremely offensive and must be denounced."

The case was essentially about group sex involving teenaged hockey players, their girlfriends and Frost, who was then a 29-year-old coach. The two women both testified in vivid detail about being involved with threesomes with their boyfriends and Frost. Exactly what they had to gain by making up stories — if they did — is anyone's guess. These girls had far more to lose than gain in this case but Griffin didn't see it that way. One witness, Kristy Boyer, was terribly uncomfortable yet remarkably graphic in her descriptions of the two threesomes she allegedly took part in with Frost, but Griffin somehow found reasonable doubt in her words.

"He called the girls liars," said Steve Jefferson. "The girls weren't lying ... The girls had nothing to gain by being here. The whole thing makes me sick."

While Judge Griffin maintained the Crown didn't succinctly demonstrate Frost's level of control over his players, he read out the dictionary definition of a cult.

But he did not seem to accept the possibility that contradictory police statements made by one of the female witnesses and some of her actions over the years were instituted while she was "inside" Frost's world and that she later changed her story when she was not.

And again, he seemed to contradict himself, saying: "They (male witnesses for the defence) did not come away as brainwashed followers of Mr. Frost."

He said that just seconds after saying their loyalty to Frost rendered their testimony as questionable. But they didn't have to prove their case. The Crown did — or in this case didn't.

Sheldon Keefe
Haunted No More

June 23, 2015

He doesn't run from his past anymore. Sheldon Keefe is well aware of the dirt he left behind, the arrogance, the skirting of the law and his past association with the hockey pariah David Frost.

The key word, in his mind, is "past."

He says he doesn't associate with Frost anymore. He says he hasn't associated with him in years. The new coach of the Toronto Marlies said he needed a clean break while coaching in Pembroke to learn about himself, to begin a new career as a coach, to become an adult and have his true character come out.

He was an audacious misfit as a junior player, rude and skilled. He was a wasted talent as a pro. His general manager in Tampa, Jay Feaster, said Keefe's career was lost because of the influence Frost had over him and his inability to act or think for himself.

"I hold myself accountable for that," said Keefe in a lengthy interview on the fifth floor of the Maple Leafs offices on Bay St.

"I had an opportunity to play there and I didn't take advantage of it. Had I performed better, I would have given myself an opportunity despite everything else. There's no question I was significantly hampered by the Frost influence and all his interactions."

When he looks back at his time when he was being coached, controlled, represented by Frost, what does he think?

"You could say embarrassed," said Keefe. "Regret. It's tough to think about that. I'm not proud of it. I don't think about it very often anymore. I just focus on what I'm doing.

"Until I went to Pembroke (to coach), I hadn't started living my own life. I was 26. It's when I started to feel a lot of pride in what I was doing, who I was, what was happening."

Thinking for himself. Acting for himself.

"My true self came out. My true character."

He started looking forward, stopped looking over his shoulder. Part of him could always look ahead. But his name kept him in the news for all the wrong reasons.

Frost went to court on wild and explicit charges of sexual exploitation. Mike Danton (née Jefferson), his closest hockey friend growing up, went to court and then to prison for trying to arrange Frost's murder. Keefe was among the people Danton contacted regularly in prison and, by proxy, so was Frost.

"I talked to (Mike), I visited him (in prison), no doubt we had a long history," said Keefe. "But even prior to his arrest, (our friendship) had become less and less. We saw each other very little, especially in the hockey season. It was such a confusing time.

"I had no idea what was happening (with him) or where things were going. Trying to be supportive and everything and trying to come to terms with it all, over time, it was exhausting. Mike became bitter. I was trying to live my life and was growing up a lot, becoming more independent. I needed to separate myself from him."

Before that, he almost came to a complete separation from his family, not dissimilar to how Danton became estranged from his own home. This is where the story gets troublesome.

In my book *The Lost Dream*, I detail younger brother Tom Jefferson's recollections of the abuse he endured when he was 13 years old and spending some time at Frost's cottage. Keefe was party to that. Photos were taken from that period. Tom Jefferson was absolutely clear in describing what he believed happened to him.

Years later, when Keefe wasn't home, his mother found the photographs. Steve Jefferson, Tom's father, believes the photos had been hidden. Keefe said if he was going to hide something, the last place he would do so would be to hide them in his home.

"I had photos," said Keefe. "I didn't hide photos.

"I had them at home for years. I believe the context around the photos has been misrepresented. And it was difficult to get my parents to understand what they saw. No question, it created a definitive rift in my family. They didn't believe in me and they had no reason to believe in me at the time."

So what would Sheldon Keefe say now if he had a chance to talk to Tom Jefferson?

For a second or two, he is silent. He is accompanied by Leafs media relations chief Steve Keogh. It is rare for a PR person to sit in on any Leafs interview. But clearly, this is complicated.

"That's tough," Keefe finally says of talking to Tom. "That's really tough. I would try and get a better understanding of what he was thinking, understand him a little bit better. Obviously, I'm only aware of the things I was there for. And the things I was there for didn't happen the way he describes them. So it's difficult for me to understand everything.

"Everything that happened with that family (Jefferson) is traumatic. But again, a lot of the stuff that I've read and heard (from the cottage) — that's not how I recall them."

Along the way, lives were damaged. Danton went to prison; Frost probably should have gone to prison; Tom Jefferson has struggled; the rest of the Jefferson family has struggled; and now here is Keefe, junior hockey coach of the year in Canada, elevated now to the position of American Hockey League coach, a highway drive away from the National Hockey League.

He is on the fast track, the one success hockey story left from the Frost years. But because of his problems in the Ontario Hockey League and at the Memorial Cup as a player, he wasn't exactly welcomed into junior hockey. The one job offer he had came from a bold Kyle Dubas in Sault Ste. Marie. And the one job offer he had to turn professional came also from Dubas, now in the front office of the Maple Leafs.

Before this year, there was no lineup of any kind to hire Keefe. He is forever indebted to Dubas for the faith he had in him and for the opportunity that is now before him.

"I'm incredibly proud and grateful that people have believed in me enough to give me this opportunity," said Keefe. "I went through this in a different way as a player. You finish your junior career and you're playing in the NHL at 20 and you think this is what's supposed to happen.

"But I've had moments in the last couple of weeks where I stop and think, 'I'm working for the Toronto Maple Leafs. The Toronto Maple Leafs.' I feel I belong here. I've been given a great opportunity and I look forward to taking advantage of it."

The coach who influenced him the most wasn't Frost. It was John Tortorella in Tampa.

"When I was playing there, things weren't good. It was bottom of the league, it was a country club, and John came in and changed the culture. He lost some

people along the way, upset some people, but when they won the Stanley Cup —
and I wasn't a part of it — I thought 'That makes sense.'

"The good, biggest thing I took away from him was to respect the game. And
for a long time, I was a guy who had no respect for the game.

"In hockey, I always worried about me. If something didn't go the way I
wanted it to, it was somebody else's fault. You need to learn to respect the process
in this game, and I didn't respect the process."

He now looks forward to training camp, to getting to know Mike Babcock
better, to coaching and learning: The better he develops players, the more there
will be for him. This is his new hockey family. His real family is together again
but hasn't always been.

Keefe admits he has a fine relationship with his brother, Adam, a pro hockey
player in the U.K., who maintains a relationship and has been business partners
with both Frost and Danton. He says that isn't tricky anymore.

"I've learned to separate the two," he said. "We don't see each other much, but
we're very close. I don't talk to him about (Frost or Danton)."

He doesn't mention either anymore if he isn't asked about them.

But he no longer hides from the questions he once wouldn't answer.

All Gilmour Wanted Was One Last Chance

September 9, 2003

This wasn't what he really wanted, no matter what he was saying and selling to a crowded room, no matter how hard he tried.

Doug Gilmour wasn't ready to retire — not here, not now, certainly not yet.

He wanted to find out if there was still something left. If his wounded left knee could heal.

He wanted one more chance to do what he had done his entire hockey life — prove people wrong.

Only John Ferguson, the new Maple Leafs general manager, wanted nothing to do with the past and, in looking to the future, snubbed a local icon.

He didn't just casually say the Leafs had no plans for Gilmour, who wanted only one more season and only in Toronto. But Ferguson, in this case, went further.

He ordered the ice time Gilmour had booked at the Maple Leafs practice facility cancelled while the team was heading off to Sweden for training camp.

The words of disdain from Ferguson's introductory news conference were the equivalent of a slap to the face to Gilmour.

The cancellation of the ice time — the new GM already displaying a smallness of character — turned out to be the career knockout punch.

"You know what? All I wanted to do was skate," Gilmour said after his retirement announcement yesterday. "I hadn't been on the ice and I just wanted to get on and skate a bit. I had some other ice booked too, in North York. But when he said what he said, and he did what he did, it was like sending me a message.

"And I'm thinking 'Forget it. What are you doing this for?'

"To be honest, I don't know if I could have come back. But I wanted to find out. I just wanted to know. Then (after what Ferguson did) it was like enough's enough. If that's what they think of me, fine. I don't need this. It's time to move on."

And so it was for the greatest player ever to play for the Maple Leafs, albeit for only a two-and-a-half-year stretch. He played parts of six seasons in all as a Leaf, although it seems like it was so much longer than that.

It's just that those two seasons a decade ago were nothing like we had seen in Toronto, before or since. He owned this town the way no other professional athlete ever has. It was his team, his game, his city.

And when you're 36 years without a championship, you hold more preciously to the special moments: the Lanny McDonald goal, the Nikolai Borschevsky goal, Gary Roberts at playoff time, the Gilmour years.

Doug Gilmour came to symbolize hope and heart and everything we seem to love about hockey. Even when he came back last spring, never has so much been said, and so much written, about a 39-year-old near the end, about what amounted to 4 minutes and 28 seconds of hockey. The last shifts he played as a Leaf, his last as an NHL player.

At least Ken Dryden, in his new position with the Maple Leafs, had the good graces to show up for the retirement announcement yesterday. It might have been nicer had he stuck around until afterwards to shake Gilmour's hand and wish him well. But at least he was there, and not to make a speech. Yesterday, that was Tie Domi's job with a new hat, transforming from tough guy to best friend and master of ceremonies.

"I wish," Gilmour said, "it would have been different. I can't say I was too happy with (what Ferguson said about me). But he's the new guy coming in and it's his hockey club. I was disappointed."

This could have been easy for the Leafs, something they're apparently good at. They could have done nothing here but wait. They could have let Gilmour rehab his knee and find out by November or December if there was anything left, and then they could have made a decision.

It would have been cheap — another thing they like — a half season's salary. That's all. Just to see if he could do what he always has, make those around him taller and stronger and smarter.

Dave Andreychuk, Hakan Loob and Joe Mullen all scored 50 goals once in their careers — all playing on Gilmour's line. None of them ever came close again. That's what Gilmour did. He elevated those around him. Even at 40, there was a group of Leafs — a bunch who went out to lunch yesterday afternoon at a posh harbourfront establishment — who weren't ready to believe this was the end.

Who wanted one more season from Gilmour with the Leafs.

"I knew," Gilmour said, fibbing only slightly, "it was time ... I never wanted a free ride ... I just wanted one more chance."

The Great Fall
of Alan Eagleson

January 6, 1998

He used to burst into a room, full of noise and bravado, shaking every hand in sight, and always as the centre of attention.

Alan Eagleson had this distinctive way about him — engaging, arrogant, loud, rude, funny, supremely confident.

And now another term: Alan Eagleson, criminal.

Today, after almost a decade of allegations and accusations, he sadly will walk into a Boston courtroom, leaving all the bravado behind, to plea bargain what is left of his life and of his reputation.

The fall hasn't been sudden. It has been dramatic. The Eagleson who will be back in court tomorrow in Ontario looks and sounds so different from the raging force we used to know — more tired, more vulnerable, quieter. This is a Richard Nixon kind of ending, a movie to be made of pathos and greed and misunderstanding. Eagleson was a figure so strong, so bright, so dynamic, so twisted, so full of himself, so fiercely Canadian and yet so unlike most Canadians, defeated first by his own ambitions and later by the law. There can be no apologizing for what Eagleson has done, just as there can be no playing down the contributions he has made to hockey.

That is the difficulty of the story and of his life. There is good and there is bad all over his résumé. There is then and there is now. And along the way, there have been many victims and many who have benefitted. No matter how you choose to total up your personal scorecard of him, there is an Eagleson story to tell and a side to take.

Only the law doesn't make those kinds of distinctions. The law is supposed to be clear. And Alan Eagleson apparently broke the law. Many laws.

He got caught up in his own importance, the way so many others of similar nature have been caught up in theirs. He was, in the end, defeated by his own arrogance, so smart, so confident, so sure of himself, there was nothing he couldn't get away with. Too many of the players who now bad-mouth him gave him the keys to their operation and asked him to turn out the lights when he was ready to leave. They asked no questions. He answered to none of them.

And even when the first verbal charges were made against him, in the late 1980s, before the legal authorities entered this nasty game, he would react incredulously, he would invite you into his office, he would welcome you. "You want to see the files, I'll show you the files," he would say.

His critics were wrong, never him. They were crooked, not him. They were out to get him. It was all loud, all forceful, all somewhat believable.

And then came the charges, first from U.S. authorities, then from Canadian. Even then, Eagleson would be apt to say: "I'd love to talk to you, but I can't. You know me. I want to clear this up. But my lawyers won't let me say anything."

He said much the same in a brief conversation with the *Toronto Sun*'s Dave Fuller on Sunday. "I can't talk," he told Fuller. "You know I would if I could."

But how does he answer now? How does he answer to the bevy of charges against him and of the lawsuits that are pending and those that are to come? After today, when he pleads guilty in Boston and then follows with a guilty plea in Toronto, there is much that awaits Eagleson.

The long battle with the law, the one Eagleson seemed willing to stretch into as many rounds as this fight could go, may come to some form of conclusion today and tomorrow. But that won't end his legal difficulties.

There are civil suits outstanding, and some to come. When Eagleson leaves his downtown condominium and his Rosedale lifestyle and his time at the tennis club behind, he will find the Mimico Correctional Centre a far cry from the accommodations to which he has grown accustomed.

Life didn't deal him this hand. Alan Eagleson always played with a stacked deck. He held the cards, he dealt them, he played the hands himself and too often he decided who won and who lost.

And then he ran out of cards and time, and the game, for him, came to an end.

On January 6, 1998, the day Alan Eagleson pleaded guilty, former NHL player Brad Park challenged the Hockey Hall of Fame to remove Eagleson from the Hall. In all, 18 former players, including Bobby Orr, Gordie Howe, Jean Beliveau and Ted Lindsay threatened to resign from the Hall if Eagleson was allowed to remain. Rather than be forced out, Eagleson resigned as a Hall member in April 1988.

In Appreciation
of Mats Sundin

July 1, 2008

If this is the end for Mats Sundin as a Maple Leaf, after all the angst, the hand-wringing and the wide variety of analysis, then this is a Canada Day unworthy of celebration.

Sundin has meant that much to the many Leafs teams he has played on, at least one of which should have competed for the Stanley Cup. The past three that weren't even able to compete at all.

He has, through the good years and the bad ones, always performed. No matter what the circumstances. No matter who the coaches were. No matter which dubious linemates came and went.

For 13 seasons — ironic, don't you think? — he always was there. Twelve times leading the club in scoring. Eleven times leading the Leafs in goals.

Nobody has ever done that before in Toronto. Nobody ever will do that again.

Guy Lafleur only led the Montreal Canadiens in scoring eight times. Phil Esposito only led the Boston Bruins in scoring six times. The incomparable Gordie Howe dwarfs them all: He led the Detroit Red Wings in scoring 18 times.

And in the seasons in which he wasn't first in scoring, Sundin was twice second on the Leafs in goals, and only once second behind Alexander Mogilny for points.

This may not feel good today, assuming that Sundin won't return to the Leafs, assuming he eventually will make a decision about whether to return elsewhere for another season. There will be anger. And if he goes somewhere else, there should be anger. But even then, if you take a step back, and you do the math on the greatest trade Cliff Fletcher has ever made, the numbers and the accomplishments indeed are astonishing.

Sundin was a straight line. He rarely wavered. He never took a year off. He had only two kinds of seasons: good ones and great ones. He didn't just lead the Leafs in scoring in all but one of his 13 seasons in Toronto. He lapped the field.

On average, he scored 18 points more than the team's second-leading scorer in the 12 seasons he came out on top. In various years, players such as Mike Johnson, Darcy Tucker, Steve Thomas, Bryan McCabe finished second to him in Leafs points.

He was that far ahead, that much more dominant. He was Mr. Automatic.

Some never liked him because of his passport. Some didn't like him because he seemed satisfied when there wasn't always reason to be. Some didn't like him because he never once had a giant playoffs.

But you don't last this long as team captain, as leading scorer, as highest-paid player, without playing the part of lightning rod. There is no one opinion of Sundin that sticks or is widely accepted. And as this past season unfolded, the more complicated his place in Toronto became.

He was captain of the team and captain of those who wouldn't waive their no-trade arrangements. Some interpreted that as selfless, others as selfish. There never was consensus with much of anything that involved Sundin. And for a man who wanted to avoid controversy, somehow it always seemed to find him.

Being traded for the wildly popular Wendel Clark made it difficult from the start. Over the years, Sundin eclipsed everything about Clark as a player except his popularity. Then this past season, as the Leafs began to bottom out and the damage general manager John Ferguson had done was apparent, Sundin found himself in a most uncomfortable circumstance.

Fletcher, who once traded for him, now wanted to trade him away. It would have been in the best interest of the Leafs' future for Sundin to go. Sundin chose the opposite, and now, should he sign elsewhere, instead of reaping a scoring winger and three draft picks for his services, the Leafs will get nothing for him.

They couldn't keep him, couldn't trade him, and in free agency, can't replace him.

Typically, Sundin is saying nothing of his own situation, just as he never talked publicly about the coaches he detested playing for, about the linemates he was supplied with, about his dislike of certain Leafs owners.

The clock will strike 12 this afternoon, and an auction on his services will begin. Whether he chooses to participate remains, like so much about Sundin, a mystery.

Tie Domi: "I Feel Like I Let So Many People Down"

May 6, 2001

Tie Domi has watched the replay over and over, each time more uncomfortably than the last, and what he still can't comprehend is the why.

Why he did what he did.

Why he ended what should have been the greatest hockey night of his life injuring a player and his own reputation in the process.

What happened in that sudden moment that caused him to lose his way?

"It's not me," he said in a one-on-one interview from New Jersey. "But it was me because I did it. I can't walk away from that fact. I did it.

"I don't understand it. What am I going to say?"

If you know Tie Domi, you know he has always spoken about the code of the tough guy in professional hockey, about what's acceptable and what isn't, about what he would and wouldn't do as a player. The code his career has been based upon.

The very code he somehow violated on a noisy Toronto Thursday night. "Words can't describe what I'm feeling right now," Domi said from his Meadowlands hotel room. "I'm just trying to make sense of everything. I keep thinking back, 'What happened?' and I'm thinking that the building was so loud, the emotions were so high. There's so much going through you at that moment.

"All I know is every time I've gone to hit him (Scott Niedermayer), he had his stick up high. I guess I just anticipated that. I don't know. I don't know why. It was a reaction to what I thought he was going to do.

"What can I say? I'm sorry? I'm sorry for all of this happening. I feel like I let so many people down. I let myself down. I let my team down. I let my fans down."

There has always been a certain double standard in the job description of NHL enforcer. Be tough, but not too tough. Be mean, but not too mean. Be dirty, but not too dirty. Gordie Howe's elbows were the stuff of legends. Tie Domi will never be granted the same kind of latitude.

Tough guys — forever skating a fine line between the accepted, the expected and the unacceptable.

Marty McSorley crossed that line a year ago, costing him what was left of his NHL career, ending up banished from big-time hockey and dragged unnecessarily through a court of law. Domi, too, has crossed the line before. This just happens to be the worst, if not most public, of his crimes and misdemeanors.

"It's funny," said the image-conscious Domi. "I try to be a role model. That's really important to me. I guess I slipped. Nobody is out there in the community getting more involved than me. This is my team and my home. I always try and be a good person. I always try and conduct myself a certain way. For this to happen, for me to do this ... I wish I could understand what happened, I wish I could."

There is, and always has been, some confusion about what constitutes a suspension in the NHL. The fans feel it. Journalists try to explain it. Players often live incident to incident, not certain about which way the penalty winds are blowing.

Mike Keenan, the veteran NHL coach, watched the Domi elbow on television that sent Niedermayer to a stretcher and concluded that a one-game suspension was appropriate. Others in the know estimated that Domi would receive anywhere from 5 to 10 games.

The NHL was far more severe than that, given the fact there was a potential of 16 more playoff games to be played at the time of the sentence.

Three playoff and eight regular-season games, should the Leafs be eliminated by New Jersey, does in no way equal two playoff rounds lost, should Toronto advance.

"I don't know what's right," said Domi, looking at precedent. "Look at what (Claude) Lemieux did to (Kris) Draper. That's two games. Look what I got. To me, that's worse than what I did. Look at what happened with (Chris) Chelios and (Luc) Robitaille. He clubs him with his stick. He gets a $1,000 fine. I don't know ... I don't know what's right."

He does know he will appeal after he sits for the mandatory three games. Oddly, he will be represented by his agent, Don Meehan, in whatever process he goes through. Meehan is also the player-agent for Niedermayer.

"The thing is," said Domi, "It's been a hard time. Everyone has been so supportive. My teammates, my friends. I just want to tell everyone I'm sorry."

Wrong GM, Wrong Time

November 29, 2007

Richard Peddie was right with what he said, wrong with how he chose to say it.

And now that he has admitted it was a mistake to hire John Ferguson as general manager of the Maple Leafs, the least he could do is correct his own error.

In a backstabbing way, Peddie has almost transformed Ferguson into a sympathetic figure. Imagine being Ferguson, and waking up Tuesday morning, seeing the front page of the newspaper and having your boss admit in large print that your hiring was a mistake.

Imagine what that must have felt like. Coming from the person who hired you, who essentially protected you when others wanted you gone, who promised you a contract extension, then pulled it from you.

First, Peddie nixed the extension (which was premature in offering). Now, he has to find a way to remove the verbal knife he has placed in Ferguson's back.

In trying to maintain his own dignity, his public persona and his sense of bravado, Ferguson maintains he has done nothing wrong, and that external forces — problematic Maple Leafs Sports and Entertainment Ltd. board members with all kinds of agendas — have prevented him from being successful with the Leafs.

A few facts that need to be examined, considering the amount of Leafs misinformation out there:

1) The difference of opinion between Peddie and Larry Tanenbaum on Ferguson's employment has been apparent for more than a year now. But that has not affected any trade, signing, draft choice or front-office or coach hiring in that time period.

2) Only once in Ferguson's time as GM has any member of the board interfered with his hockey decisions. That came in the post-lockout summer of 2005 when he was basically forced to re-sign Tie Domi. A year later, he bought out the final year on Domi's contract. The move didn't affect the progress of the Leafs positively or negatively although, for a key late-season game in Montreal during

the 2005-06 season, Ferguson insisted Domi be sat out in favour of Alexander Suglobov.

3) This Leafs team, with 8 wins in 25 games, is Ferguson's team. These are his players, his free agent signings, his trades, his contracts signed. Others, as he says, may have agendas, but he made all the hockey decisions.

So how did it all go so wrong for Ferguson? There are a few basic failings.

This is his third season post-lockout and his third different starting goaltender. First, he overpaid for an injured Ed Belfour, whom he later had to buy out. Then he traded a top prospect, Tuukka Rask, for Andrew Raycroft, who he instantly signed to a long-term contract. This year, he traded away three draft picks to acquire Vesa Toskala, whom he made the same mistake with, signing him to a large long-term contract before he had played a game for the Leafs.

If goaltending has been a problem, so has Ferguson's salary cap management. In this area, he has demonstrated weakness in two different ways. One, by badly overpaying for players, which has hindered his ability to deepen the roster. And two, by surrounding himself with inexperienced front-office people, he all but strangled the club. Who could Ferguson turn to when he needed advice?

Before the salary cap, the Leafs could buy themselves out of trouble. Since the introduction of the cap, Ferguson has spent his way into all kinds of trouble.

With the highest-paid defence in the NHL, the Leafs have allowed the most goals against. The investment in Bryan McCabe, Pavel Kubina, Tomas Kaberle has not worked out as planned. Last year Kaberle was brilliant; this year he has played horribly. Last year, Kubina looked lost; this year he was playing better before he got injured. In neither of his post-contract seasons has McCabe — paid at superstar wages — looked anything other than a flawed NHL defenceman.

And in the free agency market, the cumulative three-year signings of Eric Lindros, Alex Khovanov, Jason Allison, Michael Peca, Kubina, Bates Battaglia, Andy Wozniewski, Jason Blake, Boyd Devereaux have produced what?

The board didn't sign those players. The board didn't trade away draft picks. The board didn't acquire Jeff O'Neill or Yanic Perreault.

John Ferguson, a mistake then, a mistake now, made those moves without interference. Now, he must be prevented from making any more.

A Rare Glimpse of the Big M, Frank Mahovlich

Feburary 10, 2021

Imagine being a kid from Northern Ontario who played hockey, lived hockey and idolized Rocket Richard, and you get called up as a teenager for your first NHL game. And there you are, at Maple Leaf Gardens, all set to face the iconic Montreal Canadiens.

This isn't a children's book. This was Frank Mahovlich's life.

"Howie Meeker was the coach and, before the game, he looked at me and said, 'You'll be checking Rocket Richard tonight,'" the great Mahovlich, now 83 years old, said in a rare and lengthy interview.

"I'm 19 at the time. I think Rocket was 38. I'd read so many books on him. The first time I'm on the ice, Meeker tells me, 'Don't let him get away, he's too dangerous.'

"I'm right beside Rocket at the red line. And everything I knew about him was, if he got the puck at the red line, we were finished. I panicked, of course. I was bigger than him. I wrapped both my arms around him and held on. He got a little frustrated. At one point, we were so close together his nose was touching mine.

"'Let go, kid,' Richard said. And I'm thinking, 'Rocket Richard just spoke to me. He spoke to me.'

"'Yes, Mr. Richard,' I said, and I let him go."

That was the first shift of Mahovlich's marvellous National Hockey League career, the first of 720 games he would play for the Leafs. He would go on to win four Stanley Cups in Toronto in the 1960s and two more in Montreal in the '70s, and when the Leafs traded him to Detroit, he was the Toronto franchise leader in goals scored (296) in his career and goals scored in a season (48).

It would be another 22 years before Rick Vaive, playing in a season with more games, would pass Mahovlich with 54 goals in a season.

The records didn't end when he left the Leafs. In Detroit, Mahovlich scored 49 goals for the Red Wings, tying Gordie Howe for the most in franchise history. And he remains the single-season playoff point-getter for the historic Habs to this day, with 27 in 1971.

The sometimes-forgotten Mahovlich left his mark everywhere he played.

THE MAGICAL YEAR for Leafs fans is 1967, the last Stanley Cup season. But the magical year for Mahovlich was 1968 — the year he was traded out of Toronto, the year he escaped from Punch Imlach.

Mahovlich calls his last four seasons with the Leafs "the worst four years of my life. I wouldn't want anyone to experience that. It was a waste of time."

Whatever happened between the late Imlach and Mahovlich has left significant scars on the Big M. Mahovlich doesn't hide his dislike of the legendary coach and general manager.

"He was great the first four years. And then, if you lost a game, if you did something wrong, he'd punish you. It just became ridiculous after a while," he said. "The last four years were a disaster, really. It was laborious for me.

"You have to realize the times we were living in. We were slaves, really. When I played in the NHL, if they said, 'Jump,' you said, 'How high?' We were getting a minimum wage, rookies were getting paid $7,000 a season. Today, a first-year player gets a million up front. In our days, we were like slaves.

"At one time, Chicago offered a million dollars to buy my contract," said Mahovlich. "Imagine that today? What would that be? A hundred million? I don't know. Leafs turned it down."

But everything for Mahovlich in Toronto came back to Imlach, including emotional challenges that forced him to miss some games.

"It was one man: Punch," said Mahovlich. "Nobody liked him after a while. No one said anything because nobody did in those days.

"I remember when I was a rookie, and (NHL president) Clarence Campbell came to speak to us about our pensions. In the meeting, I raised my hand to ask a question. I was only 19. I asked about the amount of money involved.

"He told me to sit down and shut up. He didn't answer. This is what you were dealing with at the time.

"You kept your mouth shut or you might get shipped out."

On March 3, 1968, Mahovlich was indeed shipped out. He was traded to Detroit, along with Pete Stemkowski, Garry Unger and the rights to Carl Brewer in exchange for Norm Ullman, Paul Henderson, Floyd Smith and Doug Barrie.

In his second season with the Red Wings, he played on a line with Howe and Alex Delvecchio, the best line he ever played on. It was Howe's only 100-point NHL season. Mahovlich scored 49 goals, second behind Bobby Hull that season.

"Playing with Gordie was something special. He was over 40 by then. Playing on that line is a great memory."

That season, ending in 1969, saw all three members of their line in the top 10 in a scoring race that included Phil Esposito, Hull, Stan Mikita, Yvan Cournoyer and Jean Beliveau.

That's some terrific company Mahovlich kept.

A LOT OF HIS FRIENDS are gone. So many in the past few years. George Armstrong. Eddie Shack. Bob Nevin. Red Kelly. Johnny Bower. So many from the Stanley Cup teams of the 1960s.

"I'm still close with Dickie Duff and I speak to Davey (Keon) every once in a while," said Mahovlich. "He'll call from Florida. Or I'll call him. It's been tough seeing so many go. These days, I keep to myself and my family. I don't go out much, maybe for a walk, especially not now."

He doesn't watch much hockey either, although he said he might watch on Wednesday night when the Leafs play the Canadiens in Montreal. He prefers football or basketball or a little golf on television. The last time Montreal and Toronto were one-two in the NHL standings was in 1961. The Leafs haven't played Montreal in the playoffs in 42 years.

Mahovlich played seven series against the Habs with Toronto, and won three, the final victory coming in 1967. He lost in the Stanley Cup Final to Montreal twice. In the two Stanley Cup wins over the Red Wings, the Leafs beat Montreal in the first round each time. And personally, for six seasons between 1961 and '66, Mahovlich was voted first- or second-team All-Star at left wing. In a league that had Bobby Hull, that was a remarkable acknowledgment.

Today, Mahovlich says he hasn't been to a Leafs game in Toronto in more than 20 years. He doesn't know when — or even if — he'll go next. He's just not engaged with the team the way Bower or others may have been.

"I got away from hockey and I never really went back," said Mahovlich. "I don't know why. I can't really identify with this game anymore.

"I did go to one game when I was in Ottawa (he was in the Senate for 14 years), it was (Auston) Matthews' first game. He scored four goals. That was beautiful. But I haven't met anybody from this team. And I haven't seen them since."

He is appreciative, though, that the alumni association sent him a Leafs winter jacket this season — a token of appreciation.

"It's come in really handy," said Mahovlich. "It's nice and warm when I'm going for walks."

IN THE FINAL GAME of the 1970 season, Mahovlich's Red Wings eliminated the Canadiens from qualifying for the playoffs. It was the first time in 22 years Montreal missed the post-season.

The following year, Mahovlich was traded to the Habs.

"First year I get there, we win the Stanley Cup and we weren't supposed to," said Mahovlich. "Ken Dryden came in, I think he played just six games for us in the season. It all worked out pretty well."

Well, not for everyone. Al MacNeil was the Habs coach. Henri Richard was a Montreal legend. In the playoffs, MacNeil benched Richard, who came back and wound up scoring the Cup-winning goal: The benching of Richard and the furor that followed cost MacNeil his job.

"I was really upset when they let him go," said Mahovlich. "Al MacNeil was the best coach I ever had. I had a great playoffs (he led the NHL in scoring) and it all got crazy when the Pocket Rocket got benched."

When it was happening, "I asked Henri, 'What are you doing?' He said, 'I lost my temper.'" Sam Pollock was the legendary general manager.

"He hired Scotty Bowman to replace Al. I asked Sam, 'Why did you let Al go?' Sam had an answer for everything, he was that smart. He told me he didn't let him go, all he did was shuffle the deck."

MacNeil was assigned to Halifax. Scotty Bowman was brought in to coach Montreal.

Two years later, in Mahovlich's second-to-last NHL season, the Canadiens again won the Cup and the Big M finished third in playoff scoring, one point behind Dennis Hull and two behind teammate Yvan Cournoyer. That would be his sixth and final Cup.

"It's not like Henri," he said, and laughed. "He's got 11. Yvan has 9, I think. But 6 ... 6 is pretty good."

Before one playoff game that year, Mahovlich went to the ticket window at the Forum to pick up his wife's seats for that night. And who was standing there, picking up his own tickets, but Rocket Richard.

"And it struck me that day, he was picking up tickets for a game I was playing in," said Mahovlich.

They shook hands and hugged by the will-call window, differently than they hugged the first time on the ice.

Hockey lives coming full circle.

Frank Mahovlich rarely gives interviews. But somehow he was willing to talk with me at length in 2021. The day after the story appeared in the Toronto Sun*, he phoned me to thank me for the piece and let me know how many friends he had heard from in the past 24 hours. He phoned again a few days later to reiterate his thanks.*

The Kid Named Jagr

May 19, 1992

PITTSBURGH — Every morning here, you can turn your radio dial to 102 FM and listen to the sounds of Jaromir Jagr, weatherman.

Actually, it's known as "Jaromir Weather," every day on WDVE-FM, the No. 1 rock station in the Pittsburgh area. "Today ... cold," Jagr says — the station has all the weather possibilities on tape.

Change stations and you might hear an advertisement for a local sporting goods store. "Hi, I'm Jaromir Jagr of the Pittsburgh Penguins ... "

Transpose the letters in his first name and you will better understand the hockey phenomenon that has exploded in this city of steel. Play the anagram game with the name Jaromir and the answer you wind up with is "Mario Jr."

"He will be the best player in hockey," said Mario Lemieux, the best player in hockey. This playoff season, there has been no one with a more exquisite sense of timing than Jagr.

His one-man overtime dance in Game 1 of the Wales Conference final meant the Penguins beat the Boston Bruins in a game they should have lost. "It was," Jagr said, "fun."

And then he giggled. He does that a lot. He giggles and he blushes, even though he relinquished his status as a teenager this winter. "He's a kid," said Rick Tocchet, who isn't. "It's like having someone's younger brother around. He's a good kid. Everybody likes him.

"We take him to the bar with us. We sit down for a drink. He goes straight to the video games. He knows how to play every one of those things."

Hockey, we are told, he is still learning about. He is still learning, even now as a trophy named for Conn Smythe is readying for his name. He is still learning, after scoring four game-winning goals. He has learned much this season, he says: to shoot more often, to carry identification when the team travels on the road, to be defensively responsible, to drive a car.

There is something else he has learned about: teenaged girls. "He attracts a completely different age group than the rest of us do," said a Penguins player. "Teenyboppers."

Jagr, with his long hair, his European ways, his broken English and almost naive smile, has taken over as the heartthrob of Pittsburgh's youth.

He has been dating Miss Pittsburgh. Word is, he has been dating all kinds of Miss Pittsburghs.

The Penguins are anything but concerned. What they see before their eyes is an ordinary teenager with extraordinary hockey talent, someone who is 20 going on 16. He is part boy, part man, part hockey terror. Or in the words of Tocchet, speaking about the past series with the New York Rangers: "He is Jay Wells and Mark Hardy's worst nightmare come true."

Jagr is also unaccustomed to being the star, and the responsibilities that go with the mantle of Stanley Cup hero. After scoring the winner in Game 1 against Boston, Jagr excused himself from the media horde expecting a blow-by-blow description of the goal. The reason? He had friends to meet.

The day after the snub, he patiently enjoyed centre stage, supplying predictable answers to predictable questions.

No, he doesn't feel any pressure with Lemieux and Joey Mullen missing from the Penguins offence. "I don't feel anything," he said. "I'm still young."

No, he doesn't feel like the second coming of Lemieux, anagram or not. "Mario is the best player in the world. He is like my teacher. If I don't know something, I watch him. I would like to be (the best). I'm not talented like him."

And no, Scotty Bowman is not Jagr's favourite man on the planet. "Bob Johnson is my No. 1 coach. He will be forever. He was more fun."

Jagr likes video games. Bowman likes mind games. But the coach made an interesting comparison when asked if he had ever seen a player like Jagr before, who so combined speed, size, strength and finesse.

The name Bowman mentioned was Frank Mahovlich. This confused Jagr. When asked if he knew who Mahovlich was, he merely shrugged his shoulders, smiled and said, "Nope."

Lou Out as Leafs GM

May 1, 2018

Lou Lamoriello won't come right out and say he's angry about being pushed aside as general manager of the Maple Leafs.

So I'll say it for him. He's angry, he's upset, he's frustrated and he doesn't understand or accept the logic Brendan Shanahan has applied in kicking him to a consultant's curb with the hockey club.

But he won't say a word about it. Not for public consumption. Not for a newspaper or a television camera. Not even to a close friend.

Because more than anything else in his life, he's consistent, he's frustrating, he's Lou.

That means he specializes in revealing nothing about anything, least of all himself. That means there are no leaks and no one around him has a voice in Lamoriello's world. That means even when he disagrees with a decision that's been made, he sticks to his principles and won't stop being a team player. That means what is said in the front office stays in the front office.

He didn't invent that old dressing room adage in pro sports, "What you see here, what you say here, when you leave here, let it stay here," but he could have.

Lamoriello is the ultimate company man, even if the company is kicking him upstairs, likely in Leafs style for very high wages and very little influence.

There is an old Don Matthews line that describes Lamoriello in many ways: "Football isn't a democracy," the late Matthews once told me. "This is a dictatorship and I'm the head dick."

Lamoriello was precisely that in his three years with the Leafs. But when your dictatorship is run as efficiently as the Leafs were run, sometimes more of an autocracy than dictatorship — Shanahan as president, with Mike Babcock as head coach, with excellent assistants in different roles such as Kyle Dubas, Mark Hunter and Brandon Pridham — there was a place for everyone and a role that fit each man's specific skills.

But only one man in charge.

It might have been Lamoriello yesterday. Today it is Shanahan, until he names Dubas GM, whenever that becomes official.

And the earth will shift ever so slightly, with Lamoriello moving out and Dubas likely moving in. He has been the chosen one since the Leafs hired him before Lamoriello ever came from New Jersey. Dubas came in with graphs and charts and computers and has developed nicely, I'm told, into a hockey man.

Shanahan has put together a terrific, varied front office, of which Lamoriello was the centrepiece. Even at the age of 75, he showed no signs of slowing down.

If the baton is passed to Dubas, there will be questions. We know he's young, we know he's bright, but what we don't know is, can he do the job? In sports, you don't find that out until it's decision time.

Once upon a time, a lawyer named John Ferguson was given the keys to the Leafs car. Only he couldn't see and he couldn't drive and no one knew that until he took the large office.

We know who Lamoriello is, what he can do, how he conducts himself.

Lamoriello came to Toronto three years ago from the New Jersey Devils with his reputation, like that hockey team, slightly in tatters. He was yesterday's news until he reinvented himself strictly by being himself. And the Leafs went from last place to playoff surprise to possible playoff contender. And who knows what's next? The deal Lamoriello signed in Toronto was for him to be GM for three years and after that to become the senior advisor of the franchise for the next four years.

That was the deal he agreed to.

So Lamoriello knew what might be coming, even as he went to work Monday morning figuring he was still GM of the Leafs and was going to continue in that role until someone told him differently.

In their meeting in the morning, Shanahan told him differently. They shook hands. They've known each other forever. They grew up in the NHL together. And now that maybe they're together, it's more likely that Lamoriello says goodbye.

However it ends, it doesn't mean it doesn't hurt. It doesn't mean it was easy for Shanahan to make the move or for Lamoriello to accept it.

In explaining the move, Shanahan paid tribute to Lamoriello. He called his contributions to the Leafs vital. He talked about building the cultural foundation with the Leafs and the mentorship he provided for the front office.

"I thought he was the perfect fit," said Shanahan.

Then he made the decision he originally projected three years ago: He took Lamoriello's title away.

And with it the famous Lou's Rules are likely to be pushed aside — some of them team-building, some of them archaic, all of them put in place because of his deep belief of establishing a unique culture and deep belief in organizational discipline.

In his time running the Leafs, Lamoriello did more than his job. He may not have been millennial-friendly or player-agent-friendly — some Leafs felt strangled by their surroundings and the lack of personality tolerated — but over three years he exceeded whatever the job description and the expectations may have been.

Lou Lamoriello has reason to be upset. He did his job well. He hasn't lost a step.

There was no need, Shanaplan aside, to replace him now.

Sickness Cured, Kessel Gone

July 2, 2015

The hot dog vendor who parks daily in downtown Toronto just lost his most reliable customer.

Almost every afternoon at 2:30 PM, often wearing a toque, Phil Kessel would wander down from his neighbourhood condominium to consume his daily snack.

And now he's gone. Just like that. The Maple Leafs could no longer stomach having Kessel around, the first player to be both punished and rewarded for the saddest Leafs season in history. The Leafs held their breath, plugged their noses, and ostensibly gave Kessel to the Pittsburgh Penguins because they couldn't stand having him around anymore.

Really, this was as much about illness and insomnia as anything else: The Leafs were sick and tired of Kessel.

Sick of his act. Tired of his lack of responsibility. Unwilling to begin any reset or rebuild with their highest-paid, most talented, least dedicated player. He didn't eat right, train right, play right. This had to happen for Brendan Shanahan to begin his rebuilding of the Leafs. Separation between the Leafs and Kessel became necessary when it grew more and more apparent with time that everything Shanahan values was upended by Kessel's singular, laissez-faire, flippant, mostly uncoachable ways.

It doesn't matter that the Leafs didn't get much for Kessel. It doesn't matter that the players they received for Kessel are probably named "if" and "but," and the draft picks won't translate into anything before 2019. None of that matters as Coach Mike Babcock begins his new era of hope in September.

What matters is that Kessel is gone. That who he is, what he represents, what he isn't, had to be removed from the ice, from the dressing room, from the road, from the restaurants — from everywhere. They couldn't have him around anymore and be honest about the direction they intend to pursue. Everything they believe in for the future is almost everything Kessel has proven to be lacking in.

A Leafs front-office voice recently spoke about the two largest influences on any player. One comes from the coach. The other comes from the player who sits beside you on the bench. Those are the voices you hear most often.

For Tyler Bozak and James van Riemsdyk, that voice belonged to Kessel.

If the voice is negative, critical, disruptive, condescending of players, critical of coaches, critical of fans, then that impacts more than just the player doing the talking. It poisons the environment. It brings players down. It cuts into their effectiveness. It establishes the kind of mood no team wants.

The right kind of leadership can make a team greater.

The wrong kind can destroy it.

The second-half Leafs were the most destroyed team in Toronto history. The flag carrier of despair was Kessel. He played like he didn't care, insulted the jersey, the paying public, the people watching at home, the interim coaching staff. He wasn't alone.

But he was the only one making $8 million a year. He was the only one truly entrusted to make an offensive difference. He was the only one who seemed to take people down with him.

When Dave Nonis was fired, when the Leafs scouting staff was fired, when the coaches were fired, it finally turned to the players. Kessel was the first to go. He won't be the last. But sending him packing first was necessary. The message was necessary. The tone was necessary. This won't be tolerated any longer.

Even if this is a Vince Carter–type of trade — the kind that may bring next to nothing in return. Carter quit on the Raptors. In a different kind of way, Kessel quit on the Leafs before they quit on him.

Kasperi Kapanen is a Leaf now. His stock has been dropping since Pittsburgh used a first-round pick to select him. Some people consider him a future third-liner, if he has a future in the NHL at all.

Scott Harrington is a Leaf now. He played four years for Mark Hunter's London Knights. When they couldn't come away with one of the Penguins' better defensive prospects, they settled on the competitive Harrington. He is an AHL skater, scouts tell me. Maybe he'll play in the NHL. Maybe not.

The best part of the deal is the lottery-protected first-round pick for next June's draft. It's nice to have that kind of pick going forward. But expect a choice between 20 and 30. That's a long shot. Maybe three years away. Maybe more.

And you have to figure Kessel is good to score 40 goals or more playing alongside either Sidney Crosby or Evgeni Malkin in Pittsburgh. And still, this is a deal the Leafs had to make. A deal that was necessary.

They had to move Kessel out. They had to have him off the roster by the time Babcock begins training camp in September. You can't have him half-assing skating drills with a team trying to learn how to work. You can't have him being first off the ice with a team pushing to reach Babcock's lofty goals. When you have an illness, you must get rid of the poison.

The Leafs did that on Wednesday. They treated their own infection — the Penguins playing the part of antibiotic. It doesn't matter what they got for Kessel. What matters is he's gone.

When this piece originally appeared, it created huge controversy. The lede, about a hot dog vendor, was inaccurately written with the wrong address. It has been corrected here. I stand by the facts of this piece — and maintain that no story written on Kessel's departure from Toronto better explains the circumstances than this one does.

What Makes Mike Babcock Tick?

April 23, 2018

On the night the World Cup of Hockey ended, Joel Quenneville and Claude Julien were walking out of the Air Canada Centre when one championship coach turned to the other and said: "I need a vacation."

"From hockey?" asked Julien, Stanley Cup winner.

"No," said Quenneville, four-time Cup winner. "From him."

They both laughed and then they didn't. They were talking about Mike Babcock, head coach of Team Canada's championship unit, whom they had assisted in the tournament. They loved their job and all that the tournament was. Getting used to Babcock, the 24/7 coach of the Maple Leafs? Now that was an experience.

It still is. Those who know Babcock best, those who have worked closely with him, describe him to the *Toronto Sun* as extraordinarily focused, relentless, detailed, driven, dogged, harsh, honest, too often singular, rarely social, but coaching, every day, often every minute of every day: To work with Babcock, to play for Babcock, those are expected to be just like Mike. All in.

"That's Mike," said Todd McLellan, the Edmonton Oilers head coach and Babcock's longtime assistant in Detroit. "He's always on. He expects you to be always on. That's the way he's wired."

Jimmy Devellano, the longtime hockey executive, talks about the three great coaches of his career while in management with Red Wings and the dynastic New York Islanders teams and includes Babcock among them.

"Scotty Bowman was different than Mike, and Al (Arbour) was different than Scotty," said Devellano. "I worked with all three. They're all different, very effective, very affected, very driven.

"Mike can be like a race car driver. He only knows one speed and he keeps his foot on the gas all the time. He's like that, so he expects everyone else to be like that. I don't think he cares whether the players like him or not. He cares about results. Scotty was a lot like that. He didn't care what you thought of him. Mike has some of that in him."

In Detroit, where Babcock made his National Hockey League reputation, he became known as a demanding, almost obsessive, coach, not only to his players but to the Red Wings front office. At times, it was thought he tried to coach, play and manage the team all at the same time. He was forever asking the front office for players, demanding change or trades.

"He can be very disrespectful of coaches, players, general managers," said an NHL executive. Red Wings general manager Ken Holland disagrees.

Sort of. He hired Babcock to coach the Wings, and the two worked together and became close friends in their 10 years in Detroit. He knows what Babcock is, how good he is at his job, how much of a pain in the butt he can be.

"He's a great coach," said Holland. "In life, experience is a good thing. We all get excited about youth. But in the coaching fraternity, experience is very, very valuable."

He went from Lethbridge to Moose Jaw to Spokane to the Memorial Cup to the world junior to the American Hockey League. He didn't get here by accident.

"And he is consistent. No matter what time you get up on a road trip, you're going to meet with him at seven in the morning and we'll go over the tape from the night before and talk about what our plan is for the next day. It's relentless, it's day after day after day, and he does it because he believes in it. He does it because he believes in routine, and that's how he lives his life."

Babcock has had an uneven playoff series against the Boston Bruins, just as his Maple Leafs have experienced.

Early in the series, the Leafs had two penalties for too many men on the ice. He missed an offside goal and struggled with matchups against Boston. Penalty killing has been an issue all series long. So Babcock almost stepped out of himself and tossed the lineup on Saturday night, altering his lines. He threw different looks at the Bruins. He wanted to take more advantage of the Leafs' depth with the return of the suspended centre Nazem Kadri. And his changes were anything but accidental, even if he rarely makes them.

"Mike doesn't make snap decisions," said Ken Hitchcock, who worked with Babcock at two Olympic Games. "I've never worked with a person who had the singular focus he has. He does nothing by accident.

"It's the same with players with Mike. He doesn't look at a player and say: 'This is who you are.' It's: 'This is where we're going to take you.' He never looks at where he is today, it's where he can be tomorrow. He puts a plan in focus to make his players better, to make his teams better.

"And the players know, hard as it can be sometimes, that he's there for them."

Even if they don't always care much for him or his ways.

Sometimes being a Babcock assistant can be challenging enough.

Minnesota Wild personnel director Blair MacKasey tells a story about coaching with Babcock. He assisted Babcock in a junior tournament years ago. During the game, while running the defence, MacKasey walked to Babcock on the bench and told him what he thought was going on in the game. Babcock apparently snapped.

"What the f— are you doing here?" Babcock shouted at MacKasey. "If I wanted your opinion I'd ask for it. Now get the f— back to your end of the bench and coach."

Hitchcock, who is strong-minded like Babcock, didn't have a similar experience with the Leafs coach when working together at the Olympics.

He considers him a close friend and admires the way in which he does his job.

"Mike is blue-collar, he comes from blue-collar roots and he's true to his roots," said Hitchcock, third all-time in wins among NHL coaches. "The thing people don't know about Mike is, he's one of the most sincere guys I've ever been around. When you see the way he was with (the late coach) Wayne Fleming and his family. If you're ever in trouble in our business as a coach or a friend of his, he's the first guy who comes to help. And he's not one of those guys who phones once and you don't hear from him again. He stays on the path to help you. He stays with it. That's a quality that comes from his upbringing, and he's sincere about it."

McLellan views Babcock as one of his best friends in hockey.

"The first thing about Mike is, he has ethics and morals and he sticks by them," said the Oilers coach. "Forget about hockey, but just in everyday life. His personal makeup is all about family. His professional makeup, he's relentless in his approach to the game. He doesn't leave any rocks unturned. He's on players when they need him to be on them and he backs off when he needs to back off.

"Over the years, we've become very close, our families got close. We lived in the same area in Detroit. Our wives did a lot of things together. We would drive together every day, 100 miles a day, twice a day. We spent so much time together. But you look at those coaches who came to the World Cup to work with him. They're all head coaches. They're all used to doing things their own way. But there can only be one boss. Not everybody is accepting of that.

"That's how Mike is. I always appreciated how he approached the game. I learned from him and I hope he learned some things from me. We've been apart 10 years now, and when we talk, we don't talk a lot about hockey. Both our boys are in college. Our girls are in school. We talk about that, what the wives are doing, what we'll be doing at the lake. The friendship doesn't change. It doesn't matter how often you see each other or talk to each other. The relationship is still there."

The hockey, though, is always there. Paul MacLean coached with Babcock in both Anaheim and Detroit. Together, they went to three Stanley Cup Finals, winning one.

"Mike comes in every day and tries to learn something new. He's nonstop that way," said MacLean. "He's thinking about the game all the time.

"I mean, all the time. He has the ability to win and you have to know this — winning isn't easy.

"But if you don't like working, you're not going to work for Mike Babcock. He tests you. He wants you to test him. He pushes you, he wants you to push him. You don't always get along, but you're working together."

Said Hitchcock: "I loved working with him. I loved the way he was once the puck was dropped. I was so impressed with the way he went about his business. He loves people who challenge him and he won't test you on your knowledge, he'll test you on your beliefs. He'll test you all the time. I loved that back-and-forth. It's coaching at its best."

The Man Who
Lost His Way

July 29, 2005

Somewhere in time, like far too many people of power, Bob Goodenow lost his way and compromised his own integrity.

Officially, he resigned his position as executive director of the National Hockey League Players' Association yesterday, just days after insisting he wasn't going anywhere. His resignation would have been welcomed and congratulated had the idea actually been his.

But just like the recently ratified collective bargaining agreement, this was not a deal of his doing: Unofficially, Goodenow was pushed aside in the name of hockey progress by the very same and small player group that once worshipped every word he spoke. He was pushed out and paid handsomely to get lost by his handpicked executive, becoming the first non-player to get bought out in the new agreement.

This is the apparent era of player-owner partnership in hockey, and if the truth be told, Goodenow would make a lousy partner. He is remarkably adept as leader of the opposition. But if you don't want a fight, if you don't want a nasty battle, if you don't want threats and strife and tension, Goodenow is not your man. Not now. Not anymore.

His time came and went before his contract came to a conclusion.

For years, Goodenow was the players' best friend. Salaries rose more than 550% in his 14 seasons in charge of the Players' Association. That's 39% a year for 14 years.

You can't question that kind of economic exuberance. It has been unparalleled in this professional sport or any other, considering the circumstances.

But Goodenow's success — to push limits, to push players, to push agents, to push owners, to forever push — was in the end his own and his members' undoing. He pushed the league to the brink of economic survival, and the players pushed him out.

Over time, Goodenow knew only one speed: full. But then he misread his own game, his own membership, the entire tenor of this miscalculated negotiation with the NHL, and for that this lost season was far more his doing than anyone else's.

His last gift to hockey was a season not played.

He was invited to negotiate more than two years prior to the expiration of the CBA and chose not to. He was invited to hire his own auditors to make sense of league economics and chose not to. His tactic of not negotiating — and then giving up a 24% rollback along with a salary cap and along with linkage to revenues and along with the confusing escrow arrangement — exhausted whatever credibility he may have had left with his own membership. And that was apparent even prior to the ratification of the recent collective bargaining agreement.

The fact Goodenow could hardly stomach the particulars of this deal and was still willing to stay on the job is indication of having squandered his ideals somewhere along the road. That, more than anything, is what new executive director Ted Saskin must step in and fix.

Goodenow was all about money and almost nothing else. The Players' Association, for too long, has been an organization without a soul. It dealt frivolously on issues of player safety (be it helmets or visors), encouraged union members to steal jobs from others while protecting their own and, maybe worse than all of that, never once at any time spoke out against the ludicrous certification of troubled player-agent David Frost.

Saskin has a grand opportunity now to mend fences, to bring divided players back together and work with the league to grow the game.

"The future is very bright for the sport and the people involved in it," said Goodenow, who wound up doing the right thing yesterday, but for all the wrong reasons.

The Dream
Slipping Away

March 8, 2007

Almost every day is the same. A two-hour workout in the gym. An hour on the ice. An hour with a therapist.

He has no job, no income, no insurance. He lives at home, outside Toronto, with his parents.

This is Steve Moore's reality, three years to the day after the cowardly attack by Todd Bertuzzi ended his brief National Hockey League career. Tonight is his uncomfortable anniversary.

"When the day comes, it really hits you," said Moore in a rare interview yesterday. "It kind of hits home, everything that happened to me.

"In some ways, the time has gone incredibly fast. It does not seem like three years. In other ways, it seems like a long time ago. It's a bit of both. It's an unusual feeling."

We can say Steve Moore's hockey career is over. He won't or can't say it. Every day is about getting back. Every day is about getting medical clearance.

He spent his whole life trying to be an NHL player. Now he spends his whole life trying to be one again.

"It's difficult," said the 28-year-old Moore. "I try and notice the progress I've made, not being all the way back. I've made a lot of progress.

"The intensity of the workouts has grown. But it's not a perfect science. I haven't been cleared to resume contact of any type."

He doesn't know when — or if — clearance will ever come. And even when he trains at a high level, there are still symptoms of his multiple injuries to endure.

By now, others would have given up. Others would have taken the paltry insurance settlement that an NHL rookie is entitled to for having his career stolen from him before it ever began.

Moore has never been much like others. Others don't graduate from Harvard. Others don't become 10-goal scorers in the American Hockey League but still visualize the future. Others don't come from a home where three brothers find a way to be educated and all play professional hockey.

"It's not an easy road now," said Moore. "I look at it as just one of the many obstacles I've faced. My whole life was devoted to being a hockey player. I dedicated myself to that. The injury took my dream away. That devotion keeps me going.

"To have your life ripped away in such a fashion, at such an early time, in your rookie year, it's something I don't want to accept. That's what's been pushing me. You're not going to let yourself get knocked out. It becomes a commitment. I still want to play.

"I try not to get discouraged. I try not to let (setbacks) get me worked up. It can be distracting. I try to focus on what I can control ... sometimes that's hard."

He has never spoken to Bertuzzi. Doesn't want to. Doesn't care to.

"To this day, Todd Bertuzzi never apologized to Steve and never attempted to," said Tim Danson, Moore's lawyer in a civil suit filed against the NHL player. "He made public apologies when he needed to be reinstated and times like that. But that was it."

"Given the facts," said Moore, "it's pretty clear he's not someone I'd want to deal with, someone I'm interested in hearing from."

The multimillion-dollar lawsuit, like most lawsuits, proceeds slowly. An attempt to have it settled out of court with NHL arbitrators went nowhere. To date, documents between lawyers from both sides have been exchanged, but no discovery or examination has taken place.

If and when this goes to court, not only will Bertuzzi go on trial, but so will the sport, the league, everyone. It has the potential to be that powerful and that damaging.

"When you're a hockey player, that's what you are," said Moore. "Every day, from the moment you wake up to the moment you go to bed, that's what you are. To lose what you are, that's very difficult. You lose yourself."

You lose just about everything.

"I live a frugal lifestyle" said Moore. "I'd saved some money from when I played but not a lot. I have no income. The only insurance would come to me in the event my career is totally ended, and because I didn't play very long, even that would be rather limited. You realize you're not taken care of.

"That's a sad situation."

Sad today will be watching the replays again, on all the sports television programs. Steve Moore won't look away. "There are times when you can't avoid it," he said. "Still, it's painful to watch."

Painful to live.

CHAPTER 3

Summer Love

Touch 'Em All, Joe

October 24, 1993

Joe Carter looked up and saw nothing but lights. And then Canada went crazy.

"I lost it," he said of his game-winning, World Series–winning dramatic ninth-inning home run that beat the Philadelphia Phillies late on a Toronto Saturday night. "As soon as I hit it, I looked up. It looked like it was in slow motion. Then I couldn't see it in the lights. I didn't know.

"I hadn't even touched first base when I heard the noise. I couldn't believe it. How could it be bigger? Seventh game maybe, but that's all. I told Duane Ward I was going to make the last out in the field. But when we were down a run, I changed it. I said, 'This inning, I'm the fourth man up. I'm going to try to be the hero.'"

The heroes of this crazed and comical and charged World Series were many: MVP Paul Molitor, Roberto Alomar and the fabulous, tragic hero, Lenny Dykstra. But the Carter blast was a home run for the ages, a Bill Mazeroski shot 33 years later, a highlight clip for the rest of our lives.

Where were you in '93? It may not rhyme, but it will enter the memorable moments of Canadian sport. This is a videotape to pack away, a newspaper worth bundling up and saving. The Blue Jays win again. Two in a row. It is right there with Paul Henderson scoring, with Gretzky to Lemieux, with Tony Gabriel's catch. In the scrapbook of our minds, a new entry.

And here are the details: The Wild Thing, Mitch Williams, delivered a slider on a 2-2 pitch. Down and in.

"I'm a low-ball hitter," said Carter. "It was my kind of pitch."

He learned to hit the slider his father used to throw in his backyard in Oklahoma City so many years ago. They had an apple tree and Carter had a plastic bat. His father could throw a mean breaking ball with the apples he picked from the trees.

That was before Carter played quarterback at Wichita State, before a college coach named Gene Stephenson invested time in his baseball skills, saw something in Carter that nobody else saw. He used to hit the apples until they disappeared into pieces; last night, when his home run ball went over the left-field fence, it too disappeared.

"I dreamt about this in the backyard," said Carter, and this has been his season of dreams. It was a midwinter's night dream that told Carter to reject the offer he had from the Kansas City Royals and sign again with the Blue Jays. And the winning hit last night, well, that was the stuff of dreams as well.

"It's a kid's dream, and I'm just a big kid," said Carter, soaked in champagne, after being carried from the SkyDome field. "This is what baseball is all about ... I still don't believe it has happened."

This was Joe Carter's dream, but it is a dream no more. It is his own piece of history, the Blue Jays' piece, his home run delivering a second straight championship. And here was Carter, whose strength has always been in his numbers. Others have made more money, more All-Star teams, been recognized, been lauded. But not now. All that will change.

It all began when Mitch Williams came in to start the ninth inning. The two hadn't faced each other in five seasons.

"He's not throwing as hard now," said Carter. "When I saw Mitch coming in (last night), we knew something good was going to happen."

Carter was the fourth batter. Rickey Henderson was on second base. Paul Molitor was on first. One out.

"You always want to be the hero," said Carter. "You always think about that. You always hope it's you."

And then it happens. And you try to capture the moment, but it is too frenetic, too wild.

"They haven't made the word up yet," said Carter when asked to describe how it felt.

In Atlanta last year, the picture of Carter was clear. Catching the ball at first base. Jumping.

"I was jumping last year, I was jumping this year," he said. "I thought last year would be remembered. This will be remembered."

His life will never again be the same. Forever he will tell the tale of the home run that won the World Series. His home run. His personal morsel of baseball history.

"You couldn't," Joe Carter said, "have asked for a better script."

Barry Bonds and the Meaningless Records

May 4, 2008

As the agonizing home run march of Barry Bonds moves towards its inevitability, the discomfort of baseball sadly plods on.

Whether we care what Bonds does, how he behaves, how he runs from the truth, how many home runs he hits has almost become irrelevant because of the stain that he and others have left on baseball.

We don't know what to think anymore of what we've seen with our own eyes. We don't know what to make of the numbers we've read. This is what happens when you've been duped by others who were doped.

Baseball has forever been about conversation and debate — era versus era, pitcher versus pitcher, hitter versus hitter, which numbers in a world so full of numbers mean more than any other?

This is all bigger and sadder than Barry Bonds. It isn't really about Babe Ruth. It isn't really about Hank Aaron. It isn't about records broken or fans confused.

It's about deception.

It's about a trust lost.

And so much of it is about establishing context.

The top six home run seasons in baseball history were orchestrated by Bonds, Sammy Sosa and Mark McGwire, all of whom have since been tainted in one way or another. The detail of Bonds' usage of performance-enhancing drugs has been meticulously reported in both book and newspaper form.

Sosa, not so far removed from being the sport's most beloved figure, is not active or retired. He is nowhere. He isn't playing and hasn't announced he won't anymore.

As people await word on Steve Yzerman's impending announcement, Sammy Sosa disappears and there is no need for any search party.

There was one offer for his services this season, from the Washington Nationals and without a guarantee of salary or playing time. It was so terrible an offer that even the disgraced Sosa, who pretended before the U.S. Congress that he couldn't converse in English well enough to be understood, refused to accept it.

Sosa deferred to his lawyer before Congress. McGwire should have considered a similar approach. Instead, he spoke, said nothing, answered no questions, showed no remorse, and played a part in shattering his own reputation as a big-league player all in one afternoon.

In fact, as Bonds creeps past Ruth and towards Aaron — and yes, "creeps" is the correct term — there is a need to take stock and try to comprehend what it all means. Among the top nine home run hitters in history, there are Bonds and Sosa and McGwire and Rafael Palmeiro.

Two proven steroid users. Two suspected steroid users.

Two players — Sosa and Palmeiro — who didn't quit and didn't play, odd footnotes at this most disagreeable time.

Bonds and McGwire, Sosa and Palmeiro are surrounded by Aaron and Ruth and Willie Mays and Frank Robinson and Harmon Killebrew. And a game in which records meant everything now finds the greatest of records eventually may mean nothing.

There is something almost perverse about the scene around Barry Bonds this season and this spring. He despises it, but he seems to feed off it. He wants no attention but has agreed to a reality show that is filmed around him. In the least team-like of all team sports, he is nothing more than individual, isolated from those he plays with, tolerated because the San Francisco Giants made a determination that he somehow matters.

Other athletes, weaker men, less stubborn men might disappear the way Palmeiro and Sosa have, though their diminishing skills played into their disappearances. Defiant and self-obsessed, Bonds never would give baseball the satisfaction of quietly disappearing.

If he is going to be afflicted, it's almost as though he wants baseball to suffer right along with him. Really, we should close our eyes, turn the page, hold our noses.

Barry Bonds shouldn't matter anymore, no matter where the numbers end up, no matter if he's taken down for perjury or tax evasion or steroid abuse. They will get him. What they can't do is make him disappear.

So Long, Pat Gillick
— and Thanks

November 28, 1995

Paul Beeston searched for all the right words, but in the end he pulled a Pat Gillick: He broke down and cried.

He was sitting at a table behind a microphone, trying to explain the unexplainable, and searching for the candor and composure that normally is his.

"Well, it's different," he began to answer the question, and then his face started to contort, the way all our faces do when we cry and don't want to be seen doing so. He rubbed his eyes, he bit his lip, he tried to speak again, he put his face in his hands and, for almost 20 seconds, Paul Beeston said nothing. For him, that is something of a personal record, but this was a very personal day.

For two decades, they were the brains behind the Toronto Blue Jays. Paul Beeston, the business guy. Pat Gillick, the baseball guy. Together they operated the finest franchise in professional sport. One was loud and friendly and always with a big cigar. The other was quiet and unpredictable and always emotional.

"All we can say, it has been 20 great years," Beeston was saying once the words returned.

He had been asked what is was like to be sitting on this Monday and making the least likely of announcements: That Pat Gillick was no longer a Toronto Blue Jay. That he was a Baltimore Oriole now. That he was, in essence, the enemy.

Beeston never believed this day would come, but then Paul Beeston's record of predictions of late hardly has been sterling. He said there wouldn't be a baseball strike. He said the World Series would never be cancelled. He maintained through all the talk of Gillick retiring as Blue Jays general manager that he wouldn't believe it until Pat walked out the door. And for the record, he liked Western in the Vanier Cup.

But that's another story.

When the call came from the Orioles just before the World Series, asking for permission to talk with Gillick, Beeston thought it was just another of the many calls he had received over the years. A lot of teams have called in the past decade asking about the availability of Gillick. There have been many conversations.

"I didn't think any more about this one at first than any of the others," said Beeston, the Jays president.

But one year after officially retiring as GM and moving into a part-time consultant's role, it still stings and it still shocks that the man who set the standard for operating a baseball franchise has left this city. At the SkyDome yesterday, there were long faces and many words spoken, but few that made much sense.

If he wanted a new challenge, there is no challenge greater than the messy Blue Jays. If he wanted to go back full-time, certainly the Jays would have found something for him. The subtext of Gillick's departure is that maybe the architect looked at his crumbled building and decided it was time to walk away.

It was that kind of day at the SkyDome.

Upstairs, on the 300 level, Paul Beeston and Gord Ash tried to assure one and all that the roof at the Dome wasn't about to fall in. And just an hour earlier, on the field level, in a room normally utilized by Blue Jays wives and children, the former Jays vice-president was announcing the firing of Bob O'Billovich as Argos general manager and coach.

There have been four O'Billovich news conferences in the past 11 months. At the first, Obie stepped down as coach. At the second, he hired Mike Faragalli to succeed him. At the third, he fired Faragalli. Yesterday was his turn.

Four news conferences in 11 months: The Argos won only four games in the last season of his second stint with the team. There will be better days. There have to be.

The best days of the Blue Jays, however, seem at least two years in the past. They have become the Cuba of sports organizations; there are defections almost daily. Gillick yesterday. Devon White last week. Robbie Alomar soon. The two-time world champions all over the map.

"I can assure everybody we're not (crumbling)," said Ash, now owner of the general manager's job without anyone looking over his shoulder. That is either a blessing or a curse. It depends on your perspective. "The ship is not sinking ... and we look forward to putting a club on the field that is heading in the right direction."

There is no need to replace Pat Gillick in the limited role he made for himself the past season. But there never really was a way to replace Gillick. Paul Beeston knows that better than anyone.

He didn't just lose an associate yesterday, he lost a friend, a family member, a legend.

"The one thing I learned from Gillick is not to worry about crying ... I'm sorry," Beeston said.

We all are.

What Happened to the Game I Love?

August 23, 2019

The game I grew up loving has disappeared behind so much physics and geometry — two subjects I never did well in — somehow replacing the romance and suspense I adored in Major League Baseball.

It's hard to completely understand how I came to love baseball so much, knowing what we know and see now, before there was ever a team in Toronto, when baseball was something I watched on a small black-and-white screen on a Saturday afternoon, eagerly awaiting the Game of the Week. Baseball was something I read about almost daily in magazines and newspapers, and devoured every time the *Sporting News* landed in the mail.

My father was something of a baseball freak. Before I learned to read, I knew that Ted Williams was the greatest hitter who ever lived. My dad seemed to know that, even though he never saw Williams play. He just knew, and it seemed important for him to tell me that.

Years later, he told me about coming home from work, carrying his briefcase into his office, and doing what my mother thought was invoicing. What he was actually doing was scoring baseball games and listening to them on the radio. And when there weren't any games to score, he invented his own card game, his personal version of Strat-O-Matic, before there were ever card games or video games or anything to play that wasn't real baseball.

I liked nothing better than to sit with him at Maple Leafs baseball games at the foot of Bathurst St. I carried a glove, he carried a scorebook. We watched triple-A together when the stands were almost empty and the interest in the city almost nonexistent. I was 9, he was 47. We could argue which of the Leafs in 1966, Reggie Smith or Tony Horton, would be the better major leaguer.

The next year, 1967, was the last year of triple-A baseball in Toronto. The Maple Leafs were the farm team of the Boston Red Sox, who came from nowhere to win the pennant that year, managed by the ex-Leafs manager Dick Williams. "The incredible dream," they called it. Everything about baseball seemed to be just that in my youth.

I didn't see much of baseball as I inherited my father's obsession: There were no Blue Jays or Expos then. There was no nightly television sports highlights show or even much on the news about the game. There were no sports networks or sports-radio stations back then. But you had your imagination and your box scores, and you didn't need anything else.

Then the World Series came on television and you saw Bob Gibson for the first time. My dad called him the greatest pitcher ever. After the 1967 World Series and before he had a 1.12 earned-run average in 1968, I called him that too. I still call him that.

He started nine World Series games for the St. Louis Cardinals in his career. He pitched eight complete games, seven for wins. How could anybody be better than that? The more baseball I got to see, the more time I spent listening to my dad, the more I became enamoured with defence. He told me about Willie Mays' catch in the 1954 World Series and about a catch that somebody named Al Gionfriddo made off Joe DiMaggio in 1947. I never really knew anything about Gionfriddo except he made that catch. Every time I saw a great catch — like the one Devon White made for the Blue Jays in the 1992 World Series — I compared it to the ones made by Mays and Gionfriddo, and still complain about how we were cheated of a triple play that Blue Jays championship season.

I think a lot about defence now in baseball because the constant shifting and technology has robbed us of thrills that don't exist anymore. The best left side of an infield I ever saw — and my dad agreed with me — had Brooks Robinson at third base for the Baltimore Orioles and Mark Belanger at shortstop. Belanger didn't make errors and Robinson regularly took your breath away.

But the need to dive to your left and go deep in the hole — to make the kind of play behind second base Roberto Alomar would make rather easily, even though it was nearly impossible — is gone. Today, they position the second basemen in the outfield. They don't have to move very far to catch just about anything. They position themselves where they are told to position themselves. The human element is another thing gone in big-league baseball.

I wonder what we would think of Alomar playing today's game, because the plays he made — to his left, to his right, the catches, the throws — were instinctual and poetic. A graph and chart can't replace beauty and instinct. Where do we see that now? We can't see a Gibson today because of pitch counts and inning limits and the babying of pitchers that have become part of the business. There are no Gibsons anymore because the game won't allow it and sports science and agents and management have made it all but certain that Superman pitchers can't ever be Supermen again.

Baseball was more fun when it was more human. I used to watch Frank White play second base for the Kansas City Royals and didn't think it was possible for anyone to play second base better than he did. And then along came Alomar and, from a local point of view, I never saw a better everyday player up close.

My dad would talk about Willie Mays or Mickey Mantle or maybe Joe DiMaggio being players you couldn't forget. They were mostly mythical figures for me. I saw a little bit of Mays at the end when he was too old and too slow to be special. But what a giant he was, a bigger star than anyone playing today while we try to figure out why baseball can't find a way to market Mike Trout.

Everything changed for me when the Montreal Expos were born in 1969 and baseball came to Canada in a more regular way than ever before.

We could tune in twice a week on television. There were some local radio broadcasts. It wasn't anything like today, when there are 15 games on just about every night and every highlight of every game blends into one other. Devouring box scores was what I did long before anyone knew what fantasy baseball was — it used to be the only way we knew who was who and what was what.

As I got older, I came to be fascinated by the great outfield arms of baseball. Ellis Valentine sure could throw, and so could Jesse Barfield and Dave Winfield and Dave Parker and Dwight Evans and Roberto Clemente.

My dad would talk about the arms of Mantle and Al Kaline. And he never got a chance to see Ichiro throw. But man, he could throw it too.

How is it I know those names without looking anything up and can barely name the best arm in baseball today? Because there aren't really many plays at the plate anymore. It's easy to understand why, with safety being preeminent in all of sports today. But how often does someone go deep to the fence in right field, pick up a ball the way Valentine or Barfield would and fire a bullet to home plate or third base? I don't know what it says about baseball today that I can name seven or eight great arms from the '70s and '80s and barely mention one player from today. Tom Brady is like no one who came before him in football. Connor McDavid is faster with the puck than any hockey player we've ever seen. LeBron James is, well, LeBron James.

Baseball has evolved, just not in the right way. There are fewer base runners, fewer balls in play, more strikeouts, more home runs, less managing than ever before.

Wins aren't important for a starting pitcher the way they were for Bob Gibson, and RBI don't matter the way they once did for Tony Perez and the Big Red Machine. Just about anybody who plays regularly today can hit 20 home runs if he has the proper launch angle with his swing.

Nuance has been defeated, pushed aside by analytics and general managers who think computers can select talent better than scouts can. Stealing bases is a thing of the past, Rickey Henderson's career be damned.

All of this happening, or not happening, at a time — maybe a record-setting time — for young players in baseball. There is a remarkable pool of kids playing baseball today in the majors. Ronald Acuna Jr. in Atlanta heads up the sensational 21-and-under club, alongside Juan Soto in Washington, Vladimir Guerrero Jr. and Bo Bichette in Toronto, and Fernando Tatis Jr. in San Diego. All of them are learning on the job, the way Mays did at 20, DiMaggio at 21, Mantle breaking in as a teenager in New York.

The talent in today's game is more than generational. It's matching some of the greatest names of all time. This should be reason to celebrate the richest, deepest period of baseball youth maybe ever.

All of this genius youth is being strangled by a game that has allowed the computers to take over, the heartbeats pushed aside for clicks. In a 10-year period from 2009 to 2018, the number of balls in play dropped by 10,000 a season. Ten thousand? That's more than four balls in play per game, on average, gone missing.

The current Blue Jays strike out 9.11 times per game. A decade ago, they struck out 6.35 times a game. When they won the World Series in 1993, they struck out 5.3 times a game. That's an increase of 71% over a 26-year period in baseball.

The more strikeouts there are, the fewer balls there are in play; the fewer base runners there are, the fewer defensive plays made. The more teams play the shift, the less, frankly, there is to watch.

My father has been gone for 20 years. So much of baseball has changed since he passed. I still watch a ton of baseball, more than ever before, really, because it's so accessible. It's in my house, on my television, every night. But the more I watch, the less the game interests me. Sadly, for me, the romance, the magic, is gone.

And I'm glad my dad, baseball lover of all baseball lovers, never saw this game. It might have broken his heart.

I get emails — a few, usually — after everything I write. Some negative. Some positive. But always a few. When this column appeared, I was flooded with responses. The most I'd ever received for anything I'd ever written. This piece, written from a purely personal slant, hit a nerve with readers like nothing I'd written before. People usually respond when they're angry or when they disagree. In this case, the overwhelming response was in agreement with my words.

Joey Bats, the Most
Hated Man in Baseball

October 19. 2015

KANSAS CITY — From beneath the microscope that is playoff baseball, the many images of Jose Bautista are daunting and contradictory.

There may be no player in baseball more despised — not necessarily by fans, but by the rest of the game — and there may be no one player looked upon to be as all wrapped up in himself, his emotions, his purpose, his arrogance, his anger as he seems to be. Bautista doesn't have to look for a fight. Every game, for him, seems to be one. Internally and externally.

Monday is his 35th birthday. It is also Game 3 of the American League Championship Series, and if Bautista were looking for any kind of fight, he's certainly found a tough one here. The Blue Jays trail the Kansas City Royals by two games after two games.

Thus far, just days from the crazy celebration of Wednesday night, he has yet to accomplish much of anything in the ALCS. This, as many already have said, should be Bautista's time to go national, to make an impact on the other side of the border. He feels that intensely, takes all of this very personally.

The subtext of his whole life in baseball has been about proving people wrong. And along the way, he has steamrolled all over them. Obliterating the doubters. He's a fighter with a lifelong chip on his shoulder, a persona with a little professional wrestler mixed in. He is part athlete, part thespian, caught up his own character, his own brand. He is the defiant leader in victory and can be the finger-pointing heel in defeat. Few Toronto athletes have ever been as successful or complex.

But production-wise, it's been hard to look the other way. He has been one of the best players in baseball, and that wasn't enough for him. He yearns to be more than even that. He wants to be a brand. He wants the stage. He wants to win. There may be a certain humility to his slugging teammates Josh Donaldson and

Edwin Encarnacion. There is almost no humility to Bautista: He is too overt, too wound up for that.

He is an old man on this team, an old man in baseball, but on Monday night a pitcher 11 years younger than him will be asked to bring the Blue Jays back in this series while another pitcher, 15 years younger, may be called upon to close. This is their beginning on the national stage. This may be Bautista's only shot — and already he became international with his Game 5 home run against Texas, the bat flip, the body language, the debate and discussion that followed — not the biggest home run in Blue Jays history, just the most talked-about.

That matters to Bautista. Being a point of conversation. Being a baseball player who matters.

"There's a saying in baseball," said David Price, talking about how Bautista hits a fastball. "You can't sneak cheese past a rat."

And then he made sure people understood that he wasn't calling Bautista a rat.

Some have. Umpires, privately. Other managers. Fans in opposing cities. Players on other teams. In Game 1 against the Royals, he struck out on three consecutive pitches he didn't swing at. He then gave umpire Tony Randazzo the Bautista evil eye. In Game 2, he struck out again on a called third strike and basically sunk to the ground on his knees. He can't help himself, even without a hit since the Rogers Centre home run. It's always someone else's fault with Bautista — that is part of his strength, part of his weakness.

He can be the flip-the-bat playoff hero who turned on a nation and angered another one. And he can be, as he was in the clubhouse Saturday night, cold enough to look the other way, almost with a certain disdain, and distance himself from teammate Ryan Goins, who personally took the blame for the pop fly in Game 2 that landed between them.

Bautista could have played the part of supportive teammate here Saturday night, could have been a decent teammate the way Russell Martin was, the way Troy Tulowitzki was. Instead, he came across as a singular ass, which he can be at times, putting a wall between himself and the kid who is eight years younger than him. Bautista, not necessarily self-aware at times, may not have realized the impression he left after Game 2. And in his case, he probably doesn't care.

That's why he can be the most popular Blue Jay on a Monday, the least popular on a Tuesday.

He loves me, he loves me not. Fans play that game with Bautista, sometimes series to series, sometimes week to week.

Manager John Gibbons said the other day: "He's been one of the top players in baseball for the past five or six years. But we never got to the post-season. I don't think he's had a chance to show off how good he is."

That chance came against Texas in the craziest of all innings. And he was the last out Saturday night, with two on base and two out. A home run then would have tied the game. He flew out to right field and the only celebration was in the stands at Kauffman Stadium.

The game Monday night is paramount for the Jays. It's election night in Canada. It's Bautista's birthday. It's the biggest game in Toronto since last week's biggest game.

All of this matters to Bautista, which is why he was so critical of Alex Anthopoulos a year ago, publicly planning how to get the message out. And this is why he was excited like a little kid sending exclamation mark texts to his teammates this year when Anthopoulos started loading up at the trade deadline.

What the Jays need from him now isn't fire or anger or defiance: They need production.

Especially with Encarnacion playing with a sore finger. Especially with Ben Revere not getting on base. Especially after the highest-scoring team in baseball scored three runs in two games against Kansas City and usually needs five a game to win.

Only four players in the American League hit more home runs than Bautista's 40. He ended up eighth in OPS and third in RBI. He may not be the outfielder he used to be, a little slower, a little less arm, a little jump gone, but offensively he remains a tour de force in the Blue Jays' bopping lineup.

Since the home run at the Rogers Centre, Bautista doesn't have a hit. He's 0-for-5 against the Royals, who have pitched around him, walking him four times. The Jays are hitting .130 with runners in scoring position. The combination of Donaldson, Bautista and the banged-up Encarnacion are 3-for-19. Leadoff man Ben Revere is 0-for-9 in the series.

That puts the top four Jays batters at 3-for-28. A .107 batting average.

That isn't the way Jose Bautista, all bottled-up and bothered, full of swagger, arrogance and pomposity, sees this ending. He had his great moment of the post-season, one of those baseball moments that will last forever.

That's not enough for him. He wants more of them.

Omar Vizquel's
Private War

September 27, 2012

At the start of the last homestand of Omar Vizquel's big-league career, the future Hall of Fame shortstop painted a picture of a laissez-faire Blue Jays team full of promise but lacking in maturity, and of a coaching staff that doesn't address mistakes in any meaningful way.

It hasn't been a good combination for the Jays.

Vizquel, who called his only season in Toronto a personal disappointment, said he believes the Jays run too loose a ship, let too much go throughout the season and need to "jump on mistakes" more often than they have in John Farrell's second season as manager, Vizquel's only season here.

"It's part of the inexperience," said Vizquel, in his 24th and final season as a player. "If you make mistakes and nobody says anything about it — they just let it go — we're going to keep making the same mistakes over and over again. We have to stand up and say something right after that mistake happened. We have to talk about it at meetings. We have to address it in a big way in the clubhouse.

"Sometimes you have to punish players because they're making the same mistakes over and over again."

The implication from Vizquel was that didn't happen throughout the season. Vizquel didn't specifically address what kind of mistakes he was referring to, but anyone watching the Jays most of the year would know there have been no shortage of defensive shortcomings, base-running blunders and execution errors that were apparent before injuries ravaged what was left of this disastrous season.

"No doubt this is a good young ballclub," said Vizquel. "Obviously, they need some veteran leadership in here. I tried to do my best, a little helping here and there. But I think the coaching staff have a big responsibility to kind of get in there and tie things up a little, have a bit more communication with their players and try to make this thing happen the right way.

"Look, I think a lot of mistakes were let go because it's young guys. You expect mistakes from young guys. It needs to be talked about. It shouldn't just be let go and say, 'Ah, we have another day.' You have to get on it. You have to say, 'I didn't like that play' and 'Let's try and do something different.' You have to talk it over and over again and how do you call it, be on top of that."

Vizquel said he wants to see what the Jays look like next year, with "a guy like (Jose) Bautista helping out (Edwin) Encarnacion." He wants to see what a healthy Adam Lind can do. He wants to see what J.P. Arencibia can do with a full season behind the plate. He wants to see a pitching rotation that includes Drew Hutchison, Kyle Drabek and Brandon Morrow. And he wants to see what Henderson Alvarez does "when he starts thinking about the game" more.

"It's not too far away," said Vizquel. "We have enough talent here to compete ... It was too bad we couldn't do it this year."

In one way, Vizquel was like the young Jays. He left spring training believing this team was for real. "Oh my God, I was really excited about our chances," he said. "Until you start playing the games, then you realize this is not spring training anymore. This is the real deal."

The real deal wasn't kind to the Jays this summer. And as the end approaches, the end of the season, the end of Vizquel's remarkable career, he admitted to feeling sad.

"I'm feeling sad in a personal way," he said. "I was expecting much more from myself." He didn't quite know where he fit in on the team. He didn't know when he was going to play, in what situation, against what kind of pitching, or what position he was going to play. He found some of that difficult and confusing, again bringing into question the internal communications on the team.

And still, "it was a great experience being here. I love this town. I love the ballpark. The city is amazing. I made some good friends. There's nothing more that I can ask."

For 24 seasons, all he did was his job. Wednesday night the Jays' season and his playing career both come to an end.

This was Vizquel's final weekend as a major league player. Less than a month after this column appeared, the Blue Jays did the unusual and traded manager John Farrell to the Red Sox.

Losing Alex

October 30, 2015

This is how you negotiate with Alex Anthopoulos.

You ask what he wants and then you give it to him.

And then you give him a little more than that. Just to be sure.

Because you can't let him go. Because after feeding him, nurturing him, watching him grow into the Executive of the Year in Major League Baseball, you can't allow a young general manager — this smart, this creative, this Canadian, this built for the position — to walk away.

Not after the season the Blue Jays, Toronto and Canada just experienced.

Not after that three-month ride of baseball exuberance, which was like nothing we have known before. Not after a city and a country invested in a team, emotionally and financially, like they never have before.

You find a way to keep Alex Anthopoulos.

If it means control, you give him control. You find a way.

Except the Blue Jays didn't.

The great failure of this punch-to-the-gut Thursday, the day the Jays' baseball balloon deflated, was that just about everybody went off-course. The clowns at Rogers who wouldn't know a sacrifice fly from a tsetse fly were authors of their own demise. They have been tripping all over themselves from the day it was determined they would stab Paul Beeston in his baseball back. They did their own little dance of Tinkers to Evers to Chance — but in this case, that meant it went Dan Duquette to John Hart to Kenny Williams.

And eventually they settled on Mark Shapiro to replace Beeston as club president. No matter how Shapiro turns out on the job, he will forever be known as the man who couldn't make a deal with Anthopoulos.

The man who wouldn't relinquish baseball control and has now made his entrance to Toronto the great second-guess.

He needed to find a situation that would have kept Anthopoulos fruitful in his role as general manager. He couldn't work the kind of compromise that might have been necessary to allow Anthopoulos to be in charge of baseball, which is what he deserves to be in charge of.

And what club chairman and son of Ted, Ed Rogers, needed to do, after making a mess of his early attempts to replace Beeston, was get Anthopoulos and Shapiro in a room, much like a union negotiation of sorts, and not leave the room until they had some kind of working arrangement.

Because this was worth fighting for. Anthopoulos is worth fighting for. And all you have to do is break down the work he has done over his time in Toronto to understand that much.

Consider the Josh Donaldson trade, a deal for an annual MVP candidate. Anthopoulos called Billy Beane in Oakland and Beane said he had no interest in dealing Donaldson. But he called and he called and he called some more, doing the Anthopoulos thing.

What's made him so engaging a figure as a general manager has been his inability to give up on any idea that seems to be a good one.

Beane yelled at him, told him to stop calling. But Anthopoulos gets like a dog on a bone: He kept at it and kept at it and kept at it until a deal was made.

Last November, in between trading for Marco Estrada and signing free agent Russell Martin, he acquired Donaldson to play third base.

Did anyone else in baseball have that kind of month?

Did Mark Shapiro?

Then came summer, and the engine that is Anthopoulos wouldn't stop. He added Troy Tulowitzki. He added David Price. He operated the Jays like a fantasy team, adding and deleting on a seemingly daily basis.

By the end of this marvellous season, the Jays had changed their starters at first base, second base, shortstop, third base, catcher, left field and centre field — all in a calendar year. Only Jose Bautista remained in right field. The rest, with Edwin Encarnacion moved to designated hitter, was all new. Who else in baseball could do that?

Anthopoulos was that happy, that creative, that much ahead of so many of his colleagues. He needed to fix the Jays' defence at shortstop and somehow got Colorado to bite on Jose Reyes, like that was easy to do. He didn't have a left fielder who could make a play, so he brought in Ben Revere. He deepened his bullpen and his bench. Even a small move like the addition of Cliff Pennington paid off because Ryan Goins had to be moved to shortstop when Tulowitzki crashed into Kevin Pillar.

And, in doing so, the moves he didn't make were almost as impressive as those he did. He talked trade with Cincinnati for Johnny Cueto and they wanted Marcus Stroman in exchange. At the time, Stroman hadn't thrown a major-league inning in the season. He offered up a minor-league pitcher and said no on Stroman.

Two years earlier, he had a chance to get David Price from Tampa Bay, but it would have cost Stroman and Drew Hutchison. He said no that time as well. You can make a bad deal like the R.A. Dickey for Noah Syndergaard and Travis D'Arnaud trade, but you can't do that often. And you have to find a way to recover from it. That's what the best general managers do. They make up for their mistakes. They all make them. It's how they recover that distinguishes one from the other.

The general managers around baseball have been consumed by what Anthopoulos accomplished this season and the remarkable executive he has grown into at the age of 38. If he's like this now, what's he going to be like in 5 years or 10 years? And we know he's going to be around that long. His workaholic nature makes him all but certain to be a lifer. And now he's out, just like Beeston — one to retirement, the other to free agency. The Beeston exit was messy but understandable. He's done his time. The Anthopoulos exit was explained, really, by no one, in a day of spin-doctoring all around.

Anthopoulos turned down a five-year deal, probably something in the neighbourhood of $10 million, for what he called his dream job and couldn't — or wouldn't — explain why. He talked in circles about how it didn't feel right but wouldn't say what didn't feel right.

Whatever it was that was eating Alex Anthopoulos, he wasn't about to share it, although it's been pretty clear in recent conversations that he wanted to continue to have control of baseball matters and decision-making in that area. He felt he had earned that over time. He believed in himself, his staff, his players, his manager even.

He talked about how well he was treated by Shapiro and Ed Rogers, which sounded like the kind of lip service you pay while walking out the door.

But you don't walk from the city you love, the team you adore, your dream job, for something small or simple or for something not feeling right. You don't do that.

The hole had to be gaping.

The disagreement large.

The walk Anthopoulos has chosen to take could affect the employment of his close friends in the front office, of John Gibbons, the manager he is forever defending, of those he cares deeply about. You don't walk away from all that unless there is something absolutely stirring — be it ownership, be it Shapiro — that tells you it's time to leave.

"This decision is solely mine," said Anthopoulos, not expanding on the reasons.

"It's hard. It's hard to leave the staff. But I just felt it was the right thing for me at this time ... I'm a Blue Jays fan at heart. I think they're going to win the American League East next year."

When asked again why he had to leave, he said: "You have to be true to yourself."

True to yourself. Just not true to an adoring public, some of whom chanted "Thank You, Alex" in Baltimore just a few weeks ago.

He said he had every intention and desire to stay on the job.

Then he walked away without a real explanation.

His call.

His decision.

Our loss.

Anthopoulos left the Blue Jays in 2015. His teams have been in the playoffs every season since leaving Toronto, first with the Los Angeles Dodgers and then with the Atlanta Braves, who won the 2021 World Series.

Gibbons' Long Road
to the Big Leagues

October 8, 2015

The World Series ring sits in a jewellery box rarely opened, deep inside a safety deposit box thousands of miles from here.

John Gibbons doesn't talk much about the 1986 World Series, about the championship ring he hardly looks at or thinks about. When the New York Mets won that World Series, Gibbons was something of an afterthought.

He had been called up in August to replace the injured Gary Carter. He spent October as the bullpen catcher. He wasn't on the playoff roster.

When the champagne was sprayed in celebration, "I kind of stayed out of it," he said. "I didn't think it was my place to get involved. I didn't really feel like I was part of that team."

He doesn't want to stay out of it now.

The World Series ring he so desires is 11 wins away. This is his opportunity — and he knows it, understands it. His chance to be a baseball somebody. He knows he's not necessarily popular outside of his own clubhouse. He knows what some think of him — that he's never the reason the Blue Jays win, the story goes, only the reason they lose. The world isn't always sure what to make of his mumbling, his self-deprecating humour, his lack of modern-day sound bites.

This is Gibbons' first time on the big stage. His possible coming-out party.

"Yes, it could be that," said Gibbons in a lengthy and rare one-on-one interview. "I'm not looking for that, necessarily. The attention is going to be on the games, on the team, not on me.

"I know what people think ... I hear it sometimes. I want to be known as a good baseball guy. In the baseball world, I'm viewed that way. And I want to be known as a good individual. If my legacy is as a good father and husband, then that's what matters most to me."

But something else matters: winning with this opportunity. There are a lot of good baseball people who never make it to the big leagues, who never get this kind of opportunity. Gibbons thinks about them — he used to be one of them.

"A lot of times, it's luck of the draw. Right place, right time," said Gibbons. "Baseball isn't rocket science. Sure, there's something to those who win all the time — they're definitely on the ball — I would love to be in that category but I don't obsess over it.

"This would mean everything to me, but this isn't about me. I've been here a while, but not long like some people. For the franchise, the city, really the country, it's been so long.

"I don't mind staying in the background. I never wanted to manage in the big leagues just to say I managed in the big leagues. I want to manage a winner. That's the whole idea, isn't it?"

JOHN GIBBONS WON a championship in his first season managing in the rookie Appalachian League. He did it again in his second year in the Florida State League. That was in 1996. He was on the fast track as a hot guy in the Mets organization. He hasn't won a championship since.

The first year, he remembers, was the best year. Or in his Gibbyspeak, "the funnest year.

"I was the manager," he said, "but that was just part of what I did. Our guys in Kingsport, Tennessee, didn't have cars. We had a team van.

"Every game day, I would drive the van all over town, pick up our guys, and take them to the ballpark. The guy who owned our team was a big defence lawyer in town, and his one grounds crew guy was on parole. About a week into the season, he violated his parole and he was back in the slammer.

"So I would drive around town, pick our guys up, get dressed, go down the right-field line, get the tractor, drag the field, then set up the field and then we'd do our early work. There was only two men on our staff — me and the pitching coach — and a few days after we broke spring training, our pitching coach broke his throwing hand. So he can't throw batting practice. I'm basically throwing all the BP, doing all the grounds-crew work, and after the games, I'd round up the boys and drop them all at home and then go back to my place and relax.

"Crazy, when you think about it, but it was probably the most fun time I've had — my first shot at managing — my fondest memory in the game."

The reason he won the championship that first year?

"Good players," he said. "It's always come down to that. You win when you have good players."

IF BUCK MARTINEZ had not been fired as manager of the Blue Jays in May 2002, the odds are John Gibbons would never have become Jays manager.

Gibbons had gone as far as he would go in the Mets organization. He managed three years at triple-A Norfolk and was not at any time invited to join the big-league team. It was time to get another job. That turned out to be more difficult than he had imagined.

"My kids were getting a little older, I didn't want to keep dragging them around the country," he said. "The Mets offered me my job back. I told them I wasn't going back."

He called his friends Billy Beane and J.P. Ricciardi with the Oakland A's, looking for work. There wasn't anything there. Beane had been selected in the first round of the 1980 baseball draft by the Mets. One pick after him, the Mets chose Gibbons. One pick before Beane, the Expos took Terry Francona, and the pick before that, Atlanta selected pitcher Jim Acker.

"I remember calling Billy and he said he couldn't talk, something was up with J.P. That's when J.P. got hired by the Blue Jays.

"I was under some pressure. We had three kids, had just bought a house in San Antonio and I had two weeks left in my contract. It was a nervous time. J.P. called me and said he had two jobs he could interview me for. A third-base coach and a bullpen catcher. He interviewed me and Carlos Tosca. Carlos got the third-base job. And after that, J.P. said, 'I'll pay you the same as they were paying you in triple-A if you take the bullpen job.'

"I'm thinking, 'I can't do that.' I couldn't squat anymore. I flew home figuring I needed a job. But nothing was happening. I end up taking the bullpen job, going to spring training and, on my first day squatting to catch, my knee blew up on me. I was the only bullpen catcher in baseball who couldn't catch.

"So the season starts and I'm barely able to get it done. We don't have great pitching and, every night, everybody and his brother are throwing by necessity. I'm catching them all on one knee. About a month in, I figure I've got another month of this, no more. There was no way I could physically do this anymore."

Fifty-three games into that season, Martinez — now the Blue Jays' play-by-play man — was fired by Ricciardi. Tosca was named manager. Gibbons moved from bullpen catcher to first-base coach. Ricciardi hired Brian Butterfield to coach third base.

"If that doesn't happen," said Gibbons, "I don't think I ever manage a big-league game."

When Tosca was fired in 2004, Gibbons was named Blue Jays manager for the first time.

WHEN JOE CARTER hit the home run to win the 1993 World Series, Gibbons was working at the instructional league in Florida with the Mets. Coaching in the morning, fishing in the afternoon, some beer and baseball at night.

Four months earlier, the Montreal Canadiens won the Stanley Cup, the eighth Canadian-based team to become champion in a 10-year period in the NHL.

Since then, 22 years without Canadian champions.

"That's amazing," said Gibbons. "I knew how long it was for us. I didn't know how long it was for Canada."

With that to carry around, what will he say to his team as they begin baseball's post-season, many of them, including Gibbons, for the first time? He said the same as he always says — next to nothing.

"Baseball, the more you talk, the less they listen," said Gibbons. "I haven't had to have a team meeting all year. First time I can say that. I never felt a need for it.

"I know this team. They want to play. They don't want to hear from me."

The Fight to Draft Bo

September 11, 2019

You may not know the name J.B. Woodman, but he is what can happen when process and charts take precedence over old-school scouting in baseball.

The Blue Jays' second pick in the 2016 major league draft is 24 years old and already out of baseball. He was taken 57th overall.

Nine picks later, many Jays scouts held their breath on the way to selecting Bo Bichette, whom they badly wanted with their third pick of the draft. They were that excited, that nervous. They knew they wanted him but also knew that process was in their way. With the 66th pick in the second round, they selected Bichette, whom general manager Ross Atkins had never seen play.

This was Atkins' first draft with the Jays. This was president Mark Shapiro's first too. Having been through much success in Cleveland, they came up with a template of what they wanted to accomplish in that draft. The Jays' scouting staff was essentially instructed — which happens often in sports — about what kind of player to look for and invest in.

What Shapiro and Atkins didn't want — and were adamant about this — were high school players. They especially didn't want high school position players.

Woodman, a position player, played his ball in the SEC at Ole Miss.

Bichette played his baseball at Lakewood High School, a pitch and a putt away from the Jays' spring training home in Dunedin.

Most of the Jays scouts liked Bichette way better than Woodman, but that was a fight they would lose at the time. They had to pick their spots.

So here was the problem, especially for those who saw something special in Bichette a year before he was draft age. The Jays watched him regularly. Area scout Matt Bischoff did much of the background work, as area scouts often do.

Those who know this story best call Bischoff the star of the Bichette draft. He got to know Bo's habits, his high school, his parents, almost everything you could get to know about the young shortstop. Bischoff watched him play high school games, play in off-season All-Star tournaments, watched him work out at times with Troy Tulowitzki.

Then came the national cross-checking scouts. The more excited they were about Bichette, the more they watched him. The Jays paraded scout after scout to Florida. They never missed an at-bat.

Brian Parker, now with the Los Angeles Dodgers, watched Bichette play. Dana Brown, now with the Braves, watched. Chuck LaMar, the former Tampa Bay GM, watched. Ross Bove, still with the Blue Jays as special assignment scout, was an influential voice in the process.

But still there was a problem: How could the scouts convince Atkins, against his wishes, that they were going to invest a reasonably high pick in Bichette? And because Bichette had some leverage regarding college, they also had the concern they would have to overpay to get him.

This wasn't an easy conversation. Depending on who you speak to about this, there were levels of contention here. And another perception to get over: Bichette's older brother, Dante Jr., had been a reasonably high pick. Dante Jr. has never played beyond Double-A.

But the Jays' scouts had put two full years into watching Bo play. They loved his exaggerated swing and the unlikely plate discipline that accompanied it. They liked the way he played against the highest level of competition and how his game always got better in those situations. And even though he had a big swing, he was not described as a free swinger by the Blue Jays scouts.

The 2016 major league draft was not exactly one for the ages. Mickey Moniak went first to Philadelphia. Maybe he'll play one day, maybe not. The best pick, Pete Alonso, went to the Mets two picks before the Jays nabbed Bichette. He's got 47 homers and a Home Run Derby win under his belt as a rookie. The 63 players taken before Alonso have combined for 52 home runs. Bichette has hit 10 in 161 at-bats — a 30-plus pace in his first big-league campaign.

"We had great information on the kid, his makeup and his family," said a scout involved in the process, no longer with the Jays. "Through his dad (former major league player Dante Sr.), he got to know some of our players. And I think we were an attractive team to him because he had worked out with our players and because we were an attractive team because of what we were doing in the big leagues."

On draft day 2016, there was no argument about what to do with Bichette. Those conversations had already taken place. Some of them heated, we're told. By then, the scouting staff had convinced upper management that Bichette was worth the selection — even if they had to pay him significantly more than the slotted salary for the pick.

It took some massaging of upper management to get Atkins to agree to take a high school player with such a high pick.

Now the Jays have two future stars in Vladimir Guerrero Jr. and Bichette. One came via former GM Alex Anthopoulos, now in Atlanta, and with the background work of Ismael Cruz, now with the Dodgers. Outside of Bischoff, most of the others involved in the scouting of Bichette have since moved on.

Two months after the draft, scouting director Brian Parker, who fought hard for the selection of Bichette, was fired by the Blue Jays.

CHAPTER 4

Hoops!
(There It Is)

Nothing Halfway
about Isiah Thomas

May 29, 1994

It is an unbelievable road travelled, the one that has taken Isiah Thomas from the slums of Chicago, from the troubles of his youth and his siblings, from a career as an NBA bad guy to the here and now, as minority owner and vice-president of the Toronto Raptors, NBA team–in-waiting.

"It's kind of like a fairy tale," Thomas begins. "When you look at my life, coming from where I came from, and knowing what I know now. I feel like I've been blessed."

No one has ever done this before, gone from player one day to the head of an expansion franchise the next. The step is large and significant, but so have been many in Thomas' 33 years. The ninth child of Mary Thomas, her littlest boy has done more than defy the odds: He has obliterated them, beginning at home.

One of his brothers was a pimp. One sold heroin. One was an alcoholic. That was Congress Street and that was home.

It wasn't until his brother Larry picked up a bag of heroin one night, showed it to him and begged Isiah not to follow in his footsteps that his life began to change, that this child who yearned for street action began to grow up. Everyone in the family seemed to look out for Isiah, beginning with his mother.

The stories of Mary Thomas have almost become legend. She has been so much the central character in Isiah's life that a movie of the week was made about her. Those who know her best tell the same stories, over and over, always with a sense of pride.

There was the time the Vice Lords gang in Chicago tried to recruit her sons. Mary excused herself from the door, returned with a shotgun and announced: "If you don't get off my porch, I'll blow you away."

And there was the time she burst into Mayor Richard Daley's office, unannounced. They were living on welfare at the time, and the rules of welfare meant living in assisted housing. Her assistance cheque had been cancelled. "I didn't want my family in the project," she said. "I didn't think anybody had the right to tell us where to live." But after an unscheduled meeting with Daley, all was ironed out. Mary Thomas had won.

And there was the time Isiah got caught stealing a piece of fruit from a corner store. "Call the police," he told the man at the store, "but don't call my mother."

"She was a strong disciplinarian," Thomas said in two lengthy interviews this week. "She believed in heavy-handed methods. But my mother is the strongest and most inspirational person in my life."

Mary Thomas was born in Mississippi, the descendant of slaves, and was denied any formal education. "But she has a will and a determination that makes her far more successful than I can ever be in my life," said Thomas. "She spoiled me with love, not with material things. We didn't have anything. We were well below the poverty line."

Much has changed over the years: One by one, his brothers straightened out. The family is now fine. Isiah Thomas bought his mother a home in Chicago and another in Florida. "I'd like to get her one more," he said. "Right here in Toronto."

There is no middle ground with Isiah Thomas, basketball man.

He is both revered and despised, called hero or weasel, often depending on who is doing the name-calling. Some people in sport evoke no emotion or interest, but he can't avoid the storm.

"I feel like Russia," Thomas once said. "When something happens, it's always Isiah's fault."

Explaining that remark, he said: "It's like Notre Dame. People love them or hate them. That's what it's like when you're successful. When you get to the top of the mountain, people have to decide if they like you or dislike you.

"If you never make it to top, people never have to decide."

When Thomas was left off the Dream Team for the Summer Olympics in 1992, with an unhidden Michael Jordan power play in the background, few came to his defence. Frank Layden, now president of the Utah Jazz, said Thomas wasn't picked because "nobody does and never has liked him."

Now Layden will have to deal with Thomas face-to-face at NBA meetings. "I gather he's rather embarrassed about that statement," Thomas said. "Why did he say that? That's a question you have to ask him."

The wars over the years have been many. With Larry Bird. With Jordan. With Adrian Dantley. Isiah Thomas has never picked on lightweights.

Sometimes the battles have come from the outside but also from within his own team. And just as the Pistons began to become successful in the 1980s, it was clear the team had a serious split: There was the Thomas camp and the Dantley camp. Both great players. Both with conflicting agendas. One handled the ball. One wanted it more.

"I had to do something to change that," said Jack McCloskey, then general manager. "I couldn't let the team get destroyed."

This was a power play Isiah Thomas won unquestionably. Dantley was traded to Dallas for Thomas' high school buddy Mark Aguirre. Detroit went on to win two consecutive league championships.

Said Dantley's mother at the time: "I guess his royal highness got what he wanted."

The genesis of Isiah's trouble with Jordan goes back to Michael's rookie season and his first NBA All-Star Game in 1985. The players were all requested to report to practice in their All-Star uniforms. All did except Jordan. He wore his own head-to-toe Nike. Two of the players most bothered by what they saw of Jordan were old friends Thomas and Magic Johnson.

They thought Jordan's outfit showed a lack of respect to the league. Thomas, playing for the East, acted on his feeling: Playing point guard, he passed the ball to everyone but Jordan. Jordan made only two field goals in the game, finished with seven points, and was angered by the slight.

The hard feelings began there and festered over time. And even though the two have barely spoken to each other, the dislike remains strong. When asked about the Jordan situation, Thomas said: "I don't really want to get into that."

The strain, however, remained, as did the reputation of Thomas as an NBA bad boy. "I don't feel I'm disliked," Isiah Thomas said. "I was voted to 12 consecutive All-Star Games by the fans. If that's not support, what is?"

At almost every Christmas in his famous life, Isiah Thomas dresses himself down with a hat, fake facial hair and tattered clothes and then goes shopping with a large amount of cash.

In costume, he finds anonymity and bigotry. He is searching for only one of those.

It serves in his mind as a reminder of who he is and where he came from and how far North American society still has to go.

"Wearing a disguise, being out in the public, you get treated differently," said Thomas. "You realize that racism still exists, that it isn't the same for everybody.

"I wasn't treated like I'm normally treated. I was treated the way I was before I became popular. When I went to pay for expensive gifts with cash, I got a lot of looks. When I walked into certain stores, people looked at me like, 'What are you doing here? If you're not going to buy, leave.'

"That's the real world. Sometimes my world isn't so real."

Isiah Thomas can't forget and won't allow himself to forget where he comes from. The boy from the hood. From that place outside Chicago Stadium, and from the Hamburger Helper he ate without the hamburger and from the ironing board, which doubled as his bed. Now he represents companies and owns companies and this week bought himself a percentage of the Raptors.

The critics say he isn't qualified to be vice-president of the expansion franchise. But this is nothing new for Thomas. His whole life has been filled with doubting Thomases. Now all of basketball watches him again.

"It's extremely important," Thomas said, knowing well the historical significance of his new situation. "It's a task and a burden that unfortunately you have to have. I understand that if I fail at it, the chances of it happening again are highly unlikely. But if I'm successful, then I've gone a long way in breaking down stereotypes.

"If I can accomplish that, that may be the most important thing I ever do."

Welcome to Toronto

May 29, 2019

Welcome to Toronto, basketball people, and welcome to the 2019 NBA Finals.

I know you've been here before. You came for the NBA All-Star Game. You froze your asses off, just like we did. You froze — and we were embarrassed about it. You probably said then you'd never come back.

I understand. That weekend, I vowed never to go outdoors again. So there is that.

But here you are, back in Toronto, for the most meaningful basketball games of our lives, in this place not exactly known for a sport invented by a Canadian.

So for that, and more, we are sorry. We're sorry for a lot of things. It's part of being Canadian. Part of who we are. When other kids in cribs are learning to say "Mama" around the world, we're learning to say "Sorry."

That's our culture. That's so much of our identity. We want you to like us. We were born insecure about that.

Truth is, we want you to love us — and there is so much to love here. But in between our frantic anxiety over what you think of the city, our team, our cleanliness, our food, our taxis, our Ubers, we will apologize if need be, for just about anything else.

So in fairness, before the first game of the Finals, before the first chant of "Ref, you suck," which seems to be just about everywhere these days, here is a blanket apology on behalf of a city that grew up as apologists.

And we mean it. I saw Shaquille O'Neal walk into what was then the Air Canada Centre for the All-Star Game here. He may be the largest man I've ever seen up close. He was wearing the largest fur coat ever made for any man anywhere. As he walked in, with toque and scarf and giant fur, he looked like a small building in winter clothes. Or something prehistoric, like an NBA Sasquatch.

On him, you'd need an elevator to get to the second floor.

Shaq won't need that fur coat if he's here for the next several days. It's going to rain on Wednesday, I'm told. And maybe Thursday and, according to my weather app, on Saturday. At least you can go outside and your face won't be in the kind of pain it was in February 2016. That's a pain you never forget.

If you didn't bring an umbrella with you, well, just add that to the list of things we're sorry about.

In Toronto, we're sorry about the traffic, sorry that there's construction just about everywhere, sorry we have too many condos and not enough lakeshore, sorry about the blight that is Pearson International Airport, sorry that you had to clear customs to get here and really sorry if your passport has expired, which I'm sure happened to some of you.

We're sorry that our money doesn't look bland and unoriginal like your money, but yours is worth a whole lot more, which means you're coming to Toronto on the cheap, if 35% on the dollar is considered cheap.

We're sorry to ABC and ESPN that we're not an American city, that the Raptors won the Eastern Conference final. Television ratings will therefore suffer and, for at least the next two weeks, you can't go on ignoring us as you do on Christmas Day every year.

You can go back to ignoring us once the series is over. We're used to it. And only the small-minded among us — and I can occasionally be in that group — can get heated about being ignored.

We're kind of used to being an NBA afterthought. Anybody ever talk about Kevin Durant or Anthony Davis or LeBron signing in Toronto? Anybody? In the who-is-going-where conversation that so envelops NBA gossip life, Toronto barely gets mentioned. It got mentioned when Kawhi Leonard came here. It gets mentioned now because Kawhi lifted the historically disappointing Raptors to the league championship series — and we don't know if he's staying.

We are relevant today, for this moment, for as long as this lasts. But you have to understand, this is a basketball market that has been waiting to break out and flex its muscles for the past 24 years. We've waited for something big to happen. We're not used to winning around here. That's part of our sporting culture: We understand disappointment.

The Toronto Maple Leafs last won a Stanley Cup in 1967. The Raptors have never been this far before. The Blue Jays won their second World Series in 1993.

The last quarter-century, we watched championships played by other teams in other cities and wondered what it would be like if it ever happened here.

While Toronto played for zero major league championships from the time the Raptors were born — and remember, just because they call it Major League Soccer doesn't make it major league — Boston played in 22 title games with its four big-league clubs. Los Angeles was in 16. New York was in 16. Even the Bay Area, home to the Golden State Warriors, shames us statistically. They've played in 13 championship games or series. This is their 14th.

In all, 44 different cities have made it to the finals in the NHL, NFL, MLB and NBA over the past 24 years. Until now, Toronto has not been among them.

We're still determining what kind of basketball city this is. There are deep-rooted fans here. There are the bandwagon jumpers. There are computer nerds.

And this being Toronto, there are those who only appear when something is trendy. We are not yet the capital of the world. But we're getting there.

This is a breakout week for us and basketball here and across the country. But is it changing forever? As my friend Michael Farber wrote in *Sports Illustrated* years ago, "One day you will be able to shout 'Shaq!' on Yonge St. in Toronto and no one will assume you mean Eddie Shack."

If you don't know "Clear the Track, Here Comes Shack," you're either a basketball fan, a hockey hater or under the age of 40. But there was definite meaning in what Farber wrote.

All these years later, we're still searching for some kind of identity in the NBA. That's part of what makes these next two weeks so special. It's about playing for a championship and maybe winning a championship and showing off to the world what a great place we have here, what a great resilient team the Raptors have grown into.

So if you get a chance, take advantage of being in Toronto. Go to Little Italy. Take in the Danforth. Try Kensington Market. Rub elbows with the rich on Yorkville. Enjoy the bevy of great dining there is in this city. There is lots of it. Walk around the theatre district.

And if you didn't bring an umbrella, here's my advice: Go buy one. Spend your American dollars here. And enjoy the NBA Finals. There will be no weather problems here.

The games are played indoors.

More Than Two Sides
to One Ugly Story

April 23, 1996

The story of Brendan Malone's firing isn't simply the story of another coach gone wrong and another dismissal on the sporting scene.

It is a story of miscommunication and insubordination, a twisted series of subplots and nastiness that made it appear as if the Toronto Raptors were inventing ways to lose basketball games.

And it is a story with the fingerprints of Isiah Thomas all over its messy pages.

The firing of Malone yesterday smacked of managerial inexperience, could have and should have been avoided, and restored the Raptors' reputation for mud, conflict and controversy.

Brendan Malone probably would like to tell the story himself, but he can't. In buying him out, the Raptors also purchased his silence. It is a not-so-nice piece of corporate business. The franchise didn't just fire him, it also, in essence, shut him up.

But piecing together how the end came about through a variety of sources paints the Raptors as mean-spirited, and also as ethically and competitively questionable.

When it became apparent that Malone and GM Thomas were no longer on the same basketball page — that the coach was doing the unthinkable and coaching to win, and the GM wanted a continued training camp instead of trying to heal the situation — the Raptors began plotting how to get rid of Malone.

They didn't meet with him face-to-face. They didn't discuss strategy. They were never that up-front. Instead, they began sending memos: memos that threatened Malone's future as coach, memos demanding he play certain players a specified amount of time, memos that threatened the security of Malone's three-year contract and the money owed to him.

Some of the memos weren't even handed to him. Some were silently slipped under the door of Room 2539 of the Westin Hotel, where Malone lived in Toronto until checking out yesterday.

"Nobody ever sat down and said, 'Brendan, this is who you're supposed to play,'" Malone said at a news conference late yesterday afternoon. "I never had a lot of discussions with Isiah. Maybe four."

But Isiah Thomas had a lot of discussions. He spoke with his players. He spoke with the assistant coaches. One by one, the players knew which way to turn.

And then the injuries came. There is a sincere belief by those close to the team that the Raptors took advantage of the NBA's injury list, didn't dress players who could have played — the result being the Raptors lost a lot of ugly basketball games.

Malone wasn't the only victim of that; paying customers were also, and so was the NBA's integrity. After the initial euphoria of the early season, with the Raptors being surprisingly competitive, the reality of the situation set in for Isiah Thomas. The more wins the team had, the worse draft position it would wind up in. And the more competitively the team played, the less the younger players other than Damon Stoudamire would see playing time.

The Raptors lost 9 of their final 12 with Malone under threat to play not-ready-for-prime-time players. He could have compromised and not suffered from terminal stubbornness, but this was his one head coaching shot, this was his chance. He wasn't about to give in on his competitive ways. And in a colossal error in judgment, Malone flaunted his own stubbornness by overplaying his inexperienced players in a loss to Orlando.

Thomas was so angered by Malone's insubordination that he told people he wanted to "take him outside the SkyDome and beat him up." Instead, Thomas shut him down and then shut him up.

It's funny in retrospect. The team paid B.J. Tyler a full salary; he never played a game. They paid Victor Alexander; he never played. They paid John Salley; he hardly played. But they were ready to quibble over Malone's relatively small salary and use it as a threat against him.

But in the end, whatever the buyout was, it hardly begins to pay for the value Malone brought to the Raptors. Respect can't be purchased. It can, as the Raptors prove, be compromised.

And in the end, the Raptors were nothing if not small. They ordered all but one shot of Brendan Malone to be cut out of their highlight film. It is the way they choose to conduct their business.

The Life and Times of the Remarkable Wayne Embry

April 15, 2020

Wayne Embry is a walking, talking *World Book Encyclopaedia*, having made his own history and lived through almost all that has mattered in the past 83 years.

He can still see his uncles, Woody and Louis, walking up the driveway in Ohio, coming home safely at the end of World War II. "I thought about that just the other day," said Embry in a wide-ranging telephone conversation. "What a glorious day that was. We were so proud and so happy. And we had a big celebration on the hill when they got home.

"I guess, when you're home now and being safe, and there's lots of time, you have lots of time to think about all kinds of things."

Home now, like all of us.

Home and safe in his daughter's house just outside of Dayton. There are no basketball games being played. There is only so much television and so much news you can watch. There is the occasional contact with Masai Ujiri or Bobby Webster or Larry Tanenbaum. "They keep me informed," said the Raptors senior basketball advisor.

Embry has lived through World War II, the Korean War, the polio epidemic, Vietnam, the civil rights movement and, of course, his own pioneer ways as the first African-American general manager in the NBA. But nothing, he said, like the coronavirus. Nothing that has brought the world to its knees like this has.

"I don't think we've lived through anything comparable," said Embry, who has lived through almost everything. "When I was much younger, the polio epidemic was pretty bad (in the late 1940s, early 1950s). And then the vaccine came in (around 1952) and that levelled off after that. We're kind of hoping for that now.

"The wars, they were horrible. The civil rights movement was a big fight. But there's nothing comparable to this (virus). This is unbelievable. And we don't really know where we are with it. This is awful."

136

This is a different kind of frightening.

Back in 1965, when Embry was playing for the Cincinnati Royals and rooming with the great Oscar Robertson, he got a call from his wife, Terri, with somewhat disturbing news. Terri had decided to be part of the now famous civil rights march on Selma, Alabama. She told him that Robertson's wife, Yvonne, was going to march with her. She told him not to tell Oscar — to let Yvonne tell him personally.

"I asked her not to go," said Embry. "I said, 'You've got kids at home. You're not going, Terri.' She said she was going and not to tell Oscar."

A minute later, the phone in the hotel room rang again. It was Yvonne on the line. "We were really upset about it," Embry said. "We understood why. Terri told me she was doing something that she wanted to do and had to do. She said it was no big deal for us but it was a tremendous big deal. We were very upset until they got home."

That was well into Embry's career in Cincinnati. When he first arrived as a rookie in the NBA, he was the only African-American on the team. He couldn't eat in the same restaurants the team ate in. He couldn't sleep in the same hotels. He was as isolated as you can be without self-isolation. "My teammates were really supportive," said Embry, knowing he almost didn't make it to the NBA. "That got me through it."

Before he was drafted to play basketball, he thought he was headed to the marines and Vietnam.

He went with a friend to sign up to fight for his country. "We were standing in line and I got a tap on my shoulder. The guy said to me, 'We can't take you.'" Embry stepped out of the line and asked why.

"You're too tall," he was told. "We'd never find boots for your size 17 feet."

Embry did get to Vietnam. But it was years later, on a public-relations visiting tour. "When I was in Milwaukee, the State Department asked if I would take a trip to the Far East to visit hospitals. Now that was a traumatic experience. It relates somewhat to what we're experiencing now.

"I remember standing there in a hospital room and the officer walked in and asked: 'How many are going to make it?'

"And you're looking around thinking, 'How many are going to make it?' It was just awful. Vietnam was a horrible experience for the world, and that trip was one of the most traumatic experiences of my life."

And his life has been full of experiences, traumatic and triumphant. When Embry came out of retirement to play two seasons with the Boston Celtics, he wound up being hired as the head of recreation for the city of Boston. He was also doing some work for the soft drink companies, first Coca-Cola, then Pepsi. He figured that was his future. He didn't envision 50 or so more years in the NBA.

He was first hired by the Milwaukee Bucks as assistant to the president and a year later, in 1972, he was called to a meeting with ownership. "I thought I was going to be fired," Embry said. "They said, 'You're the new general manager of the Milwaukee Bucks.'

"I sat there dumbfounded, I don't know for how long. I didn't think it was possible."

The first African-American general manager in North American professional sports. He didn't realize what he was headed for.

"I got letters, hate mail, all of that. My focus was not on being African-American. My focus was on doing the job. I thought my hiring was only significant if others followed me. I had a job to do and had to do it well. It wasn't what Jackie Robinson went through. It wasn't anything like that at all.

"I knew I wasn't hired because of my colour. I was hired based on my qualifications. They felt I was qualified. And I was fortunate to get a lot of support around the league from people like Pete Newell and Bob Ferry, and Jerry Colangelo and I became very close." Embry wound up as general manager in Milwaukee and later Cleveland for more than 20 years. That's a run he's extraordinarily proud of, and Embry doesn't really like to point out his accomplishments.

He loves his current role with the Raptors, still involved after all these years, like a lot of us, in love with this current edition of the team, coming off an NBA championship and then without Kawhi Leonard exceeding expectations in a season that may not come to a conclusion.

"I never would have believed we would have a time where we wouldn't finish a season," Embry said. "We had the lockout in '98, but that was the beginning of the season, not the end. Now there's no way of knowing what goes on. And we have to be so careful. You don't want to go back too soon. It affects so many people.

"There's so many constituencies here. Players, coaches, various staff, area people, media, fans, operations. There are just so many people involved and it's all so complicated. I watch the news every day, good things or bad things. I've got to keep up, but I can't watch too much of it. I go for a walk every day. I can't go to the gym anymore because it's closed. The days are very long and there's only so much you can do. I watch some old games on ESPN, I watch NBA TV. If the Raptors send me something, I look at it.

"I try to keep up on things that are going on with our staff. We're having such a good year. I hope we find a way (to end it), but that's just hope right now. We have no way of knowing."

His health is good. His wife is still struggling from the aftereffects of a seizure she suffered last year. Both are socially distancing themselves, unsure of what might be next.

But basketball has been his life, really is his life, now into his 10th decade. "I'm doing fine," said Embry, quoting his doctors. "They tell me to keep doing what I've been doing."

And in the meantime, he is so proud of where the Raptors have been and where this season might have been taking them.

"Kawhi had a lot to do with us winning, but look at this season, the way Pascal (Siakam) has emerged as a late pick, Freddy (VanVleet) has emerged as an undrafted player. How Terence (Davis) has emerged as an undrafted player and Norm (Powell) as a second-round pick.

"I'm really proud of what our people have done. Masai has put together a staff of people and developed a culture that's remarkable. And Nick (Nurse) ... I had a little background on him before we hired him as an assistant. I knew some people who knew him, people who had coached against him. They indicated to me when we hired him that he's a sleeper. And I guess they were right.

"And as good as we are, hopefully we get to see what it means. But I don't know. I don't know if we're playing. What's going on right now, this isn't good. This isn't good at all."

Hope Arrives in Vince Carter

June 28, 1998

Glen Grunwald always looks a little uncomfortable behind a microphone, always looks like there are a thousand other places he would rather be.

But he had that slight smile last night, that draft-day smile when he came to answer questions about the circumstances that made Vince Carter a Toronto Raptors player last night.

Grunwald, the general manager, had that can't-lose look about him — and the truth is he better have that look because after all that has gone wrong, he can't afford to be wrong about Carter.

There is too much at stake.

There is this franchise, still in its infancy, still treated as a dubious curiosity by a mostly disinterested public. The fragility of the situation cannot be underestimated. Blow this pick and have another year like last year, and soon there won't be a next year and another pick to talk about — for the team or Grunwald.

He knows that as well as anyone. It isn't just his reputation on the line. He inherited the mess that Isiah Thomas left behind and inherited his job and his office in the process. What he didn't inherit was his presence, either internally or externally.

A franchise needs a face. The Raptors had one with Thomas and with Brendan Malone and with Damon Stoudamire.

But one quit, one was fired, one was traded and a silly-looking dinosaur should never be the face of any franchise. A franchise needs a face and a star.

At the same time, when Thomas left and Stoudamire left and Doug Christie's wife kept asking to be traded — she does play for the Raptors, doesn't she? — the word around the league began to spread from agent to agent and player to player. This was a place to avoid, a country with taxes higher than the CN Tower and a basketball environment not fit for a Jimmy King. Perception was becoming reality and reality was becoming perception.

And say, who was this Grunwald guy anyway?

Some of that can change now in the year in which the Raptors move into the Air Canada Centre. Some of this can change now that Butch Carter has been secured as coach and Vince Carter has been secured as a player and Jimmy Carter is no longer U.S. president.

Maybe, just maybe, Vincent Lamar Carter, he of the Michael Jordan comparisons, he of the fabled athletic ability, can be what he is advertised to be.

"We did the best thing to build the franchise," said Grunwald when explaining the choice of Antawn Jamison, who was then traded away for Vince Carter and a small wad of cash.

"I'm not going to say he's going to be a star in his first year here. But he can do some things in the air most people can't do on the ground."

For the sake of basketball in Toronto, in a season in which the Raptors move to a real home, Grunwald has to be right about Carter. In some ways, his job is banking on the pick, and so is the franchise's future. If you think basketball has all but disappeared in this city now, wonder what it will be if Toronto has another season like the last one.

Drafts, as Ken Dryden would say in one of his soliloquies, are about hope. They're about imagining. They're about belief in the future. Everybody wins on draft day. The reality doesn't hit until the start of the next season.

This was the fourth draft for the Toronto Raptors, and each has come with its own flavor and own form of intrigue. First, there was the Stoudamire draft, a rousing success until Thomas left town and Stoudamire turned sour.

Then there was the Marcus Camby draft, and two years later nobody knows what that means other than they messed up by not taking Shareef Abdur-Rahim.

And then there was the Tracy McGrady draft, and one of these years he'll be 20 years old.

Now say hello to Vince Carter, who is not to be confused with the sergeant in Gomer Pyle, and who wasn't drafted last night by the Raptors, but in keeping with the true Maple Leafs tradition of cash first, compete second, emerged as Grunwald's choice after a trade with the Golden State Warriors.

He can jump. He can shoot. He can write poetry. And his dunks have become regular highlights on the nightly news. And on a team where everybody who's a somebody has asked to be traded, he's happy to be a Raptor. "I'm ready to contribute right now," he said.

"The job can get done if I shoot the ball."

Glen Grunwald is banking his reputation on it. His reputation and that of the Raptors.

The Mother of All Trades

June 11, 2004

When last we saw Mats Sundin's mother — or better yet, the actress playing her in the commercial — she was serving soup to her hungry son.

When last we heard from Carlos Delgado's mother ... well, truth is, we've never heard from Carlos Delgado's mother.

So why is Vince Carter's mother, Michelle, everywhere?

Why is she at courtside, and on all-sports radio, and too often the unnamed source, inadvertently embarrassing herself and her son and the Raptors all at the same time, spreading the Vince message to whoever cares or whoever will listen.

Why is everything always about Vince?

The Raptors search for a general manager: What does Vince think?

The Raptors hire a new management team: Will Vince like this, or will he ask to be traded?

The Raptors need a new coach: Wonder who Vince wants?

Vince wanted Dr. J to be the GM, so the Raptors interviewed Julius Erving twice. Had Vince wanted Dr. Dre, he probably would have been granted an interview also.

It's hard to determine what is more annoying, Vince's mother becoming the official spokesperson for everything that bothers her son or Carter being party to his mother playing the basketball version of Bonnie Lindros — and we all know how well that worked out for Eric.

Carter is getting married soon. Maybe this will be the best thing to happen to him. Maybe this will distance him, at least professionally, from Mommy.

Maybe the kind of responsibility that marriage brings will make him a more responsible athlete to both his teammates and to the Raptors organization.

Maybe. Or maybe not.

This is year seven for Vince Carter if he makes it to the fall as a Raptor. And the team has won just one playoff series during that time. The best ball he played was four seasons ago. The best the team ever played was the playoff run it made without him three seasons back.

In the meantime, the Raptors have made the mistake of treating Carter, contractually and otherwise, as though he is one of the greats in basketball history. He is not a bad person, just not necessarily a strong one. And ownership, almost from the beginning, has worshipped this idol rather than worked with him.

Ownership believed if it made Mommy happy, it would be making Vince happy by extension. The owners gave her a voice and him a voice, and they tiptoed around when they had to. The same strategy of bowing down to Antonio Davis and his wife, Kendra, ended up blowing up badly for the Raps.

Instead of earning confidence, the Raptors found themselves taken advantage of.

Now Rob Babcock, the new GM, is supposed to walk on some kind of eggshells because he wasn't Carter's choice for the job, and the whispers — most of them coming from Mommy — are that Vince may ask to be traded.

Babcock, when he sits down with Carter, should make a few things clear. One, that Carter works for him and not the opposite. Two, that he will communicate with Carter and his agent, but there is no hotline for Mommy. Three, that if Vince doesn't like this setup, there is the door and don't let it hit you on the way out.

Babcock, obviously, will be more diplomatic than that. But is there any other player he will be forced to make peace with? And you have to wonder: What works with Vince Carter?

Kevin O'Neill rode him hard. That lasted about 20 games. Lenny Wilkens gave him free rein and Glen Grunwald asked his advice on almost everything, and Carter took advantage. Butch Carter used the tough-love approach, and sometimes it worked and sometimes it didn't.

If I'm Babcock, I'll keep the player and see if I can't trade the mother and see how everything works out in the end.

Canada's Greatest Hoopster

September 27, 2000

SYDNEY — Listen to the changing sound of these Olympic Games and all you hear is drugs.

There is a scandal over here and a scandal over there, and once again Olympic idealism has taken a drubbing and the sporting world seems forever turned upside down.

It is that way when you search only to find a professional athlete, owner of a $48 million contract, who seems the most Olympian of Canadian athletes here, the one who understands what this event is supposed to be, and can be.

Away from the crying C.J. Hunters, and the gymnasts who took the wrong cough medicines, and the weightlifting cheaters, you will find a skinny, wealthy, long-armed, fuzzy-haired, smiling Canadian who doesn't just symbolize all that can still be right about the Olympics but is living it here every day.

Meet Steve Nash, and instantly you'll feel better about yourself, about Canada, about the Olympic experience. Meet Steve Nash, and spend a few minutes listening to him, and you can dream the way he dreams, believe the way he believes.

"This is the pinnacle of my athletic career," said Nash, the kid from Victoria who against all odds — wrong country, wrong size, wrong colour — made his way to the NBA.

"This is the greatest thing I've ever been to."

And in the second week of the Olympics, long after Simon Whitfield's gold, and before Caroline Brunet's final-day kayak runs, and in the midst of all the drug whispers, the best and most uplifting Canadian story is about how one basketball player has lifted himself, carrying a team and his struggling country with him, into the rarest of stories here.

A Canadian story of overachievement. The story of the little guy who could. We love a Canadian story with promise and hope, a story you have to be proud about. And a story about a rich guy who is humble and modest and, dare we say it, Gretzky-like.

Steve Nash has become the face of Canadian basketball at a time when Canadian basketball needed a face. He is the poster boy for the unspoiled athlete; playing here hurt, doing everything for everybody else, tossing a few anonymous dollars in the direction of his less-than-wealthy teammates, living the athlete's Olympic Village life while his NBA friends from America are off in some posh hotel, with major security surrounding them, ordering room service.

A quick Nash story: When the low-budget Canadian team had to travel to Montreal for an exhibition game this summer, there was some concern they weren't exactly doing it NBA-style. The team took a six-hour bus ride to Montreal and stayed the night at a Days Inn before returning home.

"This is very different from the NBA," Nash said. "The NBA is a business, part of the entertainment industry. Everything is flash. This is much closer to the game I played as a kid. This is what I always wanted to do and it's everything I hoped it would be.

"I love it. It's just like college to me. You're in the dorms. You're hanging out together. You're going around meeting people in the Village. I pretty much fit right in."

What Nash is capable of — as he showed in the shocking upset of heavily favoured Yugoslavia that put Canada first in its round-robin pool — is winning a game on his own. This Canadian team is the antithesis of the Canadian athletes here — unwilling to accept mediocrity, willing to push as far as they can push, reaching for the impossible. And Nash is the leader, making everyone around him a little better than they already are.

The ride so far has been exhilarating and bumpy with moments of elation and moments of doubt. But as the playoffs are set to begin, you have to go along with Nash for the ride, you have to see the Olympics through his wide eyes and his big heart. There is one playoff game, then another, and then the gold medal game.

All that seemed impossible is now possible, except a win over Vince Carter and the Americans.

"Sports always comes down to the same intangible," Nash said.

"Sacrifice. It doesn't matter what sport you're in or how you play it. You have to sacrifice something."

He gave up his summer and his health to be the focus of a team so much in need of focus.

Canada hasn't won a medal in basketball in 64 years.

So forget the drugs and the poor performances; keep your eyes open and dream along with Steve Nash. "I'm leaving here," he said, "with something to remember."

The Anger Subsides in Kyle Lowry

December 26, 2014

It happens before every home game — the special meeting by the Raptors bench.

Kyle Lowry and his three-year-old son, Karter, informing each other about their respective days.

"I like to see him before a game," said the Raptors' star point guard. "It makes me whole. He doesn't watch the game out there. He watches in the back. For me, I tell him I love him. He tells me good luck. We have a talk. You've got a good thing like that going. I give him a kiss. You have that in your life, what have you got to be mad about? You go out there and do your job with ease.

"For your pride and joy. Makes my job a lot easier. I don't see him enough. He gets up, goes to school. I don't want to wait all day to see my son again. I miss him. Now it's something we can do together. He wants to see me before games, I want to see him. It's my pride. It's who I play for."

"What have I got to be mad about?" Lowry repeats that question several times as we sit in the players' lounge at the Air Canada Centre for a rare one-on-one interview. Explaining how anger has been so much a part of his life. He hasn't always understood it, where it came from, why it was him. He understands it damaged him enough that he can now separate the then from the now.

He opens up in a way he doesn't often, upon learning he is the 11th winner of the George Gross Memorial Trophy as *Toronto Sun* Sportsman of the Year, seeing Roy Halladay's name on the list of winners before him: That one caught him more than any other.

"I'm from North Philly," he said with a smile. Halladay means something in North Philly.

But the anger he talks about consuming him is in the past, and while he may play basketball with a chip on his shoulder, the little guy in a big man's game, his life has never felt more complete, more certain, more controlled.

Marriage did that to him. But fatherhood — that changed everything. "He's done more for me than I've done for him," he said of his son. "He's a bigger influence on my life. It's made me more of a man. It's made me more of a grown-up. It's made me more mature. It's made me understand that life is bigger than just basketball and being mad about things. I've spent a lot of my life being mad. I'm never mad (anymore). Off the court, I'm never mad. On the court, that's a different story.

"I don't know why I was like I was. I was always mad. Things don't always go your way. You make mistakes. You make them out to be bigger than they are. You build them up. At the end of the day, you're mad, then you're mad at yourself. It's no way to be.

"The last two years have been a very peaceful, very happy time. I've never been more stable. I've never been more understanding."

And the content Kyle Lowry never saw any of this coming.

A day after the Raptors failed to sign Steve Nash as a free agent, Bryan Colangelo brought Lowry in from Houston in a trade for a first-round pick and somebody named Gary Forbes. Lowry remembers his emotion on that day.

"Two and done and I'm going home," he said.

He wanted nothing to do with the Raptors.

"I figured two years and I'd be a free agent and go somewhere else. This wasn't where I wanted to be. I tell people that all the time: You can't predict your future. You have to live it by the day.

"Two years ago, I would not have envisioned sitting here and talking to you about an award Roy Halladay won, but I'm happy I am. Things have worked out perfectly. I love the city. I love the organization. I love being here. I love where I'm at. It's interesting how things happen.

"Our season last year was a helluva story. I was traded (to New York). Essentially, I was gone. My best friend (Rudy Gay) got traded. It was all messed up."

From that came the most memorable Raptors season in years — this helluva story; a budding, growing, electric fan base; a last-shot chance to win a playoff series; a team now dominating the Eastern Conference standings; talk of Lowry as an All-Star (he's never been one before), and an MVP candidate (he's never been mentioned before); a $48 million contract and now this, a new beginning for Lowry in his ninth NBA season — a new place for him in the star-driven NBA.

How would he react post-contract? That's always a question for any athlete. Especially one with potholes on his résumé.

Some take the money and run. He's taken the money and run the offence.

"I'm motivated," said Lowry. "I'm more motivated than I've ever been. It wasn't about getting a contract. I was going to get that. It's about me fulfilling my contract, doing my duties. It's about winning. It's about working harder. They gave me the money for a reason. It's about being a professional.

"I have a lot more to give. For me, it's not just about right now. It's about next season and the season after that. It's about the future. I don't satisfy easily. There's a long way to go."

He doesn't view himself as a star. When he talks about the stars of the NBA, he talks of them with a certain reverence. He mentions Anthony Davis and LeBron James. He mentions Chris Paul and Kevin Durant and Russell Westbrook and Marc Gasol and Dwyane Wade and Blake Griffin.

"Those are MVP-type players," he said. "The beauty of the NBA is everybody has their own special talent. None of those two players are the same. Everybody has that unique thing about them. In this league, you have to find your unique talent.

"I'm not one of them."

But he may be underselling himself. With the Raptors' only All-Star, DeMar DeRozan, out of the lineup, Lowry has become one of them. In the first four games without DeRozan, Lowry scored 29, 27, 39 and 22 points, which are hardly point guard numbers. He then had 13 assists, followed by 14 assists, and in the past five games, has had his time reduced because of relatively easy wins for the Raptors. An invitation to this season's All-Star Game will represent another new start. While settled, Lowry certainly has gotten used to change, not just in himself but with those around him.

"It's extremely crazy what's gone on," he said. "I lost my boy in Rudy, but I was gaining a boy in DeMar. It's funny how basketball brings guys together that would never be friends. This kid's from Compton, California. I'm from North Philadelphia. We're 3,000 miles apart and we're very similar and very close.

"When you're young, you don't really understand what's going on in your life. You have to go through a process. I'm older now, I'm wiser. I've got a family and a wife. I've got a team that counts on me every single night. It wasn't always like that.

"Back then, I was young, sassy, didn't like to do interviews, wouldn't sit here and say this, wouldn't speak out loud, wouldn't incorporate everybody. Now I know how important it is to have friends, to have people who can say, 'Let's go to dinner.' To have people to talk to. To trust people.

"I've got a great back-court mate in DeMar. We talk every day. Rudy's my guy, my best friend. But having DeMar here has been great. We've taken this friendship to a whole new level."

Lowry has everything he needs in Toronto: His family. His friends. His team on the rise, along with his career. And his relationship with Masai Ujiri, the general manager who had him traded away but made him understand what he was capable of being. This isn't one-and-done for him. This is year nine in the NBA for him — and it's really another beginning.

It's why he doesn't consume himself with the last-second shot that never happened against Brooklyn in Game 7. He doesn't even think about it. There is not much else to do.

"Kobe Bryant missed a game-winning shot last night," he said. "I'll tell you one thing: If he gets one tonight or tomorrow, I'll bet you he's going to shoot it with the same confidence.

"I have to think the same way. I've missed two potential game-winning shots this season. Give me another one. I'm going to take it and I'm going to make it. That's just the way I am."

Champion Raptors
Are a Team for the World

June 15, 2016

OAKLAND — The decision maker is from Nigeria. The coach is from Nowhere, Iowa. The general manager is from Hawaii.

There's a woman making basketball decisions in the front office. There's an emerging star from Cameroon and a cooking show maven from the Congo.

There's a new father who is too short and was passed over in the draft who made all the key shots in the fourth quarter of the championship win. There's the quiet, proud man from Spain, who spent last summer rescuing refugees. There's the even quieter man from Los Angeles — the glue, the difference maker, the superstar who would rather not be noticed, wearing a scuba mask.

These are your NBA champion Raptors. Toronto's team. Canada's team. And in the words of the visionary Masai Ujiri, the world's team.

Now, he was chuckling amid the noise, the spraying of champagne and all of the Thursday night celebration that went well into Friday morning, that maybe ABC will have to broadcast them on Christmas Day this year.

Chuckling and not chuckling. There's nothing that bothers Ujiri more than a lack of respect or a perceived lack of respect.

"Do you get the Christmas Day invite now?" he was asked.

"I don't know," he said, then laughed at his own words. "It might still be in question. It might be."

But he thinks it's more than time for respect for his Raptors, owner of the second-most wins in the regular season, the most in the playoffs. Time for respect outside Toronto, outside Canada.

"We're not Canada's team," said Ujiri. "We're the world's team."

And it's time to relish, embrace and celebrate the most unique champion the NBA has ever had — maybe the most unique champion North American professional sport has ever known.

This is Ujiri's science project.

It may be just one year. It may be more than that. In the lab, with all of his associates, Ujiri put this together, added pieces and more pieces, replacing a legendary coach with an unknown. He replaced, tinkered, prodded and added a mysterious superstar who played offence and defence better than anyone else in the NBA.

When did Ujiri know the Raptors could win an NBA championship? "To be honest, as soon as we got one of the best players in the world (Kawhi Leonard), you know you have a chance," he said. "You don't know how the other things are going to be. At the trade deadline, I could tell Kyle (Lowry) was tuned in, and bringing in Marc Gasol (he called him the final piece).

"And Nick (Nurse, the first-year coach). Nick is good. I'll tell you that. We went through a process in hiring him. I really want to give credit to my staff, Bobby (Webster, GM) Dan (Tolzman, assistant general manager), Teresa (Resch, vice-president of basketball operations) and Keith (Boyarsky, director of research) for that. Everybody said we were giving him the job since day one. But that's not what happened.

"(Nick's) unbelievable. I'll tell you what: So many things came together. It takes a lot of luck. Some of their players got hurt. But you know what? That always happens."

The good fortune came when Leonard's bouncing jump shot at the buzzer bounced its way into the basket for a series-winning shot in Round 2 against Philadelphia.

It came when VanVleet, who looked irrelevant and small against the 76ers, played so well against Golden State and received a vote for playoffs MVP ahead of the MVP, Leonard.

It came when the selfless ranged from great to uninvolved and back, the way Norm Powell did, the way Serge Ibaka did, the way Danny Green did, the way Pascal Siakam did in the final series.

And on the night they needed Lowry to take over, he did, on the road, on the final night of basketball at Oracle Arena — this sometimes polarizing figure, his reputation on the line, brilliant on a championship night his team needed him to be brilliant.

Lowry's career has always been about being close. He played in two high school championships, lost two. He played two years at Villanova, didn't have the tournament he wanted. He has spent 13 years in the NBA waiting for this great opportunity, and then he left his mark. He left it forever.

And across Canada, the people left their mark. There were 59 different viewing stations, many in the least likely of basketball locations.

This is how the Raptors grabbed us, pulled us in, made the disinterested interested. Social media did its part as well.

If it looked like fun watching this team from Jurassic Park, even when it was cold, even when it rained, then that spread across the country, even into the United States, where they had a gathering in Kansas to watch VanVleet play Game 6.

"If there were 59 viewing parties across the country, I'm not even going to tell you how many viewing parties there were in Africa," said Ujiri. "They (ABC) made a big mistake five years ago. Whoever it is, they wouldn't put us on TV. We continue to grow. We continue to persevere."

Ujiri remembered back on Thursday night to the day he was hired. He promised a championship for Toronto, for Canada. He remembered that I challenged him on his words in 2013.

"You didn't believe it," he said. "I told you we'd do it in your lifetime. And we did."

The parade is Monday morning. Toronto is so deserving, in need of a celebration of this magnitude.

Ujiri changed four of his five starters in a year and put out a championship lineup. A team with so many dimensions. A team that went through the playoffs going 8-2 in the final 10 post-season games against Milwaukee and the dynastic Golden State Warriors. The team with the best record in the NBA and the two-time defending champion.

"These guys are so resilient," said Ujiri of his team. "There's a sense of calm (about this team). I don't know if it's Kawhi, Nick, Gasol, we just had a different sense of calmness, even in adversity. When things got tough and rough for us, they overcame. They always had the strength to overcome."

And then he complimented Alex McKechnie, director of sports science, the now-five-time NBA champion, who set out the plan to have Leonard ready for the playoffs after missing one out of every four games during the season.

"Everything came together, working together, and that's not bullshit," he said.

What he wasn't about to address — and may not go public with in his approach — is how to convince Kawhi to stay. And that this isn't a one-and-done championship run.

"I don't think I can think good enough right now, but we are going to be who we are," Ujiri said. "There's no oversell. We just wanted to show that we could be as good as anyone in every aspect in the NBA. His teammates, medical, the organization, the country, the fans, the media, the coverage — and he was unbelievable. He was the MVP."

Either way, Leonard delivered. He brought a championship to Toronto in concert with Ujiri and friends. He could bring more if he chooses to stay. He could go somewhere else and probably be MVP again. Really, it's his call.

During most games, Ujiri doesn't take a seat. He walks around, watches a little, gets nervous, watches some more.

"At one point I couldn't watch (Game 6)," he said. "I did a Jerry West. I went outside. People will tell you I was out in the parking lot. Sometimes I had to pretend I was on the phone because they wondered, 'What the hell are you doing here?'"

At the end of the night, today, tomorrow, yesterday, he knows what the hell he is doing here. He knows, because there is always interest in him to go elsewhere. The latest comes from the Washington Wizards. In an NBA in which winning championships is truly exclusive, the Raptors have now entered that magical club.

But the job remains the job, and his dedicated work for Africa remains his passion, and he rushed home from the NBA Finals for his young daughter's graduation. That's Masai, forever multidimensional and big-hearted and, when he has to be, coldhearted.

All that coming after he rushed to California on the day of Game 6 after a free-agent camp in Toronto. "And we don't have a pick until 59th."

His staff made sure he was at a camp he really didn't want to be a part of. You don't leave a stone unturned.

Ujiri now more than understands the history of the moment, the culture of the company he works for, the 26 years between big-league championships.

I asked him if he'd ever met Joe Carter.

He smiled and said, "He came to my Nelson Mandela event in December."

They have since developed a relationship of sorts. There is now a sporting string that attaches the 1993 Blue Jays to his 2019 Raptors. Champions to champions.

"I'll send him a text tonight," said Masai Ujiri, with a broad smile, from one legendary home-run hitter to another.

The Bitter Split of Casey and Nurse

November 14, 2018

No one will come out and say it directly, but a still-hurt, still-angry Dwane Casey returns to Toronto on Wednesday night to coach against a former colleague and friend, Nick Nurse, who certainly is not a friend anymore.

Time may heal these wounds, but not enough time has passed yet. Casey was the coach of the year in the NBA and was shown the door by club president Masai Ujiri.

Casey's and Ujiri's final days together were not good days. Their relationship had deteriorated to mistrust and bordered on dislike.

When Ujiri fired Casey, he made it sound like it was the hardest thing he had ever done, firing a family member, putting on a show. It looked from the heart.

It was terrific acting on Ujiri's part. Anyone close enough to be aware of their collapsing relationship knew what really went on.

And what made it all worse, from Casey's perspective, was the hiring of Nurse, whom he had brought into the NBA, with whom he had worked side by side for five seasons, growing together, learning together, winning together.

Losing your job is hard enough to handle. Losing it to someone you believed was a friend makes it very difficult to swallow.

They used to speak every day, the way coaches on the same staff speak every day. Then Casey was fired and Nurse was hired, and they haven't spoken since.

When asked about his relationship with Casey afterwards, Nurse did a tap dance of sorts on Tuesday morning.

"Good," Nurse said. "We have five years together. We had a lot of success and a lot of battles and a lot of long hours working hard. I've said this before. He took a team from relative obscurity, from the hinterlands, to relevance. That may be the hardest thing to do in this league."

But what about their communication? "Well, my communication with whoever is between me and whoever I'm communicating with. Whether it's Kyle (Lowry) and me or Kawhi (Leonard) and me or Casey and me, I keep that to myself. I'm looking forward to seeing him tomorrow."

When I asked directly if he had spoken to Casey since the Raptors fired him — and it's usual for a fired coach and his assistants to remain close after a dismissal — Nurse wouldn't exactly answer.

"My communications are between me and him," he said. "I'm looking forward to seeing him."

Just a piece of context, a recent exchange of text messages between OG Anunoby and Nurse, was made rather public by the coach. So I suppose some of his communications are private — just not all of them.

Toronto wasn't just a basketball team to Casey. It had become home, even as he went back to Seattle each summer. He had made many friends here. His family was grounded here. His kids played soccer with Kyle Lowry's kids and he had built tight bonds with the city and fans and media — which is highly unusual in professional sports at any time — so his firing seemed like the extended family was missing something.

The wins, the losses — they were one thing. Casey was like a part of us, a part of the town, a part of the story, a reach back in history to a time when the Raptors were an NBA embarrassment. He grew, they grew and we grew alongside him. He and Ujiri fought through all that — not always together; management and coaches aren't always together — not always on the same page, but fighting nonetheless. And for the most part, they succeeded against everything but LeBron James.

Casey was fired before James went to the Lakers and before Kawhi Leonard and Danny Green were traded to Toronto. Nurse has a new team and a different way and has experienced early and impressive results with how the Raptors are playing.

Veterans Kyle Lowry and Serge Ibaka have never been better. Pascal Siakam is looking like an All-Star and Anunoby doesn't seem to be a sophomore at all. Jonas Valanciunas has never played less and been more efficient.

And Leonard, well, is what he was advertised to be — an elite player in the NBA.

This is already Nurse's team.

Casey is being paid way more money with way better terms to coach the Pistons, but that's the contractual stuff, not the human stuff. Casey is being paid life-changing money in Detroit, but once the season begins, money becomes less relevant than wins and strategies and preparation for coaching lifers.

Nurse is a coaching lifer himself. He started to hear his name mentioned last season for head coaching jobs in other places. He believed this would be his year.

"I thought my opportunity was coming," Nurse said. "I didn't think it would be here."

Now he's off to a flying start with the Raptors, Casey doing as much as you can do with the middle-of-the-road Pistons.

Casey once had to go to Japan to reinvent his career. Nurse coached at obscure colleges and in England before finding his way to pro basketball in North America. He was brought to the NBA by Casey. Once upon a time, they each came from their own place called nowhere, and maybe one day they can be friends again.

Would it bother Nurse if he never repaired the relationship with Casey? His answer was muddy, yet rather clear.

"My first and foremost concerns are I do this job here to the truest of my abilities, right, that I can serve my family first and my players next. I do the best job I can. Again, I have a lot of respect for the guy. I really like him. That's all I can say. I don't really give it much thought."

The First Retirement of Michael Jordan

October 7, 1993

CHICAGO — There were no tears, no voices cracking, none of the usual sounds and sights of retirement emotion.

There was Michael Jordan, dressed in a business suit, his voice icy, some bitterness to his tone, sitting at a table in the middle of a basketball court saying some very cold goodbyes.

The night before, a city began to deal with the trauma of the retirement of its greatest sporting star, but the morning after seemed more like a frigid shower, both shocking and uncomfortable.

Surrounded by 51 television cameras and hundreds of reporters, Jordan sat, his wife on one side of him, Chicago Bulls owner Jerry Reinsdorf on the other, all three appearing devoid of expression.

"You ride a roller coaster for years, it's time for me to ride something else," said Jordan.

He spoke like that a lot. In short phrases we've all heard before from the clichéd sporting world. Some of his words were meaningful, some not, but from someone who played his game with so much passion for nine wonderful seasons, there seemed so little in his parting words and some reason to doubt the sincerity of what he spoke.

"I conquered a lot," said Jordan. "I practically achieved everything I could from an individual's standpoint and from a team's standpoint."

Over and over again, he said he had nothing more to prove, nothing to motivate him, no reason to continue.

And listening, in the place where the Bulls practice, I wanted to believe him, wanted to applaud him, wanted to see a Jordanesque curtain call. But there was little introspection, no final number. A story was being told, but too many of the chapters seemed missing.

Apparently, Jordan told Reinsdorf, the Bulls owner, that he didn't want to play anymore: That conversation took place a year ago. Reinsdorf's response at the time was for Jordan to think everything out first before making such a final decision. They met again a week ago and Jordan reiterated that he wanted to quit. "I asked him not to make a hasty decision," said Reinsdorf.

A meeting was set up at the home of Jordan's lawyer, David Falk. That meeting took place last Sunday. Jordan reaffirmed his decision. He wanted out.

Before finalizing the decision, Jordan spoke with Bulls coach Phil Jackson. He asked Jackson if he had anything more to prove. Jackson, who is never at a shortage for words, had no response. "I knew then it was time to quit," said Jordan.

And still the timing seems odd. He is still, clearly, the best player in the NBA, maybe the best basketball player ever. Ted Williams left with a final home run and George Brett with a base hit, but both were at the end. Not since Jim Brown left the Cleveland Browns has any professional athlete quit in his prime. And as dominant as Brown was, his impact was not the same as Michael Jordan's.

Speculation had him quitting because he hadn't fully recovered from the tragedy of his father's murder. But yesterday, Jordan said his father's death only convinced him he was making the right decision.

"My father has left us ... he saw me play my last basketball game. That means a lot to me," said Jordan. "He asked me to retire after my first championship, but I still had a lot to prove. I wanted to win more.

"One thing about my father's death. It taught me there's still a lot of things for me to attend to — family, friends. I've been very selfish in my career. Now it's time to be a little unselfish, for my family, for my kids. I wanted to get back to a normal life."

And later he contradicted himself: "I don't think I'll ever have a normal life."

He lived the circus life of a celebrity, always in the news, rarely private. It made him rich and infamous and occasionally miserable. It meant too much of his life became known, and he came to resent the attention.

Yesterday, he was never confronted on the issue of his gambling troubles, but NBA commissioner David Stern said the matter has yet to be resolved. And I couldn't help but wonder if somehow this is the unspoken side issue here. A story behind the story.

And the coldness of this warm Chicago day was altered only by the possibility that the retirement of Michael Jordan will be brief. When questioned, Jordan did not rule out a return to the Bulls.

"Will I ever unretire?" he asked. "I don't know. The word *retire* means you can do anything you want. Maybe that feeling, someday down the road, will come back. I don't believe in never."

Michael Jordan retired in 1993, saying he was tired of basketball. After a stint in minor league baseball, he returned to the NBA, racked up three more championships with the Bulls, then retired again in 1998. He stepped down from his post as president of basketball operations for the Washington Wizards at age 38 to join the team's roster in 2001 before retiring for a third and final time in 2003.

CHAPTER 5

A Football Life

The Faded View
of Terry Evanshen

November 19, 1993

The photo albums of Terry Evanshen's life are of people he no longer knows or remembers. The stories of his past are told to him by his wife, Lorraine, and he listens and too often he forgets.

Five long and exasperating years have passed since a car crash sent Evanshen into a coma he miraculously came out of, and still every day is an ordeal and every hour a challenge.

The problems are not so easily solved, not by the phenomenal support of his family, not by a court that this week awarded Evanshen a $1.6 million settlement, an amount that comes after five frustrating years of battling the legal system and the insurance industry.

"No amount of money in the world will give my husband his life back," Lorraine Evanshen said yesterday. "If I could trade all that money back, I would do it in a minute.

"I wasn't celebrating in court. I'm just glad it's over. It was like, 'I'm tired now. I just want to go someplace and sleep.'"

Terry Evanshen caught 600 passes in a brilliant Canadian Football League career. He remembers none of them. It isn't only the football. It's his marriage. The birth of his three daughters. His life.

"Any of that, I don't remember," he said. "You don't know what that's like. You don't know what it is to start over."

They are sitting in the living room of their lovely farm home, Terry Evanshen on one couch, Lorraine Evanshen on a chair, trying to convey how a careless accident changed their lives. Terry talks, Lorraine corrects. Lorraine talks, Terry listens.

"Sometimes, I feel like I have four kids," she said. "Sometimes you get frustrated, but you can't live like that all the time. I've pulled a lot of strength from looking back at his life, knowing all that he accomplished. He was so strong. It was my time to be strong."

He used to talk a mile a minute, which is almost as fast as he ran. And you look at him now at 49, after the accident, and he still has that boyishness that made him so special. Part of him is gone forever, but somehow a part of him has remained.

"One of my doctors told me that we don't know where character comes from," he said. "She said, 'You won't lose who you are.' She said that I'll react a certain way and say certain things and she told me not to question it.

"We talk a lot about the way it was, how I reacted to things, what I did. I still don't have much memory. I write things down on my calendar and then a week from now I look back and read them and see if I remember them."

The difficulty comes from daily life. From meeting people he used to know. From trying to relate experiences to his children when he cannot recall his own. "Sometimes, it's totally embarrassing," said Evanshen. "You meet somebody and they say, 'Good to see you,' and you don't know who they are. I've learned to say, 'I'm sorry, I don't know your name.'"

On the worst days, Lorraine Evanshen gets into her jeep, drives down a country road, stops and just listens to silence. And sometimes, Terry Evanshen goes for a walk, talks to the dog, tries to distinguish right from wrong and yesterday from today.

He still speaks in football phrases, though he admits the nuances of the game confound him. "Life and football are a lot the same," he said. "You need a good team around you. You need a coach and a quarterback. Bernie Gluckstein was my coach and Fern Silverman the quarterback. They were my legal team. They treated me like I was their son. If it hadn't been for them, I'd be in psychiatric care now."

The lawyers helped and so did the local bank, getting the Evanshens through five years without income. "You come out of this realizing you're just a number to the insurance companies. They don't care about you," said Evanshen. "Without the proper legal team, I wouldn't be here. Everything starts there. You don't know how vulnerable you are when you've had a head injury. A head-injured person can make bad mistakes and not know he's doing it.

"I'm a victim here, but what people don't always realize is, it isn't just me. My family has been a victim too."

The Buffalo Bills' Drive for Five Has Begun

August 20, 1994

FREDONIA, NEW YORK — The pretty roads wind around the green campus of Fredonia State University in this sleepy Western New York town. This place is far from the real world, removed from the wise guys and the cynics and the football comedians who love to make jokes at the expense of the Buffalo Bills.

This is their quiet training camp home, where the only cries of 'Oh no, Buffalo' are heard from the outsiders who stopped here for a day and then moved on. This is the training camp of the four-time Super Bowl losers, the football dandruff that won't go away — the team that almost everyone wants to stop ruining its championship game.

"I have two words of advice for anybody who thinks that way," said Jim Kelly, the Bills' quarterback. "Beat us.

"You don't want us in the Super Bowl, then someone is going to have to beat us first. As far as I'm concerned, I say to hell with it. I'm going for No. 5."

Here at Fredonia, where the Bills are almost a family unto themselves, the cynicism is kept to a minimum. The television trucks are lined up on the campus, dispensing the nightly news on three different channels. They sit beside the radio trucks, where nightly call-in shows on two competing stations go head-to-head. The spin is always on the positive. If there is any feeling that the football world is sick and tired of the Buffalo Bills, then it remains unacknowledged here. Coach Marv Levy and general manager John Butler have worked hard at the psychology of Being No. 2.

"If everybody is against us, I think that works in our favor," Butler said. "This team likes to have a cause to rally behind. Give them a cause, and I say we'll be a better football team. From what I've seen of this camp, I don't want to say this out loud, but I like our chances.

"I believe in what Marv Levy says. You don't start the season as one of the Super Bowl favorites, and every year there are about five teams capable of winning the Super Bowl. You want to be one of those teams. I believe we are one of those teams."

Beneath the peaceful exterior and all the flowery verbiage coming from management, all is never peaceful with the Buffalo Bills. Thurman Thomas, the star running back, has gone through a tumultuous camp, verbally sparring with local media members, warring with *Buffalo News* columnist Jerry Sullivan and trying to comprehend why five great seasons of running have been overshadowed by some Super Bowl mishaps.

What people remember, even in rah-rah Buffalo, is Thomas' fumble against the Dallas Cowboys, which altered the outcome of last January's game. They remember him pulling himself from the game with supposed leg cramps, even though it appeared as though he was quitting on his team. They remember the symbol of the misplaced helmet against the Washington Redksins: the sign the Bills were not ready to play.

You lose four Super Bowls and you need to find a scapegoat. And with a chip on his shoulder and an attitude just waiting to go wrong, Thomas has become the easy and natural target.

"This city can close in on you real fast," Thomas said in one of the rare interviews he has granted since training camp began. "Everything is football here. The entire focus of this city is on football. That way everything is magnified.

"I look at what I've done since I've been here. Tell me, who in football has done more? Who on this team has done more? But all you ever hear is 'Thurman did this and Thurman did that.' To be honest, I'm tired of it. My attitude is, I'm just going to shut up and have another good year. That's the only way I can deal with it.

"I hear them on the radio. 'You've got to get rid of Thurman. You've got to trade Thurman.' It's crazy talk. I'm 28 years old. I'm in my prime. I don't miss games. I run the ball. I catch passes. You tell me, what's the problem here?"

Said Butler: "The good thing about Thurman Thomas is the more he's challenged by people, the better he'll play. That's what I like about him. And that's what I like about this team."

At practice in the afternoon, Butler stands on the sideline, watching, joking, almost always enjoying himself. Ask him about his team and he lists his assets the way a mutual funds manager would.

"This is why I like this team," said Butler. "I've got Jim Kelly, I've got Thurman Thomas, I've got Bruce Smith, I've got Darryl Talley, I've got Cornelius Bennett. They're not just my best players. They're the best-conditioned guys. Bruce Smith has 5% body fat. That's like a wide receiver's body. And they're my hardest-working guys. They set the tone for this camp and everybody else follows.

"Look at Kelly over there. Have you ever seen him looking better? I've never seen him looking better."

Those illusions come in a melodic training camp setting. While Kelly does have a tone to him that has rarely been seen before, his health remains one of the largest questions at Bills camp. It remains a question because of the glaring hole the Bills have on their offensive line.

While no one wants to admit to the problem, it is there. In the past two seasons, the Bills have lost All-Stars Will Wolford and Howard Ballard to free agency, while saying goodbye to a very credible lineman in Jim Ritcher.

According to Chuck Dickerson, the former Bills and one-time Argos coach, who now dubs himself "the Coach" on his WGR radio talk show, the Bills' offensive line is "a boil on the ass of creation."

"It's an absolute disaster area," said Dickerson. "They're trying to say it's not, but what else are they going to say? Kent Hull, the centre, is hurting. John Davis is always hurt. John Fina's just a second-year guy and the other guys have never played before. Listen, Jim Kelly is not a mobile quarterback. Playing behind this offensive line, he could get killed."

When asked what he thought of his offensive line, Levy quipped: "They're big."

When asked the question again, he answered the same way. "They're really big."

The translation, in Levyspeak, is he doesn't know and wants to find out through camp. The Bills were quick to claim Canadian offensive lineman Mo Elewonibi off waivers from the Washington Redskins when he was a salary cap victim.

"That tells you how bad it really is," said Dickerson. "They bring in a guy like Mo who's hurt all the time. He comes into camp and right away he's going for an MRI."

Still, the tone doesn't change. There is no room for negativity here. All Bills punch lines must be checked at the door.

"Every day I get asked the questions," said Levy. "'Are you concerned about this? Are you concerned about that?' I've got to be honest. I'm concerned about everything. You're always concerned when a guy feels like I do when I wake up in the morning.

"That's why we have training camp. That's why we play pre-season games. You find out and you go on. That's what football is all about."

The screams in the off-season came for change, but not the kind of change that was witnessed. Ballard left for free agency, as did All-Star cornerback Nate Odoms. Two other starters in the secondary, Kirby Jackson and Mark Kelso, are gone. But the core players remain the same. Kelly at quarterback. Thomas in the backfield. Andre Reed catching passes. Smith sacking quarterbacks. Talley and Bennett doing the linebacker thing.

"People ask me, 'Why haven't you replaced any of those players?'" said Levy. "I believe in the George Allen philosophy: If you're rebuilding your team, you'll always be rebuilding. You replace players when they can't play anymore. If they can still play, why replace them?

"It's a misconception that this is the same team going to the Super Bowl every year. It's not. We've had to part with a lot of valuable veterans, and that isn't always easy. Guys like Fred Smerlas, Art Still, James Lofton, Joe Devlin, Mark Kelso — quality, quality guys. I don't see the wisdom of seeing a guy and saying he only has two years left and trading him. Play him for those two years, and then we'll find someone else to take his place. That's what we believe in here."

They believe in themselves, even though hardly anyone else wants to. It is the same old story, one year later, and one year older. The Bills against the football world.

The drive for five has officially begun.

Jermaine Gabriel, from Homeless to Grey Cup

November 25, 2017

OTTAWA — He doesn't remember how old he was the first time he was homeless.

Or the first time he was starving.

Or the first time he was penniless.

Or the first time he threw a punch in frustration — although he thinks it might have been in Grade 4.

It all is something of a blur to Jermaine Gabriel, growing up angry in the area known as Chalkfarm, that small stretch of North York high-rises not far from Wilson and Jane. He knows what happened, he knows how it happened, he knows where he came from and how he got to the Grey Cup.

And along the way this football kid, who refused to give in, will start in the defensive backfield of his hometown Argos on Sunday night, a personal tribute of sorts for a story you couldn't invent.

Gabriel had no father to speak of, was brought up by a poor single mom in one of Toronto's most troubled neighbourhoods. He studied guns and gangs and violence in his own way, the way some kids his age studied math and science. And he knew it wasn't the life he aspired to.

He took a most unconventional route in winding up with the Argonauts. After playing football at Cedarbrae Collegiate, there was no scholarship offer awaiting Gabriel. He had to find his own way in football. He went to Bishop's University in Sherbrooke, Quebec, as a walk-on, made the team, and started playing right away.

The football part worked. The rest didn't.

He was at university and admits now he didn't buy a single textbook in his two years there. He couldn't afford any. When there weren't team meals to eat, he regularly dined on what he refers to as syrup sandwiches: One piece of bread folded in two. Pancake syrup playing the part of meat and lettuce, mustard and tomatoes.

He left Bishop's after two seasons because he couldn't pay tuition anymore and was supposed to transfer to St. Mary's, but just as he arrived in Halifax, the head coach and the athletic director at the university were fired. It turned out there was no money there for Gabriel, either.

Instead, he took a job at a local mall as a janitor, cleaning tables in the food court. It paid some bills, but it didn't get him any closer to the football field.

And this is where football took over, at least the community of football. Somebody familiar with Gabriel and his athletic ability was also familiar with a junior football coach in Calgary. Gabriel wound up playing for the Calgary Colts. He hoped at the time, not knowing the rules, that if he played well enough, the local team, the Stampeders, would notice and sign him.

There was only one additional difficulty here. Because he had already played at Bishop's, he couldn't go from junior football to the CFL. He had to go through the draft. And with the 17th pick in the 2013 draft, the Argos selected Gabriel, and the celebration began.

"After such a long road, a long journey, to get brought back to Toronto was amazing," said Gabriel. "As soon as the draft happened, my phone blew up. My mom called as soon as I said hello, she was just screaming in the phone. And my sisters were screaming in the phone. And everybody was screaming in the phone.

"It was such a great feeling to hear all that after all the work I'd done."

It didn't come without a cost along the way. Gabriel lost friends, some to prison, some to funeral homes — too many goodbyes for a man so young.

"I always wanted to make something of myself," said Gabriel. "I'm not lying to you. Growing up was rough. It was a rough lifetime. We were homeless a few times. We lived in a shelter for a little bit. I wasn't leaving Toronto because of gangs and struggling and all that. It was personal for me, I was trying to find my way out."

He needed to get out to get back in.

"A lot of kids growing up didn't have the belief they could get out," said Gabriel, 27. "It can get to you. They thought there is no way for them. It only takes one to show them the way.

"If I can be that guy, great. I always looked up to professional athletes, knowing I had ability, thinking, 'Why not me? Why can't I do it?' I just focused on that.

"I needed to stay focused. That was challenging sometimes. My goal was, every day, not to stray from my ultimate goal, to make it out. You have some ups and downs, but you have to stay at it. I just wanted to get drafted. I just wanted a chance to play. I thought once I got that, the rest would take care of itself."

The rest has taken care of itself.

In his fifth CFL season, Gabriel will play in his first Grey Cup on Sunday.

Then he will go home. To the Mississauga home he moved into while preparing for the Eastern final. His new home. Home and settled, finally.

What Was Pete Carroll Thinking?

February 2, 2015

GLENDALE, ARIZONA — Pete Carroll was talking fast, and talking nonsense, and pacing in circles, trying to explain how it was he made the coaching gaffe of his life, costing the Seattle Seahawks the Super Bowl.

Really, it was hard to explain, and he wasn't helping himself.

Carroll tried more than once to be clear in speedy tones, clearly aggravated and agitated, with no logical answer for how he prevented his team from a second straight football championship.

"Let me tell you what happened," said Carroll, coach of the Seahawks.

Yes, tell us.

There were seconds to go in Super Bowl XLIX, the ball at the 1-yard line, the Seahawks a touchdown away from victory. There were seconds to go, the NFL's most prolific runner, Marshawn Lynch in the backfield, having just run for four yards the play before, in Beast Mode, with the best rushing quarterback in football, Russell Wilson, also in the backfield.

There were three downs to get one yard. There was time left. There were timeouts left.

There was one yard between the Seahawks and a championship, and really nothing in between.

Everything pointed to a Seattle win. And then Carroll made the bad call of the ages, or maybe Darrell Bevell the offensive coordinator did but Carroll was saying it was his call.

He took the blame for the defeat. He will be known for this forever, a blight among blights, an oversight among oversights. The coach who cost his team the Super Bowl.

The Seahawks decided to pass the ball, and I can hear every football coach I've ever known saying the same thing: Three things happen when you throw the football, and two of them are bad.

Wilson made a quick goal-line throw. A pass that never should have been thrown was intercepted. Lynch, with the ball nowhere near him, never moved on the play, never got his chance to be Super Bowl MVP.

And at the New England Patriots bench, Tom Brady, who has watched the Super Bowl losses come on catches made by David Tyree and Mario Manningham, wouldn't look up after Jermaine Kearse made another of those inexplicable catches for the Seahawks. Turning a loss into a win. Except there was no win. If Brady was going to lose another Super Bowl, he just didn't want to witness it. He never looked up.

Now he's a four-time champion with a record-setting number of Super Bowl completions, and it's the Seahawks who don't want to ever see that final play again.

Carroll said he first wanted to use a running play on second down from the 1-yard line. Then New England put in its goal-line defence. So the coach or the offensive coordinator he's covering for decided to cross them up and pass the ball.

With Lynch in the backfield?

With Wilson in the backfield?

With a timeout left? With the whole stadium tilting his way?

"The whole game comes right down to it," said Carroll. "Everything that happened before is meaningless. We were going to win the game. We knew how we were going to do it.

"We had our plays to do it. We had sent in our personnel. They had sent in their goal-line team. It wasn't the right matchup for us to run the football.

"On second down, we threw the ball to kind of waste a play. If we score, we do. If we don't, then we'll run it in on third or fourth down. No second thoughts. No hesitation."

He said Wilson wasn't to blame for the interception. Wilson said Carroll wasn't to blame for the call. Wilson said he cost his team the game by throwing the final pick.

But here's where it gets confusing.

Carroll said Wilson knows to throw the ball away if the play is covered. He didn't. Wilson said he was throwing for the touchdown, had no intention of throwing the ball away. The miscommunication between quarterback and coach — either on the field or after the game — wasn't clear.

"It's not a throwaway," said Wilson. "It's not a throwaway play. It was a chance to make a play. The guy (rookie Malcolm Butler) made a great play. It wasn't a throwaway kind of play.

"On that play, there wasn't really a way out of it. They made a great play. I thought it was going for a touchdown. I didn't question (the call). I think we've done a great job in those situations all year."

"There's really nobody to blame to me. I told them that clearly. And I don't want them to think anything other than that," said Carroll, willing to take the blame, unwilling to say the call was ridiculous.

"We were going to run the ball to win the game but not on that down. That was it."

Carroll, still stunned, embarrassed, embattled, called it a wasted play to win the Super Bowl on third or fourth down.

Wilson said nothing of the kind.

The resilient Seahawks trailed in the second quarter, tied the game at the half, took over the game in the third quarter, almost lost it in the fourth and then had a chance for history.

"We were going to run the ball to win the game," said Carroll, "but not on that play."

Yeah, that's his rather sad story, and he's sticking to it.

The Brady-Belichick Championship Tag Team

January 30, 2015

PHOENIX — Once a week for 15 seasons, Bill Belichick and Tom Brady have met over coffee just to catch up, touch base with how the other is doing and work on taking the next step forward.

It sounds rather simple, really, this easy communication. But it doesn't happen anywhere else in football — or in professional sports, for that matter — that the head coach and the star player get together on schedule and just talk.

"It's pretty amazing watching them," said Josh McDaniels, the offensive coordinator of the New England Patriots. "They have a unique relationship. They meet, talk about different things, about things that can make us better as a team.

"They never look backward, only look forward. What can we do better next week? How can we do it better?"

For 15 football seasons, no one has done it better than Belichick, the ultra-serious and sometimes stoic coach, and Brady, the model-like quarterback who is married to an actual model. Together, the two men are the most prolific combination in football history. You can debate best coach and best quarterback fairly and openly — that kind of talk is endless — but never has there been a duo so successful that their history is so grand that it trumps and swallows all of the cheating allegations that forever surround the Patriots.

"No one," said McDaniels, "has ever done what they've done. Probably no one will ever do it again."

This is the sixth Super Bowl Week for Belichick and Brady. No coach or quarterback has ever done this before. Brady has played for only one coach in his career. In the games he has started, the Patriots have a 180-55 won-loss record. They have shared in three Super Bowl celebrations and probably would have had one or two more had David Tyree not made a catch that defied physics and Wes Welker not dropped a catchable ball.

This is Super Bowl No. 6 for Brady, who is now 37. Terry Bradshaw played his entire career with Chuck Noll in Pittsburgh and won four times. But that's highly unusual by sporting standards to stay in one place with one coach. Joe Montana played for two teams and won four Super Bowls, but played for three different coaches in his career. John Elway won two Super Bowls and played for three coaches on the same team. The continued excellence of the Patriots with Brady and Belichick has come at a salary-capped time, with rosters forever changing, with free agency prominent, when sustained success is challenged in a way it has never been challenged before.

Brady grew up a huge fan of the 49ers and talks about it now with a smile. Long before he had any idea he'd ever play an NFL game, his heroes were named Montana and Steve Young. Like Belichick, he doesn't much care to talk about the history of the moment or the circumstances that link their greatness, but he will go back to his younger days.

"I never imagined in my wildest dreams doing this," said Brady. "As a kid, I just loved to go out and play with my friends. You don't think about where you're going or about your future. To get a chance to play in the Super Bowl, I never thought I'd play in one. So it's pretty unbelievable to be able to play in six.

"It's amazing just sitting here, thinking this is the sixth time I'll be doing this. It's really a privilege. I've been lucky. When it first happened, I was so young that I didn't really understand what this was all about and how challenging this is because everything happens so fast."

And all the time, he never stopped being the sports fan he was as a kid.

"I've always been a fan of sports," he said. "I've never lost that. I (admire) a lot of athletes. Derek Jeter. LeBron (James). Kobe (Bryant). There's a lot of great football players that I look up to. Peyton (Manning) for one ... I admire Aaron (Rodgers) for what he's been able to accomplish and how he does it. Those guys, I really look up to."

To put Brady's playoff success into perspective, consider this: He has won 20 playoff games quarterbacking New England. Twenty-one teams in the NFL have yet to play in that many playoff games, let alone win that many.

And yet his game is somewhat understated. He's thrown for 16,000 fewer yards than Peyton Manning, thrown 138 fewer touchdown passes, but the statistic that best measures him is victories.

"He doesn't act like a big shot," said Rob Gronkowski, the superb tight end. "He doesn't walk around saying, 'I'm Tom Brady and I've done this.'

"He just does it, quietly, and he does it in a way that makes you want to do it that way. Because you don't want to disappoint Tom Brady."

Belichick grew up as something of a football nerd, son of a coach, a somewhat obsessed consumer of football information and news, who started watching film at a very young age. The game became his obsession. Belichick grew up in awe of what Vince Lombardi represented to America, who Tom Landry and Don Shula were, and now his name is alongside theirs and others. You don't win 76% of your games by deflated footballs. The cheat stories are the small picture, not the big picture here. He is the modern-day Lombardi, in a modern world where much is known and historical figures are flawed.

"It's not my place to talk about history," said Belichick, when asked the obvious question. But who's done what he's done?

These aren't the days of Chuck Noll and the Pittsburgh Steelers, with set lineups and no player movement, with nine Hall of Fame players on all four Super Bowl–winning teams. The constants for the Patriots are the coach and the quarterback. The lines, offensive and defensive, change. There is no Franco Harris; the running backs change regularly. There is no Lynn Swann or John Stallworth; the receivers are annual. The All-Star cornerbacks are new this season. This is how you play in today's NFL: week to week, game to game. And all Belichick, forever in his uniform of hoodie and jeans, does is win.

"There's a consistency to Bill (that) you come to appreciate," said Brady. "He doesn't change in approach. Whether it's one win or one loss, we focus on getting better. That doesn't change. He's incredibly consistent that way."

Brandon Browner, who played for Pete Carroll in Seattle and now with Belichick in New England, was clear when asked the difference between the coaches.

"One of them was fun," said Browner, "a player's coach."

He didn't have to say what the other one was.

The relationship with Brady isn't like the relationship with most disposable players. In a way, they have made each other great. It's possible neither could have accomplished what they've managed without each other. Brady, the unexpected superstar, the late-round draft pick; Belichick, who had a 41-56 record before Drew Bledsoe went down with an injury with the Patriots.

Belichick's winning percentage before Brady: .418. His winning percentage since then: .765.

"To me, to be able to sustain this level of success has been an unbelievable thing to witness and watch," said McDaniels. "There's never satisfaction with what they've accomplished, it's always on to the next thing. How do we do this? How do we do that? Always looking forward.

"Their attitude is, if you're satisfied for too long, you'll never advance. There is no complacency with them. The way they come to work is a really neat thing to see."

Said defensive lineman Vince Wilfork: "Just to see (Belichick) work and see what he does on a daily basis is amazing. I don't care if it's a bye week, the off-season, he is always working, thinking, chopping away at something. He never stops. I don't think there's anyone else like him."

John Elway's
Final Act

February 1, 1999

MIAMI — There was one play and a few seconds to go when he began the walk across the field, with his eyes dancing, his arms in the air, his wide grin shining like the Florida sun.

It was a walk he'll remember for the rest of his life.

"That's the one you dream of as a kid," said John Elway, Super Bowl champion once again. "Nothing feels better than this."

There was one play and 40 seconds left when his coach called him to the sideline, when he took the walk that all champions should take. There was a wave to the crowd, a standing ovation, the hugs from teammates by the bench.

John Elway, maybe, was saying goodbye. Probably was saying goodbye. Noncommittal on this wondrous night, with the Denver Broncos winning the Super Bowl again and this time with Elway as Most Valuable Player.

He cried as he stood on the sideline before the game even began. He cried as he heard Cher singing the U.S. national anthem, probably thinking about 16 football seasons flashing in front of him, looking around the stadium, taking in everything — possibly for the very last time.

"I got a little emotional," Elway said, while leaving open the possibility of a 17th season. "I'm not going to talk about retirement right now. I'll cross that bridge when it comes around."

Elway pushed his way through all the cameras when it was over, deking through the mob, searching for his family, searching for his wife. It was their vote that convinced him to return for a 16th season. The vote was 5-1; he was the lone dissenter.

This was his championship, his Most Valuable Player award, his greatest of five Super Bowl appearances. But this was theirs also. "This is just thrilling,"

Elway said. "This is what you play for. To be able to do this two years in a row, at this stage of my career, is unbelievable."

At precisely what stage of his career? That is the question. His coach, Mike Shanahan, figures this was the last of Elway and maybe the best. Some of his closest teammates also figure there is more pain in his body than he will let you see in his eyes. "If he leaves," linebacker Bill Romanowski said, "he leaves like Michael Jordan. I just feel fortunate to have been able to play with him."

Last night, he looked more like the old John Elway than *an* old John Elway. He stood tall, strong, moving in the pocket, conducting the orchestra, forever in control. He threw for one touchdown. He ran for another. He came within a miscommunication of a Super Bowl record for passing yardage.

He was the show.

The only mistake on his résumé yesterday was an Atlanta interception by Ronnie Bradford on a pass Shannon Sharpe should have caught.

"I don't remember the last time John played like that," Romanowski said. "I don't remember the last time we needed him to play like that."

This is the way storybooks are supposed to end, with the great ones walking off as champions, the good guys winning. This is the way we want our heroes to end up, with a career wrapped and packaged with a ribbon. Michael Jordan hitting a jumper to win a championship. Ted Williams hitting a home run in his final at-bat. Wayne Gretzky winning the MVP of an All-Star Game. For us as much as for them.

And now there is another name, another file for the memory, a Super Bowl game of little consequence other than sentimentality. "The old man," Sharpe said, "still has the gift left in him. He is going to sit down and talk about what he is going to do, but we would love to have him back another year."

That is the question and that is the challenge. Last year, Elway wanted to retire; his family wanted him to keep playing. This year, the idea of winning three championships in succession, something no Super Bowl team has done, will be put before him. The lure will be there. Is that dream walk across the field enough to satisfy a lifetime? Or does an opportunity to go where no quarterback has gone bring Elway back for one last season?

"I'm biased," Broncos coach Mike Shanahan said. "But whether he comes back or not, I think he's the greatest of all time."

Through a voice hoarse from celebration and with a smile that would not end, Elway wouldn't speculate about his future and wouldn't discuss his place in history. The historical references, he said, were for others to determine. The future is up to him.

"Right now, I just want to enjoy this," John Elway said. "Last year was unbelievable. This year is unbelievable. Nothing feels better than this."

The Rocket at Argos Camp

June 8, 1991

GUELPH — It was overwhelming.

You knew it was overwhelming because everyone kept telling you how overwhelming it was.

Wayne was there. And Wayne's wife. And Wayne's kids. And the Rocket. And John Candy. And owner Brucie.

And there was security. A lot of people disguised as Bob Dylan's bodyguards.

Out at the University of Guelph, there was time for photo ops and sound bites, autographs and hand-shaking. It was a bar mitzvah without the service, a wedding without the bride or groom.

"Training camp was never like this last year," said Argos general manager Mike McCarthy.

No fooling, cowboy.

Just who were all these people in Guelph, and what were they doing celebrating the opening of the Argos' camp, like it was a day of significance or something? There were nine television crews, twice that number of photographers and representatives from every newspaper in Southern Ontario. But there were more people, lots more people. People lined up outside a fence to watch Gretzky catch a football or to get a glimpse of Rocket Ismail. Future veterinarians skipped university classes just to get a look at this. Some people held signs. And some people came just to watch John Candy sweat.

For the record, Candy does sweat a lot. And for the record, Bruce McNall does not.

This I want explained to me, being an overweight person and all. It was hot yesterday and it was humid. I was wearing light cotton pants and a short-sleeved top. And sweating. A lot.

McNall was wearing a suit and tie yesterday, and I even checked to see if his top button was done up. It was. I was sweating just looking at what he was wearing. He wasn't.

Indeed this is an incredible man, owner of this brand-new hit called the Argos. He has transformed Argos football into breakfast with Bruce. Orange juice and croissants. Freshly squeezed and freshly baked. None of this Harry Ornest day-old stuff.

Training camps aren't supposed to be like this. The least comfortable-looking people at this football party yesterday were the football people, the coach and general manager of the Argos. Their job is winning. Everybody else is on the entertainment side.

Training camps are supposed to open with questions. Who'll play shortstop, Manny Lee or Eddie Zosky? Will it be Mark Whiten or Glenallen Hill in right field? And what about that fifth starter?

There were questions yesterday. Penetrating questions. Wayne, how old is your daughter? John, what's your next movie? Janet, are you still acting? Rocket, can you lend me a few bucks?

Nobody asked about James "Quick" Parker, legend of Canadian football, about to give it one last training-camp shot.

Nobody asked about the new contract that should be coming for the phenomenal Pinball Clemons, who is paid less than some of the reporters covering the club.

Nobody asked about Adam Rita, new Argos coach, in his first year on the job as a head man.

No one asked about improving a defence that kept games close last year when the Argos were scoring at record pace.

Issues? Who needs issues when you have croissants and orange juice?

I suppose this has become the sporting version of the Cannes Film Festival. Nobody really cares about the movies, do they? It's all about people watching, networking, gawking. That kind of thing.

These are the new Argos. Training camp is now open. Excitement is everywhere. I know this because people kept telling me it was so.

Two-a-days start Sunday in the heat. Competition. Hitting. Grunting. Heads smashing. The usual.

Everyone will be sweating. Everyone except Bruce McNall. You'll be able to recognize him. He'll be the one standing on the sideline, wearing a tie. Looking round but cool.

Memories of a
Best Friend Gone

November 21, 1998

WINNIPEG — The game was over and Mike Morreale sat at his locker at Ivor Wynne Stadium and began to undress when he was handed a typewritten note by a man in a Tiger-Cats jacket.

"The first thing I saw was the Argos letterhead on the page," Morreale said. "I didn't have to read a sentence. I knew."

He knew Norm Casola had passed away.

"Everything just froze at that moment. I wasn't thinking about the game or the score or what was going on around me. I just sat there, stunned, thinking about Normie, thinking about all we'd been through.

"He made me a better man."

That was two months and one day ago, and on Thursday night, as Morreale accepted the award for the top Canadian player in the Canadian Football League, he softly ran his fingers over a pin he wore on his left lapel and dedicated his Grey Cup performance to his former teammate and closest football friend.

Mike Morreale first met Norm Casola in the Argonauts training camp of 1995. The two were a lot alike. One from Hamilton. One from Sault Ste. Marie. They were about the same size, played the same position, didn't start and had to struggle to keep up, let alone make the team.

"Out of competition," Morreale said, "our friendship was born. He was always pulling for me and I was always pulling for him. We had many conversations and sometimes we felt each other's pain. A bond grew out of that: him pushing me, me pushing him, competing for the same things."

In the season in which Norm Casola succumbed to cancer, Mike Morreale made it as a football player. He caught 67 passes for the Ticats, scored six touchdowns and went over the 1,000-yard mark. A year ago, his highlight of Grey

Cup week was playing in the media touch football game. This year, he's not only starting in the Grey Cup, he's one of the game's featured players.

"The last time I spoke to Normie, he told me he was proud of me," Morreale said. "That really meant something to me. I can take so much from what I saw from him. I can take his never-give-up attitude, never quit, because it's never good enough.

"You know, he wasn't the fastest guy in the world and he didn't fit the proto-type model. He took a lot of hard knocks and he would always get on my back about being tougher. He was calling me, telling me he wanted this so much."

This football life.

"There are a lot of guys like us it doesn't come easy to," said Morreale, who was cut by the B.C. Lions in 1994 and played two unspectacular seasons in Toronto before finally emerging in this, his fourth CFL season.

"You take your lumps, you think you deserve better. Sometimes you complain to yourself about it. That's what happens when you're a Canadian player.

"But what people need to understand is what he went through, how much he wanted to play this game. I'd like to see an award named in his honour. He epitomized the Canadian in the Canadian Football League. He never made a lot of money. He wasn't flashy. He just went and played hard, good old-fashioned football."

And tomorrow, when Mike Morreale sits in the locker room and does his final preparation for the Grey Cup game, the spirit of Norm Casola will be with him.

"I don't think many people fully understand how tough it was for him, how big it all was," Morreale said. "Imagine, playing football on morphine. He did in his last year. He was in that much pain. But he wouldn't stop. That's how much he loved playing football.

"I knew what it meant for him to play. To him, it wasn't about catching a winning pass or running for 100 yards. That's not how he thought about the game. It was about getting something out of yourself and not letting your teammates down. When I think of a guy who does everything for everyone else, I think of him.

"This wasn't just a man having cancer. It was in that sensitive (genitals) area. His very manhood was being questioned."

The other night, with a national television audience watching and so much to say, Morreale knew he had to talk about his friend, knew he had to find the strength to do so.

"I almost lost it," Morreale said. "It was touch and go. If I had more time, I could have gone on all night talking about him. But I had to hold it together. It's not that I have anything against crying, but I never heard that guy cry. Not once. Not ever.

"This one I'm playing for him."

A Fond Farewell to the Cleveland Browns

December 18, 1995

CLEVELAND — Long after it was over, in the place they call the Dawg Pound, people stood with sad eyes, sobered by circumstance, staring straight ahead but barely moving.

A woman in Section 49 tried to stop crying but couldn't. Beside her, old friends hugged, promised to keep in touch and wondered when and if they'd see each other again.

"Look around, look at these people," said Tim Phillips, who has sat in the same Dawg Pound seats at Cleveland Stadium for the past 16 years. "None of them want to leave. None of them knows where to go.

"These are people from all over the state. Good, successful people who have been coming here for years. They get in here, in the Dawg Pound, and they let some steam off, they have some fun. Where are they going to go now?"

This is how it ended for the Cleveland Browns yesterday, with emotion and sadness, with anger, destruction and disgust. This is how it ended after 50 years of football, with a canned announcement thanking fans for their support, and an unscheduled renovation of a stadium in need of one.

In the Dawg Pound, behind the end zone, where the loudest and most ardent of Browns fans are found, they passed around saws and pliers and screwdrivers, taking apart the wooden benches in the stadium piece by piece.

"We started a few weeks ago, loosening the bolts," Phillips said. "I decided, I'm taking my seats with me. This is my own personal seat licence. I paid for the seat. I'm taking it. It's going into my basement."

In Section 42, not far from the Dawg Pound, where the seats are actual bolted-in chairs with backs, the final minutes of the final game were a race of stadium destruction. With each broken row of seating being passed down and tossed on to the field, the cheer went up. "This is for you, Art Modell!" But this was not the kind of stadium improvement he was asking for.

When the game ended with, ironically, a sharp 26-10 win over the Cincinnati Bengals, Cleveland safety Dana Hall was the first of many players to race the length of the field and pay homage to the fans in the Pound.

"I have seen every kind of fans in sport, but I've never seen ones like this before," defensive lineman Rob Burnett said. "That's why I wanted to go down there. It's strange, not all of this that we're leaving has even kicked in yet.

"Going to the fans, it was just something I felt. It wasn't planned. It wasn't anything we talked about. It was something I needed to do. I wanted to thank them personally. It's sad. I told them, 'You guys are the best.' It choked me up a bit."

It choked up so many in the crowd at the stadium, where the most complete Browns performance of this incomplete season seemed lost in the eerie scenery. Julie O'Boyle of Green, Ohio, grew up in Detroit and married into a Cleveland Browns relationship. Wearing one dog-bone earring and a small Browns helmet in the other ear, she hugged her husband closely as the game and an era came to an end. Together they left, carrying a piece of their seat in hand.

"When we got married, he said, 'You marry me, you marry the Browns,'" she said. "We've still got our marriage."

But divorce proceedings on the football team already have been set in motion.

The poetry of Ohio was found in the signs and T-shirts and hats worn throughout Cleveland Municipal Stadium yesterday. THE GRINCH WHO $TOLE FOOTBALL, read one sign. GO TO HELL, MODELL, read another. WE SHALL HAUNT YOU FOREVER. read yet another.

You get the idea.

And in the end-zone stands, where the barking grew quiet and the eyes of the Dawg Pound were misty, the only sounds were of the stadium seats being taken apart for souvenirs or simply for kicks.

These emotions, however destructive, were the purest of fan emotions, inspired by hurt and brought on by football injustice. NFL commissioner Paul Tagliabue should have been amongst the fans, hearing their words, studying their eyes, watching their faces. So should have every owner of every team in professional sport.

All they want here is a football team, their football team. All they want is for things to remain the same.

A man named Tony Schaefer arrived as he always arrives at Browns games. He drove the 22-seat school bus from Sandusky that he has painted in Browns colours, filled with friends and fans and memories.

"I think I'm going to cry," he said as the time ran out on the Browns in Cleveland. "I think I'm going to be emotional. I was here for the championship game in '64. I was here when Brian Sipe threw the pass. This is what I do and where I go."

Then he walked slowly out of the stadium, like so many others, perhaps for the very last time.

In 1995 owner Art Modell announced he was moving the Cleveland Browns to Baltimore. That was supposed to leave one of America's great football cities without an NFL team. It did for three seasons. In 1999, an expansion version of the Cleveland Browns began playing in the NFL, correcting one of the great wrongs in football history.

The Day Toronto Shocked the Football World

July 11, 2017

Imagine Tom Brady, Rob Gronkowski and Julian Edelman leaving the Super Bowl champion New England Patriots to sign with an upstart football league — to play in Toronto, of all places.

As far-fetched as that may sound, something similar, just as stunning, happened 43 years ago: the day Toronto shocked and owned the football world.

"I guess we made history back then," said Hall of Fame running back Larry Csonka on a long-distance line. "It was shocking. We were shocked. Everyone was shocked."

"To use an overworked phrase, we were made an offer we couldn't refuse," said Hall of Fame receiver Paul Warfield on a cellphone.

From the visionary mind of the late Johnny Bassett, owner of the World Football League's Toronto Northmen, came the notion: Why not start a new franchise in a new league and go after the best players on the best team in professional football, the two-time Super Bowl champion Miami Dolphins?

Why not stun the sporting world?

Bassett, partnering with his general manager, Leo Cahill, and his lawyer, Herb Solway, decided to target Super Bowl MVP Csonka, his backfield running mate Jim Kiick, and the elegant wide receiver Warfield — all stars on the most popular and successful team in the most popular and successful league, the National Football League — and make a serious pitch for all three.

"That was Johnny. He didn't think like other people thought," said Solway. "He was a brilliant entrepreneur. If he wanted to charm you, he charmed you. He had great ideas and crazy ideas, and this one was both of those things."

On March 31, 1974, the Toronto Northmen announced the signing of Csonka, Kiick and Warfield to a three-year, $3.86 million deal in a most unusual way. "We did it on the Howard Cosell show, live on ABC television," said Csonka, who was friendly with the legendary Cosell. "We were in Toronto on a camera and Howard was in New York. The next day, it was front page of the *New York Times*." *TIME* magazine called it "the deal that astonished the sports world."

"Johnny was so excited about this," said Solway. "I wasn't nearly as high on this as Johnny was. I was his lawyer, I was paid to worry. I didn't know where we were going to play. I didn't know how we were going to pay these guys. Johnny was a visionary. He was a brilliant visionary. When you think of the things this guy did — he brought *Hair* to Toronto, he financed films, he owned the Toros, he owned the Tampa Bay Bandits. Johnny was always looking forward. It scared me because he wouldn't see the downside of things. If he jumped off a building, he expected you to jump with him. He was jumping about the signing ... I wasn't so sure."

Johnny Bassett passed away in 1986 at age 47. He was only 34 when he signed Csonka, Kiick and Warfield.

This was one of the great adventures of his amazing life.

ED KEATING REPRESENTED CSONKA, Kiick and Warfield, and when he arrived in Toronto for a meeting at the Bridal Suite of the Sutton Place Hotel he was carrying a number of copies of a neatly typewritten book: his treatise on what it would take to sign the three football players with the Northmen.

The demands, considering the times and the modest salaries paid to professional athletes, were somewhat outrageous. But Keating was known for being precocious: He worked for Arnold Palmer exclusively before branching out on his own in the sports agency business.

"If you want these players, this is what you're going to have to pay," the late Keating told Bassett and Solway.

"Word had kind of leaked out that these guys were coming to Toronto and I think it was Dick Beddoes in the *Globe and Mail* who wrote 'Hell would freeze over' before we ever sign these guys." After seeing the figures proposed in Keating's book of demands, Solway didn't disagree. "I looked at the book and thought, 'He wants everything.' You can't believe what he asked for. It was way more than we could afford."

After the initial meeting with Keating — at the time, the players were being wined and dined in a downtown restaurant by GM Cahill — Bassett and Solway met privately.

"To be honest, I'm more shocked by the (demands) than anything I've been shocked by in my life," Solway remembered. "I said to Johnny, 'We can't do this. We can't give them these things.'

"And he looks at me like he's not listening and says, 'Suppose we say yes?'

"If I remember, there were 86 separate items in the book, all kinds of clauses, and I'm looking over all of them nervously and Bassett says, 'What's he going to do if we say yes?'

"And then before I give him the lawyer's answer, he says, 'Let's do this.'

"I said, 'You're not serious about this, are you?'" said Solway. "And Bassett said, 'I'm absolutely serious about this.'"

They then returned to meet with Keating in the Bridal Suite for a different kind of marriage. "We walked into the room and Johnny sticks out his hand to Ed and says, 'You've got a deal,' and Keating took his hand back so fast you wouldn't believe it."

Keating said: "I have to speak to the boys."

Bassett said: "You said we had a deal."

The three men left the hotel and headed to the restaurant to meet up with Cahill, Csonka, Kiick and Warfield, at least two of them nervous in their own way.

CSONKA WAS PAID $55,000 to run the football for the Miami Dolphins in 1973. It was the famed season in which O.J. Simpson rushed for 2,003 yards with the Buffalo Bills. Csonka ran for half that many but scored two touchdowns in the Super Bowl victory by the Dolphins. The three-year offer to sign with the Northmen was for a guaranteed $1.4 million over three seasons, more than eight times what the Dolphins were paying him per season back then.

"The money, it was like nothing we'd ever seen before," Csonka said. "It was hard to comprehend how much it was at the time."

Free agency in the NFL didn't begin until 1992, almost 16 years after it started in Major League Baseball. And there wasn't any kind of free agency in the NHL or the NBA until 1995.

"By today's standards, this deal seems like nothing," said Solway. "Arguably, though, this was the start of real big-money free agency in American sport."

Csonka was going to be paid the most of the three departing Dolphins. Warfield's deal was to pay him $900,000 over three seasons, while Kiick's was in the $700,000 range. The total deal was reported as U.S. $3.86 million.

"We thought we were heading up to Toronto for the weekend to meet with Johnny Bassett but we wound up spending a lot more time with Leo Cahill than we did with Bassett," said Csonka. "In fact, I hardly remember seeing Bassett very much at all."

Keating was doing the contract negotiating. Cahill was selling football in Toronto.

"I liked Leo," said Csonka. "How could you not like Leo? He believed in what he was selling you and you couldn't help but believe in him. I had this connection with Leo. He seemed to know all about me. He knew about my school days. He knew about my college days. He was a real football guy. But I wasn't nervous about any of this because, really, I didn't think I was going to take any of it seriously.

"And they didn't have to sell me on the city. I knew the city already. I'd been up there a number of times fishing. We didn't really know much about the World Football League or anything, we were just there to listen and see. And then we met Leo, and he did all the selling, and he really knew his football. One time, he pulled out a chalkboard and started showing us how we were all going to fit in."

After dessert came the offer, almost with a cherry on top. And with it came excitement and fear and consternation and another drink. It was all happening so fast.

Csonka, being the least certain, was the last to agree. He was extremely close to Miami coach Don Shula. The players used to jokingly call him "Shula's son." Before Csonka would agree to sign with the Northmen, he wanted one more conversation with his coach.

"We used to say, 'Hey, your dad called' when Shula called," Jim Kiick told the *Palm Beach Post* in 2014. "We called Shula, (at least) Csonka did. And Csonka talked to him and said, 'Hey, we want (owner) Joe Robbie to call us.'"

This is where there are various versions of the story. Csonka waited for a call from Robbie that never came. Cahill has long told a story that while Csonka was waiting for a Shula call he called down to the front desk of the hotel and told them that under no circumstances were they to put any calls through to the suite. There was a timeline attached to that call.

Csonka said he talked to Shula, then waited for Robbie.

That call never came. And if it did, it never got to Csonka.

The blocked call, if there was one, eliminated the last impediment to this crazy agreement.

After returning to Miami for his final NFL season in 1979 — long after the WFL had folded and Csonka had played elsewhere — Robbie wanted little to do with Csonka.

"Joe Robbie never understood (what happened)," said Csonka. "At first, Shula was completely rattled by what happened. It took him a long time to calm down about it. But years later, I think he understood better. He once said to me, 'This isn't college football. You're not playing for the Gipper anymore. This is a job.' But with Joe Robbie, he was never very nice to me after that. I don't think he ever got over us leaving."

In Super Bowl VIII, Csonka ran for two touchdowns and 145 yards and was named Most Valuable Player. Miami hasn't won a Super Bowl since.

Shula was asked to interview for this article. Through the Dolphins media relations staff, he politely declined.

WARFIELD WAS NO STRANGER to Toronto. He grew up in Ohio, played for the Cleveland Browns and had made the drive north on numerous occasions.

"My wife and I visited Toronto often when we lived in Cleveland, and we enjoyed it a lot," said Warfield, in a phone interview from his home in Rancho Mirage, California. "I was excited about the thought of going to Toronto initally, for the visit, but it was never my plan to sign there."

He was late in his career — "back nine," he calls it — and seeking a new contract in Miami. "I was thinking about my future and my family's future," he said. "I didn't have a lot of years left. We had been to the Super Bowl three straight years. I thought I brought a lot of value to that team. Honestly, I thought that going up to Toronto would be a way to bring the Miami Dolphins to the negotiating table. In those days, we didn't have any leverage. There was no free agency."

Right after Super Bowl VIII, Warfield instructed his agent to write a letter to the Dolphins indicating he was prepared to sign a new contract immediately. There was no response to the letter. Not even a phone call. What the players were eventually told was: Miami wouldn't be signing any contracts until after the 1974 NFL Draft and until they had draft picks signed.

"They were putting players who hadn't played ahead of those of us who had. And I was put off by that," said Warfield. "What the Dolphins were saying was, 'We'll get around to you.' Deep down inside, I must admit my sympathies and feelings were remaining in Miami."

The weekend in Toronto didn't go as planned. "It was a wonderful, wonderful offer," said Warfield. "My first phone call was to my wife. I told her, 'You wouldn't believe what's going on here.'"

The contract was written by hand on Solway's legal pad. The trio signed it in the Bridal Suite of Sutton Place. "I was nervous about fulfilling the contract," said Solway. "Johnny was a promoter. Leo was a promoter. And I'm thinking, 'How are we going to pay these guys?'"

CSONKA SIGNED FOR THE MONEY, but he also signed because he wanted to play in Toronto. He loved the city and what Cahill was selling. The same was true of Warfield.

It just never happened.

It was a different time, a different Trudeau as prime minister. And the government of Canada, with a protectionary health (sport) minister named Marc Lalonde, basically prevented the WFL from doing business in the country. It was all in the name of protecting the Canadian Football League.

"Marc Lalonde was our executioner on this," said Solway. "We had made this big splash, I thought he was unreasonable and we had to move the franchise."

The Toronto Northmen moved their operation and became the Memphis Southmen. "That wasn't what I signed on for," said Csonka. "I wanted to play in Toronto, not some other place. A lot of our hearts weren't in it once they moved to Memphis."

"I was extremely disappointed by the events back then," said Warfield. "I understood the concern of Canada, wanting to protect the Canadian Football League. But I was hoping I would have been able to play for the new league up in Canada, and I was very excited about the possibility."

"We tried to fight the government on this," said Solway. "We didn't get very far."

Csonka, Kiick and Warfield remained with the Dolphins for the option year of their contract before they joined the Southmen in the second season of the fledgling World Football League. The league folded in 1975 after Memphis played its 11th game: In all, the Southmen played 31 games, winning 24 of them. They were 7-4 with the three high-paid recruits in the lineup.

Bassett tried to turn that WFL team into something more. He went to NFL commissioner Pete Rozelle and asked for an expansion franchise. He had the three Dolphins under contract. He thought it would be enough to get his foot in the door. When the NFL turned down his request, he had no choice but to let Csonka, Kiick and Warfield out of their deals.

The three players returned to the NFL the following season, Csonka to the New York Giants, Kiick to Denver, Warfield back to Cleveland.

Csonka retired after the 1979 season, two years after Warfield stepped away at the age of 35; Kiick barely played after Memphis, rarely carrying the ball in his two final seasons. He was done by the age of 31 and is currently in poor health.

Cahill also is in poor health in his 89th year, living with family outside Atlanta. Keating passed away in 1996 at the age of 59, but not before signing Frank Robinson to a contract as baseball's first African-American manager. Solway, who played a significant role in Toronto acquiring a Major League Baseball franchise, is still seen around the ballpark and still practicing a little law at age 86. He was recently honoured by the University of Toronto.

All this happened in a flurry of activity in 1974 and Solway remembers so much of it, with one great regret.

"We're in Memphis for the opening ball game. I'm down there with (friend and law partner) Lionel Schipper and others and Johnny (Bassett) excuses himself from our box. And he doesn't come back," said Solway. "At the end of the game, Johnny joins us and tells us he was sitting over there, with Elvis (Presley).

"I said, 'Where's Elvis?' and Johnny tells me he's gone. We were pissed as hell about this. We never met him, never saw him, never got within 15 feet of him. In the end, we lost our football team and a chance to meet Elvis Presley."

CHAPTER 6

Gone, Just Never Forgotten

There Was Only
One Badger Bob

August 31, 1991

PITTSBURGH — With long faces and with great pain, they say they will continue. They say they will play. They say that it matters.

To Bob Johnson. For Bob Johnson.

And just a few blocks from today's Canada Cup opener, the hockey tournament seems far less important than a single human life.

Johnson, the coach of Team USA, the coach of the Stanley Cup champion Pittsburgh Penguins, is in an intensive care ward at Mercy Hospital, his life in a state of peril. Johnson underwent emergency surgery yesterday morning to remove a "good-sized" brain tumour from just above his right ear.

Though he's out of danger for now, Pittsburgh executive Paul Martha offered this solemn assessment: "The prognosis is not good," he said.

Once again, a cold slice of reality has intruded upon sport. And the two have rarely been a comfortable match. But here it is different, here the lines are even less distinguishable.

Bob Johnson is hockey and hockey is his life. There is no separating the two. There is no understating what Johnson means to hockey or what hockey means to him.

And for those around him now, trying to deal with the human dilemma of sport and tragedy is challenging by the minute.

"It is very hard right now, very hard to maintain a meaningful focus," said Gary Suter, the Team USA defenceman who played his best hockey for Johnson in Calgary.

"Words can't describe how I feel, how any of us feel about what's happened. You think, 'We've got to play tomorrow, and right now who feels like playing?'

Then you realize, 'What would Badger want us to do more than anything?' Today he would have wanted us to have a great practice.

"I think we tried to do that. I don't know if it came off."

Bob Johnson started feeling odd the past couple of weeks, those close to him now say. He was tired. Less himself. The bouncy enthusiasm that has been his trademark wasn't coming naturally.

"We all noticed he wasn't himself," said Penguins general manager Craig Patrick. "He was aware he was having some kind of problems."

He didn't know what. Johnson was slurring some words. He thought his problems were dental. The team dentist told him to see the doctor. And when he returned home from a Team USA road trip his wife, Martha, was so shaken by his appearance, she immediately took him to the hospital. That was Thursday.

"I just thought he was really tired," said Mike Eaves, his assistant coach and a close personal friend. "He seemed to be mumbling a lot. It wasn't like him. I thought, long season, not much of a summer, it must be getting to him."

The hospital scheduled a series of tests for yesterday. The tests were never taken.

After leaving the hospital Thursday, the Johnsons went out for dinner. Midway through their meal at a downtown restaurant, Badger Bob had to be rushed to the hospital. A neurosurgeon operated early yesterday morning. The doctors figure the growth was cancerous.

And today a sense of shock remains, for those who know him and for those who don't. Other people get old. Other people get sick. But not Bob Johnson. He's 60 going on 16. He's the Energizer bunny. He's nonstop.

"I never thought anything would go wrong with Badger," said Suter. "He just never left you the impression anything was wrong. He's so full of fun, so upbeat, every day was so positive for him.

"To me, he appeared to be a little tired lately. But I say that now, with hindsight. I didn't really notice it at the time. I'd see him sitting on the bench in practice instead of being involved. That wasn't Badger. But I never gave it a second thought then."

The silence in the Team USA dressing room yesterday was almost deafening. No music played. No jokes were exchanged. Everywhere you turned, there was a sense of sadness, a hockey void.

And today, Team USA must play Team Sweden in the Canada Cup opener, whether they feel up to it or not. This is not a great day for hockey.

"I can hear Badger Bob now, saying, 'Canada Cup. World class players. Best competition in the world,'" said Brett Hull. "His spirit is incredible. He lives for these things.

"We came to count on that spirit. And every one of us needs that spirit now."

Three months after this column was written, Bob Johnson passed away at the age of 60.

Mr. Hockey, Gordie Howe

June 11, 2016

The nickname was perfect and simple, descriptive yet succinct: Mr. Hockey.

You didn't need any other description.

That was Gordie Howe.

That will always be Gordie Howe.

The Big Fella with the warm smile and the giant handshake.

His nickname was short, just like his hockey stick. It was compact, the way his rounded shoulders and elbows seemed to be. It was basic and easy, comfortable, just like his personality. Mr. Hockey: Forever alive in our memories and our hearts, the once-in-a-lifetime talent dead at the age of 88.

Gone, but never, in a country consumed by hockey, forgotten.

He was born in Floral, Saskatchewan, in 1928, which isn't really a place anymore as much as it is an intersection on the outskirts of Saskatoon.

There's a corner and there used to be a silo, and that was pretty much it. With a HOME OF GORDIE HOWE sign. And from that frozen prairie province came the warmest of hockey stars, the contradiction of all contradictions. Never has anyone played better, harder, meaner, tougher, been friendlier, easier, more generous with his time, so much in love with his wife, his family, and the sport he helped make famous.

"He never acted like a star," said Norm Ullman, who was fortunate enough to play 13 seasons with Howe in Detroit, some of them with Howe as his right winger.

"He didn't big-time anyone. He was a great player, the greatest I ever played with. But he was a great big, friendly guy.

"He didn't put himself above anybody. That wasn't what he was about. He was just one of the guys, you'd go to his house for dinner. There was nothing big about him but his game.

"These days they'd call him a power forward. I don't know when they started using the term, but he really defined it. He was strong, big, his arms were the size of my legs, and he was really powerful, really skilled. Back in those days, everybody had to look out for themselves. There was nobody protecting anybody.

"You had to fend for yourself. Nobody fended better and tougher than Gordie Howe."

And nobody lasted longer.

He played 25 seasons for the Red Wings, six out of retirement with his son Mark, a Hall of Famer, in Houston and New England of the WHA — those four Houston years included son Marty too — and then a final NHL season in Hartford, with a Mount Rushmore lineup that included Bobby Hull, Dave Keon and Mark.

To put his talents into modern-day context, consider this: Howe scored 49 goals and 95 points in 1953 in a 70-game season in an NHL with fewer goals per game than any season of the past 63 years. No other player scored more than 30. No other player had more than Rocket Richard's 61 points. That season, Howe scored 50% more goals than anyone on the other five NHL teams and more than 50% more points.

When he first retired in 1971, he led all of hockey in games played, goals scored, points, games played for a single franchise and elbows thrown. Out of respect but not for history, the combination of a goal, an assist and a fight in a game later became known as a Gordie Howe Hat Trick — even though he had managed to do that particular triple only twice in 2,186 professional games.

"To put Gordie in context as a hockey player, it's pretty inarguable that there are four names that come to mind: Wayne Gretzky. Mario Lemieux. Bobby Orr. And Gordie. The four best players of all time. The order doesn't really matter. You can do it any way you want. They all belong," said Jimmy Devellano, the longtime general manager of the Red Wings, who watched Howe closely in his career as a fan and scout but got to know him personally after he retired.

"Of those four, two of them, Orr and Gretzky, call him the best ever. Those are the big four names of hockey. And now we've lost one of them, and that's very sad."

Devellano tried to define the Howe he knew.

"What struck me so much about Gordie was his simplicity — and I say that in the most complimentary of terms. It was his lack of what I'd call big-shot-itis. He treated the parking lot attendant the same as he would treat the owner of an NHL team."

He had that way about him.

"I loved that he made you feel comfortable being around him. There wasn't any pretense to him. You expected him to have some kind of swagger, because he was Gordie Howe. But he never had that. And that's what so many of us loved about him.

"On the ice, and Mark Howe and I used to talk about this all the time, there was an instinctive meanness about him. He would say, 'Oh my goodness, when my dad played, he used to terrify me.' Thank goodness people knew to be careful around him or they knew what they'd get. And then you'd meet him after and he was this great big gentle giant."

Howe won four Stanley Cups for the Red Wings and played in 11 Stanley Cup Finals. In one 16-year span, he scored more than a point per game in 15 seasons. A top 10 scorer through those seasons would often finish with 50 points. Howe would regularly score more than 70.

In 1959, in the first game Gordie Howe ever played against his former roommate, Red Kelly, he put his arm on Kelly's shoulders near the Maple Leafs net and gently asked, "How's your wife?" The two had been great friends. "We lived together, bowled together, played together, danced together — Gordie loved to dance — did everything together," Kelly, the Hall of Fame defenceman and forward, said Friday.

"Twelve and a half seasons together, four Stanley Cups, seven league championships.

"Pretty incredible run when you think about it. In that game, he puts his arm on me and I turn to answer. Before I know it, he almost put me through the end of the boards. I mean, that's how hard he hit me. He was cute that way. You didn't always see it coming. That's just Gordie. That's the way Gordie was."

When he stopped in the middle of the game to ask about Kelly's wife, Red certainly understood the conversation part and maybe even the context.

"I met my wife because of him."

This goes back to the days before Howe met and married Colleen, his wife and business partner of 56 years.

Back then, he was smitten by the legendary Canadian figure skater Barbara Ann Scott. The newspapers had written a little about it, even though there wasn't much of a relationship at all.

"Gordie heard she was going to be at a restaurant at Grand River, by the Olympia in Detroit for dinner," said Kelly.

"He wanted someone to go with him because he'd never met her. This would be his chance, he figured. He asked Ted Lindsay to go and he said no. He asked a few others, they said no. I said, 'Oh, I'll go with you.' So we went off to the restaurant and the head guy told us she wasn't there. But he said that some of the others from the Hollywood Ice Revue were sitting over there. He asked if we'd like to meet them. Gordie said sure."

Seated at the table was Andra McLaughlin, who had been hired in the skating show to replace the famed Sonja Henie. Andra met Red Kelly and Gordie that night. Eight years later, she and Red were married.

"If it wasn't for Gordie," said Kelly. "I don't know how my life would have turned out."

Gordie Howe and Rocket Richard were the giants of their generation. The first megastars of the NHL.

One was large and physical and skilled and occasionally vicious. The other was electric, the first to score 50 goals in 50 games.

When Howe played against Richard, it was an event — even though they were rarely on the ice together. Montreal had a checking line play against Howe. Detroit had a checking line play against Richard. But one night, they happened to be on the ice together, and all of a sudden there was Howe and there was the Rocket, gloves on the ice, ready to fight.

"Everyone just stopped and circled them and watched," said Red Kelly.

"King Clancy was the referee, and he just let them go. We all stood there watching and both guys landed some blows. And then Rocket swung and missed Howe and he lost his balance and fell to the ice. "What's a matter, you finally met your match?" Howe's centre, Sid Abel, jeered at Richard.

Richard got up swinging but not at Howe. He was so mad he broke Sid Abel's nose. "He wouldn't go back at Gordie. I don't think he wanted that."

The two generational superstars never fought again.

When Gordie Howe lent his name to the Scotiabank Pro-Am hockey tournament in Toronto, the incredibly successful fundraiser for Alzheimer's disease, it brought a certain credibility to the on-ice event. Howe's wife, Colleen, died of Pick's disease, a neurological disorder that causes dementia. Years later, Howe developed his own dementia. But before that, he put in his time with the Baycrest Hospital event.

Howe wasn't just a spokesman. He would show up on draft night to be with the fundraisers. He would shake every hand, pose for every photograph of the common man, do so much while smiling even as he grew older and slower and somewhat less aware.

A few years ago, at the event put on by Baycrest Hospital, Howe stood against one wall posing for photos with fans while Johnny Bower sat at a table signing autographs.

It was a time capsule of sorts: the most popular Red Wing hanging with the most popular of all Maple Leafs. And it was clear there was a relationship of more than respect between the two men.

"As a hockey player and a person, he's one of the best guys I've ever met," Bower said Friday. "I got to know him and he became part of the family. He used to come up to the lake, we'd go fishing together, we'd go golfing together, he'd come for a barbecue. He was a wonderful person. And what a fighter he was.

"He fought to the end. I thought he'd be gone six months ago. I thought a few other times too. But that's Gordie. He fought and fought. It's what he knew. On the ice, he had a mean streak. Off the ice, nothing like that at all.

"Even on, he was good to me. I remember going behind the net to stop a puck and he came flying to check me. But he warned me first. I heard him. He could have really got me. But he let me go."

The Leafs played Howe's Red Wings in the 1948, 1949, 1963 and 1964 Stanley Cup Finals, and each time Toronto won. Bower was in goal in '63 and '64.

Howe was his obsession. "You had to watch him all the time," said Bower. "He was so great a player, and boy, he hated to lose. A lot of those games were very close. He played with an aggressiveness that no one else played with. But through it all, we had this friendship. He'd wave to me sometimes. I'd wave to him. We'd shake hands when it was over.

"I told him one day, 'If you're ever in town, give me a call.' And he did. It could be lunch, golf, fishing, we got together a lot." Was he the best Bower ever played against?

"Gordie was No. 1 and Mr. (Jean) Beliveau, he was right behind him."

Tough as nails on the ice, Gordie Howe was something of a softy off the ice. So much so that the Red Wings and the NHL took advantage of him for years by underpaying him.

Howe didn't seem to notice or care back then.

"You signed your contract and that was it," said Ullman. "Nobody knew what anybody made in those days and nobody talked about it."

Even though he lived through the attempted formation of the NHL Players' Association and was linemates with union organizer Ted Lindsay, Howe seemed content with his rather meagre contract.

"Ted was a big organizer on our team and there was maybe five other guys in the league involved. The rest of us really paid no attention to what they were doing," said Ullman.

But in 1968, former Leafs defenceman Bobby Baun was traded to Detroit and he berated Howe for earning $45,000, which was far less than Baun, an above-average NHL player, was making. It was upon that revelation that Howe's wife, Colleen, began to manage Gordie's financial business.

She did so quite successfully until she became ill in 2002. She passed away seven years later.

Gordie Howe leaves behind three sons — Mark, Marty and Murray — and a daughter, Cathy.

And leaves a sporting world with yet another broken heart.

The Wade Belak
We Never Knew

September 1, 2011

In this sad, sad summer of sporting deaths, another good man we thought we knew is gone.

And all I keep thinking about is that bright red face, those large eyes, that childlike smile that seemed forever present and the words that usually made somebody laugh, if not himself.

That's the Wade Belak I got to know in a dressing room sense during the years he played for the Toronto Maple Leafs. If you wanted someone to dance for a video, he would dance. If you wanted someone to deliver the punch line, no matter what the gag was, he would deliver it with aplomb. If you needed an appearance by a player, a hand to shake, a kid to take a picture with, he was happy to be that guy. If you wanted to make a hockey reality show, all you had to do was ask. He did a cameo in my son's bar mitzvah video and he always seemed so damn happy, so damn funny, so thrilled to have lasted 13 full years in the NHL on what he knew were marginal skills.

And now he's gone and we can't begin to understand or comprehend why one of the most gregarious, internally beloved, bighearted, giving athletes this city has known chose to take his own life. He turned just 35 last month, was getting ready for a stint on the popular television show *Battle of the Blades*, had auditioned for some national broadcast spots and got a job calling games for the Nashville Predators, his last NHL team. From the outside, the only side we ever truly see, he looked to be making that transition from player to nonplayer about as seamlessly as you can.

But as much as we think we know players, we watch them on the ice, we see them grow into men, we get to know how they will respond to a post-game question and a dressing room quip; we don't, and can't, ever know what's inside their minds or their hearts. Sometimes with a man like Bob Probert, with a man like

Derek Boogaard, the demons are apparent from the outside. Their issues were public. Their deaths, difficult, tragic, complicated, were not stunning in a way that Belak's passing is stunning.

Sometimes you can see a train wreck before the eventual crash. But who saw anything here? Who didn't feel like they were out of breath, punched in the gut, wanting to scream but not knowing what to scream, when learning about Belak on Wednesday afternoon? His friends had to feel that way. His teammates, the same. And I can't begin to imagine what this must be like for his wife and the children he would talk about, joke about.

"I'm going home to see if they hate me today," he'd say with a big grin. And then he would tell you some story about Andie and Alex and his eyes would light up. And in every story with his kids, he made himself the punch line.

Belak is the second Toronto athlete of consequence to take his own life recently. Mike Flanagan, the former Blue Jays pitcher, was not a clubhouse clown in the Belak sense. He was more the one-liner guy. No matter what was said, he had a humourous retort. One seemingly happy hockey player, one bright and comedic pitcher. The last people we would ever expect to be gone like this.

But then, really, we only thought we knew them.

With Belak, I think of one night more than any other: at the Air Canada Centre, March 20, 2007. Maybe his proudest night as a Maple Leaf. The Leafs were playing the New Jersey Devils after Cam Janssen had knocked out Tomas Kaberle with an injury, and revenge was in the air. Someone had to take on Janssen as part of the ubiquitous hockey code. That someone was Belak.

The fight lasted one minute and 35 seconds. That's a marathon for a hockey fight. "Now it's done and we can move on," Belak said afterwards, after the ACC crowd provided him with a long and loud standing ovation, maybe the only one of his career.

"It's nice to have 19,000-plus fans screaming your name," said Belak. "It makes it worth it. And I'm still beautiful, right? I tried not to get hit. I want to have that modelling career when I'm done."

There was always a zinger with Belak, self-deprecating in life, now tragic in death.

Pat Quinn — a Giant Man, a Giant Life

November 24, 2014

Pat Quinn always made a difference.

Sometimes you didn't know how. Sometimes you didn't know why. Sometimes the Mighty Quinn seemed both giant and caricature — loud, endearing, with hands that made yours disappear during a handshake, while carrying a huge cigar, always a huge cigar.

Everything about him seemed larger than life from his expansive shoulders to his choice of steak, to his pinstripe suits, to his unending presence.

You can't always define what presence is, but Pat Quinn had it.

He was in many ways a hugely successful walking contradiction of charming old-school and newfound theories. It didn't matter if you agreed with him or not, he always made you think. He was that smart and that funny.

He was the best interview I've come across in 35 years on the job, and yet he disliked almost every moment of it, and disliked most of us asking the questions.

Quinn, who succumbed to a lengthy illness on Sunday night at the age of 71, was the most compelling Toronto sports figure of the past two decades, coaching in 80 playoff games for the Maple Leafs — imagine that, by today's diminished standards — so full of personality and blarney, so easy to embrace, so damned smart and so damned stubborn.

And for much of the time, so behind in his ways. He was more thorough than modern, but they were his ways, and he wasn't about to change them for anyone, because he believed his ways worked.

"His love for the game was a real one," Bill Watters, his assistant general manager for most of Quinn's time with the Leafs, said from his Florida home. "He wanted to be creative. He wanted the puck moving and the players moving, and he always talked about that. All his theories centred around the beauty of the game, and it was something he was so passionate about. He really believed in the beauty of the game.

"Our first priority was to win, but not at the expense of the game. He felt that way from the bottom of his heart. He wasn't going to use the trap or the left-wing lock or anything that sucked the life out of hockey. He wanted to speed the game up, never slow it down. And we talked about all of that, a lot."

Quinn's ways worked, although his systemic stubbornness might have cost him the Stanley Cup he never won. He won just about everything else, though. Olympic gold, world junior gold, the under-18s. And as coach — he loved coaching but was never crazy about being a general manager — he won more games than all but four coaches in NHL history.

Players enjoyed playing for him. He wasn't much for meetings. He protected his players off the ice, they took care of him on the ice. And even when he had teams divided, like some of his Leafs teams, he found a way to bring players together when it mattered most.

Quinn lost with Philadelphia in Game 6 of the Stanley Cup Final in 1980 on a controversial offside call that may have led to his passionate referee-baiting for the next 18 seasons.

He went to the final minute of Game 7 with Vancouver and he thought his Leafs team in 2002 should have played for the Cup rather than succumb to Carolina. That wasn't all he lost in that playoff year in which he was hospitalized. That was the season in which he said goodbye to his beloved cigars.

He would carry them from then on. Just not smoke them.

Quinn, a man's man, became in many ways his own hockey encyclopedia. He coached Bobby Clarke in Philadelphia; Marcel Dionne in Los Angeles; Pavel Bure in Vancouver; Mats Sundin in Toronto; John Tavares and P.K. Subban on Canada's junior team; Mario Lemieux, Steve Yzerman, Brendan Shanahan and Martin Brodeur on one of his two Olympic teams.

He did so running the most basic of drills and the least sophisticated of practices. He did so avoiding video if he could — he called it the jukebox — and he thought line matching took the flow out of the game. That was for other coaches, not him. And every once in a while, like most coaches, he called a guy by the wrong name.

The older he got, the more he used the generic "son" for some of his players. While coaching Canada's junior squad, he once started the wrong goalie because he couldn't remember the other goalie's name. With the Leafs, he more than once forgot to tell the goalies who was starting. And while that would undermine some coaches, it never seemed to hinder Quinn.

The players played for him. They didn't always understand him or his methods — once, in a playoff game, Robert Reichel got more ice than Mats Sundin — but mostly they respected him, his communication skills, his sense of humour, his odd analogies, his overall success. Quinn was known as a people manager: There is and always will be a certain skill in that.

"When the lights come on, do you want to be a cockroach or an ant?" he would say to his players.

And they loved the question, even laughed about it, even though most of them never knew what the right answer was.

Quinn's firing was one of the great mistakes of Richard Peddie's run as CEO of Maple Leaf Sports and Entertainment, maybe the greatest of a mistake-filled time. Peddie didn't want the same man as coach and GM of the Leafs. So he asked Quinn to pick which job he wanted.

Quinn stayed as coach and Peddie hired John Ferguson Jr., whom Quinn greeted with the words, "You're not qualified for the job."

The two didn't last long together. Ferguson stayed. Quinn was shown the door. Pre–salary cap to post–salary cap, the Leafs have never been the same since.

"The firing hurt him," said Watters. "He knew he didn't deserve it. He was shocked and upset by it. He'd say, 'Look at the record. Do I deserve this?'"

Quinn's Leafs played in 13 playoff series, making the playoffs six of seven seasons, winning seven rounds and 41 games in his time in Toronto.

Since letting Quinn go, the Leafs have won just three playoff games, no playoff rounds. Quinn missed the playoffs in only 4 of his 20 seasons coaching in the NHL. Again, by comparison, the Leafs have missed six of seven seasons since he was let go.

"I talked to Pat a while back," said Watters. "He said, 'Willy, when you get to our age, a lot of parts need to be replaced. That's what they're doing with me.' That was our last conversation."

Recently, Quinn stopped taking calls.

"I wish I had called him again," said Watters.

AFTER A NINE-YEAR playing career as a slow but rugged defenceman, Quinn worked first for Fred Shero as an assistant in Philadelphia, began his head coaching career in the NHL as a 36-year-old and ended it with one awkward final season in Edmonton at the age of 67.

He never thought about being a coach, he told me once. It just happened. He took the job in Philadelphia with Shero, thinking it would last a year or so. At the time, he was finishing law school. He graduated but never did take the bar exam.

"I thought I was going to be a labour lawyer — that was the plan. Somehow I became a coach," Quinn told me in an interview before the 2000 All-Star Game. "It was never about me (as coach). I put the onus on the players. The largest obligation they have isn't to me or to themselves, it's to the other players in the room. When you have confidence that the people can do the job and know what they're doing, great things can happen."

He said it and he lived it. For almost all of Pat Quinn's life — in and out of hockey — great things did happen.

The Greatest Olympian You Never Knew

January 15, 2021

Kathleen Heddle was telling a story and laughing, which was a story in itself.

She was sitting in a chair in Atlanta in 1996, wearing her latest Olympic medal — her fourth — and trying to explain how it felt to be referred to as the most accomplished Summer Olympian in Canadian history.

She was revelling in the moment, being a sort of celebrity, being loose and talking about watching herself on television the night before.

She and her partner, Marnie McBean, were viewing a televised replay of their gold medal rowing performance when the announcer called them the greatest Olympic athletes in Canadian history.

"We just looked at each other and we both laughed," Heddle said. "And I'm thinking, 'That can't be.'" It can be and it remains. Kathleen Heddle, one of only two Canadians to win three gold medals in the Summer Olympic Games — along with her rowing partner, Marnie McBean — passed away on Monday. She was only 55, and out of the spotlight — never a household name, which was how she preferred to live her life. She was never as well-known or as much of a celebrity as she could have been, considering her accomplishments.

Some Canadians — such as Donovan Bailey, such as trampoline star Rosie MacLennan, such as synchro swimmer Carolyn Waldo and a sprinter from another century, Percy Williams — were skilled or proficient enough in their pursuits to win two gold medals. That sets them apart in a country that doesn't win often at the uber-competitive Summer Games.

McBean and Heddle, though — it was always Marnie's name first, the way Kathleen preferred it — they won three.

It's quite likely no one will ever win four.

When she passed away the other day, there was a small mention on the nightly news. Most people wouldn't have noticed or remembered who she was or what she had managed to accomplish.

"She's the best (female) rower in the world," said McBean back then, who is known for her success on the water, her rare frankness away from it and her TV commercials throughout the country. She's also an author, a speaker and still a major force in Canadian sport.

"If she rowed in the single sculls, she'd beat Silken (Laumann), she'd represent Canada and she would win the gold, but she doesn't want to. It's not her personality."

Heddle's quiet way kept her out of the headlines and her partner in them during the two Olympics in which they competed. She only raced four times as an Olympian — and was on the podium each time. Hoping each time that someone else would get noticed for the victory.

She was, and in those Olympic years — 1992 in Barcelona, 1996 in Atlanta — she was only getting over her painful shyness. That was a long fight for her. It was easy and natural to be partnered with McBean, comfortable even. It was Marnie's team, Marnie's words, Marnie on television. If you paid attention to rowing, and mostly we do for three weeks every four years, you would have thought it was the team of McBean and McBean.

That didn't happen by accident. That was the way Heddle wanted it, even if the team should have been called Heddle and McBean.

There were rules to their partnership.

"If we were at a dinner or something and kids came up and asked me for an autograph, I'd sign it," McBean said. "But if Kathleen was standing right beside me, I wasn't allowed to introduce her. I wasn't allowed to say, 'This is Kathleen Heddle. She won gold medals. She's my partner. Do you want her autograph too?'

"I did it once. She told me, 'Don't do that again.'

"There were other rules, things I could do, things I couldn't do. Kathleen likes things a certain way."

Heddle retired after Barcelona. Training to row at the highest level is painful and arduous and challenging. For Heddle, so was retirement. It left her listless and depressed at a time when mental health issues were not shared as often as they are today. She never talked about it much, but those who knew her best understood. She was not unlike so many Olympians: She couldn't stand being one and she couldn't stand not being one.

At the age of 30, some 25 years ago, she walked away from rowing as a legend. And now, a legend gone too soon. She found a way to defeat almost everything in her life, but brain cancer and melanoma took her. She leaves behind her husband and two children.

She also leaves behind a reputation for hard work, integrity and achievement. Once upon a time, she was the rock beside McBean's outgoing granite.

It used to be, if you'd asked Heddle a question at a news conference, Marnie would answer it. That too was part of their partnership.

"I did all the interviews," McBean said back then. "She didn't want any part of that."

Now Heddle leaves us far too young as the great Canadian Olympic champion hardly anyone really knew.

The Don of Football

June 25, 2017

Don Matthews was called every name in the book, and then some, during his lifetime in the Canadian Football League.

He was his own football thesaurus: Brilliant. Egotistical. Intimidating. Driven. Singular. Successful. Nomadic. Chauvinistic. Mistrusting. Caustic. Abrasive. Acerbic. Extraordinary. All of them like the man himself — a walking, talking, winning contradiction.

The greatest coach in CFL history, who was maybe the largest personality, maybe the most controversial figure, passed away Wednesday at the age of 77. The man known as the Don was probably the most despised, most intriguing, most successful, most annoying and most fascinating coach the league has ever known.

"He's the greatest coach ever," said Jim Popp, general manager of the Toronto Argonauts, who worked with Matthews in Baltimore and Montreal and was first hired by him in Saskatchewan in 1992. "He was the best and he brought the best out of everybody. He didn't just coach his players. Most great coaches coach their coaches too. Don did all of that. He controlled the environment. I learned so much from him."

Matthews controlled just about everything around his football teams. "This," he told me years ago about coaching football, "isn't a democracy. This is a dictatorship and I'm the head dick."

Indeed, he was. Mostly loved by his players, often loathed by the media that covered his teams and difficult to work with at times with others in the front office, Matthews was part of 10 Grey Cup–winning teams — five as an assistant, five as a head coach — and he was a five-time Coach of the Year in the league.

Years ago, I wrote of him: "He has 10 rings, six Grey Cup, four wedding." That was the life he led — he was a wanderer; impatience played a role in all of his success. He made eight different stops coaching in the CFL, three times coaching the Argos, also having terrific runs in Montreal, Baltimore, Saskatchewan, Edmonton and British Columbia.

"He touched so many people," said Popp. "When you were with him, or worked with him, you saw another side of Don. He cared about people. He helped people. He did things for people he didn't want anyone to know about.

"Deep down, he was never that person (the media portrayed him to be). He did what he needed to do to win. If he took something too far, he knew what he was doing.

"Sometimes, he'd say: 'I'm going to do this today,' but everything was calculated. Everything was for the team. When he walked into a room, he had a real swagger to him, a confidence. He was the leader and everyone knew it."

One regret Matthews had was he never got a chance to coach in the National Football League. He came close to being hired by New Orleans in 1997, but the legendary Mike Ditka was chosen ahead of him. Before that, he thought he was being hired by another legend, Tom Landry, in Dallas in 1989.

Landry brought Matthews to Dallas, picked him up at the airport, asked him to diagram his CFL pressure defence and to explain how it would work with one fewer player on the field. Landry was so sold by the presentation he offered Matthews a coaching job right on the spot. The two shook hands on the deal.

Four days later, Matthews turned on his television set to see the stunning news: The Cowboys had fired Landry as coach. "I never heard from him again," Matthews told me in 2006.

Not coaching in the NFL meant Matthews had time to travel the world in the seasons away from football: He made stops in Fiji, Greece, Israel, Peru, Egypt and other African countries. With Matthews, he couldn't help his "my way or the highway" style. That's how he operated. He also loved the highway for another reason: It was a place he could ride his beloved motorcycle.

Matthews was an educated man of culture who often acted the opposite of that.

In his first days coaching the Roughriders, he got a call at 1:00 AM, from a clerk at the Regina Inn hotel. Matthews answered the phone with: "Someone better be dead."

It turned out, one of his players had been caught climbing the balconies of the hotel, trying to get from his room to his girlfriend's room. The player's name was John Bankhead.

The next morning, Matthews asked his personnel man if they had a John Bankhead on the team. The answer came back yes.

"Not anymore," said Matthews.

One time, when preparing his team to play the Edmonton Eskimos, where Matthews cut his teeth as an assistant coach in the dynasty years, the coach told his players: "This is an ass-kicking contest — and the Eskimos are supplying the ass."

That was his career. A lot of ass-kickings. He coached the Doug Flutie Grey Cup seasons in Toronto, ending up 34-6 over those two record-breaking years that will never be duplicated. He coached the all-American Baltimore Stallions, probably the most talented team in CFL history, to a Grey Cup title. He won 231 games as a head coach, which was the most in history when he walked away in 2008 under difficult health circumstances.

"I talked to him all the time," said an emotional Popp on Wednesday. The last time was less than a week ago. "He couldn't communicate, but he could hear. He could raise his arm. We needed some kind of closure. I'm sure going to miss that man."

Bill Goldsworthy's Final Days

March 30, 1996

We spoke on the phone for more than an hour on the last day of January, and Bill Goldsworthy didn't want to hang up. What he hated most was to say goodbye.

He had already been told how much time he had left, and his voice quavered as he tried to explain how that felt. "This is so hard," he whispered. "This is so unfair."

He wanted to play another game of hockey, or go for a brisk skate, something to feel special again, something to feel athletic. "That's what I've been doing all my life," he said. "But now I don't have the energy for it."

Bill Goldsworthy died yesterday morning at the age of 51, losing his battle with AIDS not all that many months after going public with the news he had the HIV virus. He went public, and then slowly he closed his doors, put on his answering machine, shut out most of his friends and most of the world, until his time was up.

"I don't have the strength to talk to people, to be with people," he said. "It wasn't like I was dying of cancer. It was like there was something wrong with me that people couldn't deal with."

Bill Goldsworthy played 14 seasons in the National Hockey League, was the first expansion team player to score 250 goals. He had his number retired by the Minnesota North Stars long before the franchise was retired. He played, scouted and coached in Minnesota, with a loud bellowing voice and a style that made him unforgettable in the early years of a growing franchise.

"I'm a hockey player," he said. "To some people, that makes me important. But because I was a hockey player, and because I had HIV, more people want to talk to me. They want me to do things I can't do. I don't have the strength, mentally or physically.

"All I'm trying to do is cope myself."

Goldsworthy knew something wasn't right in 1994 when he was coaching a minor-league team in San Antonio.

Finally, on a road trip in Memphis, he decided, reluctantly, as any athlete would, to go see a doctor. He thought he might have pneumonia. He found out he had AIDS.

He left Texas, left coaching, went home to the Minneapolis area and tried to find a way to live out his final days. He lived in an apartment with his girlfriend, saw his son and his daughter occasionally, saw his ex-wife and hardly anyone else.

"The toughest thing to deal with is the time," Goldsworthy said. "You don't want to waste the time, but there's not much you can do. So you think about the time, especially when you're alone, you think about the time."

There was, in his final months, some anger in Bill Goldsworthy, and it wasn't about dying or his physical pain; it was about AIDS and the perception of it.

He hated the way people looked at him, the way nurses treated him differently from other patients, the way doctors, with all their compassion, kept him at arm's length. He hated the hypocrisy of the system and the double standard that is rarely spoken about: The same people he saw wearing AIDS ribbons were the people he saw putting up road blocks when someone else's disease got too close to them.

"I don't like that people are afraid of me," he said. "I'm not someone to be afraid of. We're not lepers, but sometimes I feel like one. People don't understand, and when you don't understand, instead of trying to learn about it, they get scared."

Goldsworthy was particularly upset in the early days of Magic Johnson's comeback with the Los Angeles Lakers. He had spent time with Johnson just prior to his return. And he feared for Johnson, not because of the silly public fears and ignorance but because he worried about how much strength Magic would have left, knowing how much of his own had disappeared.

For all that had happened to him, and for as much as he had shut out his friends and former teammates, Goldsworthy was thankful for the support he received from the hockey community. He mentioned Brian O'Neill, the former vice-president of the NHL, and current vice-president Brian Burke, for all they had done for him. He mentioned Tom Reid, the former Stars defenceman, who was one of the few people he remained in contact with.

"They told me how much time I have left," Bill Goldsworthy said on the phone almost three months ago, and then he began to cry. "But don't feel sorry for me. There are lots of people worse off than me, people who don't have anyone to tell their story to."

The Brothers McCrimmon

June 2, 2018

LAS VEGAS — Kelly McCrimmon was sitting at his desk in the front office of the Brandon Wheat Kings when one of his colleagues interrupted him on an early September morning almost seven years ago.

"What team is your brother with?" he was asked, and the question just didn't seem right in the moment.

"Yaroslavl," said McCrimmon, and within minutes he knew something was wrong. Everyone knew. The details were sketchy and didn't come in quickly. There had been a plane crash in Russia.

"I went to get my wife, went home right away, feared the worst," said McCrimmon, the assistant general manager with the Vegas Golden Knights. "My mom and dad were on a golf holiday in Scotland and we were kind of frantic because we didn't have contact information for them. We knew they were with (former NHL coach) Terry Simpson and his wife. We finally got through."

The hardest phone call he ever had to make — Kelly McCrimmon had to tell his mom and dad that his older brother Brad had died in the airplane crash that killed 43, including all but one member of the entire Lokomotiv Yaroslavl team. Brad McCrimmon, 52, one year older than Kelly, his brother, his best friend, was the head coach.

"The next morning, Maureen (Brad's wife) and I headed to Russia to do all the things you had to do," Kelly said. "The devastation, I don't think I'll forget that. You had to go over and identify the body. You don't expect to be around a tragedy of this magnitude. We're in Russia, we don't speak the language, we don't know what's going on, and we're trying to make sense of everything, and you see everything around you. It's the saddest thing ever."

They grew up on a farm in small-town Saskatchewan, somewhat isolated, outside of a place called Plenty, population 164. The big city, Rosetown, was 50 miles away.

Dad farmed. Grandpa farmed. Brad and Kelly lived the farming life almost from the day they were born. They had no neighbours, no kids on their street. They had each other. Eighteen months apart. They played, they fought, they wrestled, they helped Dad and Grandpa whenever they could. And just as their father did, they loved and lived hockey.

Brad had more talent, enough to play 18 years in the National Hockey League, enough to pair with Mark Howe on the best defensive unit in hockey, enough to win a Stanley Cup with the Calgary Flames in 1989. Kelly had enough talent to get a hockey scholarship to Michigan. He was enough of a leader to be captain as a senior, just not good enough to play beyond that level.

Kelly figured he was going home after college to a farming life, because that's what McCrimmons did.

"I'd come home every summer and farm, Brad would come home every summer and farm. That's what we did," he said.

Only, like his dad, he started to coach. First with a local senior team. Then in the Saskatchewan Junior Hockey League. And before long, he was coaching the Wheat Kings in the Western Hockey League.

One day, as a relatively young man, at the age of 31, Kelly was offered a one-third stake in Wheat Kings ownership. He jumped at it. The farming life was over — and his father, who raised cattle and farmed grain, completely understood.

"Everything always revolved around the farm," he said. "Brad came home every summer and helped out. But there came a point when I was in Brandon and couldn't get home to help out anymore."

Brad was making it big in the NHL. Kelly was making it big in junior hockey as a coach, general manager and owner.

"We were each other's biggest fans and best friends," Kelly said. "We were really close because of the way we grew up. Any success that either of us had meant so much to the other one. When he won the Stanley Cup, I remember I couldn't be any happier or prouder of him. I think I know every game Brad McCrimmon played in, I know the score, I know what he went through. I was always his biggest fan."

"He was the same with us," Kelly added. "He played for the Wheat Kings, and when I got involved owning and running the team, he came whenever we had something big going on, like being in the Memorial Cup. As long as it didn't interfere with his season, he was there."

Three years ago in Red Deer, Brandon played in the Memorial Cup.

"I miss him so much. That week, I really felt it."

This week, the Golden Knights are pushing towards a Stanley Cup. They may win, becoming the greatest hockey story of all time. And it didn't really occur to Kelly until I brought it up to him — at least that's what he says — that he may end up with a Stanley Cup ring from this miraculous season, and that would make two rings for the McCrimmon family. One remains in Michigan with Maureen. Maybe one will end up with McCrimmon in Las Vegas, his new home, after finally giving up the junior-hockey life to become George McPhee's right-hand man with the Golden Knights.

"I think he'd be really proud of what we've done here," Kelly said of his brother. "Not just being in the Stanley Cup Final, but the whole opportunity I had, how well the team has done, how we built the team. He would be proud of all those things. He loved to talk hockey and talk hockey detail. And he had a great mind for it."

There has been no shortage of difficulty for the McCrimmon family, but you would almost never know it from Kelly's upbeat personality. He lost his brother in 2011; his parents moved from Saskatchewan to High River, Alberta, where twice giant flooding robbed them of a lifetime of memories and keepsakes; the Golden Knights season started just days after one of the giant shooting tragedies in American history devastated Las Vegas; and a few months before that, the Humboldt Broncos bus crash that killed 16. All of that touched McCrimmon personally and professionally.

"I felt connected to Humboldt," he said. "For so many reasons. I know what happened to Brad's team and how difficult that was for everybody. And as someone who put on a lot of miles riding buses in the Saskatchewan Junior League and the Western League, just looking at those pictures, and in them there was this bright blue prairie sky in the background, and I'm thinking, all those kids, all those families, and you know, I always used to worry about bad roads and bad weather. It's the saddest thing ever for those families.

"My dad felt the same way I did. He said to me, 'I know how those families are going to feel.'

"It isn't something you ever really get over."

The Pioneer, Bernie Custis

February 24, 2017

I used to sit with Bernie Custis sometimes, usually before Argos games, and ask him to tell me stories about his remarkable life in football.

He would talk softly, almost without ego, about the history he made, and it struck me then, just as it strikes me now with his passing at the age of 88, that he never cared to be any kind of celebrity or pioneer. He was a quiet man who appreciated the path just not necessarily the politics. And what he wanted, more than anything else, was to play the position he was most comfortable playing: that was quarterback.

That was what mattered to the young Bernie Custis.

Only one problem: He was Black.

One year after Jackie Robinson, Custis played quarterback at Syracuse University, the first African-American to start at the position at a major American university.

After Syracuse, where he had a later-to-be-famous roommate named Al Davis, he was drafted by the Cleveland Browns and on his way, he believed, to being the backup quarterback behind the famed Otto Graham. That didn't happen. At the conclusion of his first and only training camp with the Browns, the legendary coach Paul Brown called him into his office. He didn't want to cut Custis; he wanted him to play another position, maybe defensive back, receiver or running back.

Brown wasn't ready for an African-American to play quarterback. Maybe America wasn't either: The NFL didn't have any Black players at any position between 1934 and 1946. Without coming right out and saying so, Brown told him he couldn't have a Black man playing quarterback.

Custis understood as much as he would allow himself to understand.

Brown also told Custis he wasn't going to release him to sign with another NFL team. He was too talented, too athletic and too valuable to just be given away. The only way Brown would release him was if he could place him in the Canadian Football League.

And Brown made a deal with Hamilton, basically selling him to the team closest to the U.S. border. That season, 1951, history was made.

Four years after Robinson broke the colour barrier in baseball, Custis started at quarterback for the Tiger-Cats in a game against Montreal.

It wasn't the big deal it should have been back then, but there was nothing big-deal about Custis: Only his accomplishments, his deportment, his character, all of which were magnanimous.

The Canadian Football League changed football forever — maybe the CFL's most important role — with the manner in which it welcomed African-American quarterbacks long before the NFL would alter its vision.

Custis led to Chuck Ealey, who never lost a college game at Toledo, to Condredge Holloway, who was Russell Wilson before there was a Russell Wilson. Holloway led to Warren Moon, who changed just about everything about the way football viewed Black quarterbacks and most recently, Damon Allen, who broke records that will never be broken, passing the baton to Henry Burris, who won a Grey Cup in his 42nd year.

Custis took stock of what mattered in his football life, never stopped loving his game, looked back at it with a sense of humility and honour. You met him and you liked him almost instantly. There was something almost magical and soft about his ways, his words, his smile.

After football, he taught and became a principal and scouted and coached Tony Gabriel in junior football, coached collegiately in different Ontario stops and was a fixture often on the Tiger-Cats sideline during training camp practices.

Davis never lost track of his roommate. He'd offer him job after job with the Oakland Raiders, but Custis would turn them down year after year.

He'd left the United States. He hated to fly. He'd found a home in Canada. Here, he had discovered a place where his colour didn't seem to matter much, in football or in his professional world.

It took more than 30 years after Custis' trade for the NFL to be in any way welcoming to African-American quarterbacks. And that was just a beginning. But after Moon, there has been Doug Williams and Donovan McNabb and Randall Cunningham and Michael Vick and Cam Newton and maybe the best since Moon, Wilson.

Progress has to start somewhere: It started in Hamilton with the quiet man, Custis, who, like a lot of Americans who played in the CFL in those days, settled in nicely into Canada after his career, making a mark on the field and in education.

The pioneer should have been a household name, but Bernie Custis was just fine being in the background, letting others tell their stories. He was a first in college football, a first in pro football, a giant of a figure without ever being a giant.

For a long time, he was all but forgotten. Now he is gone: Bernie Custis is someone worth remembering forever.

The Little General

September 19, 2008

For almost five decades of Canadian football, a lifetime and then some, you couldn't miss Ron Lancaster.

He was everywhere.

He was playing quarterback in my youth on a black-and-white television screen: In the park, we all tried to roll out and throw on the run like the Little General. He was coaching some of the best and worst teams anyone had ever seen. He was a friendly face and friendly voice in almost every press box.

He was in the broadcast booth alongside Leo Cahill — the greatest team of analysts and entertainers the Canadian Football League has ever known. He was the coach who answered his own phone, unless he was busy, and then he would apologize for being that when he called you back.

He was all that, and now he is gone. On Hall of Fame weekend in Hamilton of all things. A legend succumbed to lung cancer and an apparent heart attack yesterday at the age of 69 while we celebrate those who came after him. And hopefully, we celebrate the life Lancaster brought to everything he touched. A life worthy of celebration and remembrance.

Lancaster was a smile on the worst of days, hanging on to a bankrupt franchise in Hamilton. He was a story waiting to be told. There was always a happy greeting, a joke to pass on, a firm handshake, a piece of wise analysis. He was comfortable in and around the CFL, like an old piece of furniture, an antique you were always proud of.

You were proud, and in his aw-shucks, semi-humble, non-quarterback kind of way, he was proud as well. He just didn't show it much. He didn't have that air about him. He didn't have to.

There was a certain CFL humility to Lancaster: the essence of why we still grasp on to this game when there is every reason to turn elsewhere. He didn't walk around telling people who he was or what he had accomplished. As he once told me in a lengthy interview a few years back: "I didn't expect any of this ... I've had a ball. I couldn't have had a better life..."

"Whatever happens, I've had a great run and enjoyed every minute of it. I've been fortunate. I've never had to get a job. The jobs have always come to me."

The Canadian part of the story began in Ottawa 48 years ago, when Lancaster kissed his young wife, Bev, goodbye, and told her he would be home "when they send me home." But the opposite happened: They never sent him home. Instead, he sent for his wife. And a few years later, they sent him to Regina.

"Russ (Jackson) was the quarterback (in Ottawa)," Lancaster once said. "I returned punts, kickoffs, played defence, did whatever they told me to do. When Russ got hurt, I played the rest of the season. The second season, we shared time. The next year, they traded me for what I call a broken helmet."

It wasn't actually a trade. The Roughriders had claimed Lancaster on waivers from the Rough Riders.

For a man who later became synonymous with this franchise, Lancaster wasn't exactly open to the idea of going to Regina.

"It was different than any place I'd been," he said. "You come from the Steel Valley part of Pennsylvania and go to Ottawa, you can handle that. But Regina, there's a town that took some getting used to. The first year, I didn't bring my family. I hated that. I didn't like it after the second year, either.

"But it turned out to be the best thing that ever happened to me. I played there for 16 years and spent three more coaching there."

Upon retirement, Lancaster owned virtually every passing record in Canadian football. He went from legend on the field to legend in the broadcast booth — skipping only a few beats and tripping when he tried to coach the terrible Saskatchewan team he had retired from. But he hit the trifecta later, coaching both the Edmonton Eskimos and the Hamilton Tiger-Cats to Grey Cup titles, which made him a champion player, champion analyst, champion coach. A man who did everything imaginable in the CFL. Except live forever.

"Our league has lost its Little General," CFL commissioner Mark Cohon said yesterday. "And our country has lost a giant of a man."

Or, to repeat Lancaster's own words: "I've had a ball. I couldn't have had a better life."

CHAPTER 7

The Fight Game

The Greatest of All Time

June 5, 2016

Who will we love now?

Muhammad Ali, the most important athlete of our lifetime, is gone. He was everything we wanted and needed. He made us smile, he made us laugh, he made us think, he made us cry: He made us make hard decisions about religion, about politics, about government, about war, about sport at its absolute best.

He gave us something to talk about — all the time.

Ali was part boxer, part artist, part dancer, part poet, part thespian, part social commentator, part comedian and yet barely educated — and all of that coming from a pulpit that no longer exists. The most important title in sports: When the world heavyweight champion mattered, he mattered even more as heavyweight champion.

He transcended his game and every other one. And now he is gone at the age of 74, after too many years of suffering from what was first called Parkinson's syndrome and was later described as Parkinson's disease. Over time, he lost his ability to speak as his hands and head shook, and his expression grew more blank, as his ability to entertain vanished as did all his athletic gifts.

He was, in his own words, both "the Greatest" and "the King of the World." He said both of those after beating the ogre-ish Sonny Liston for the heavyweight championship in 1964. He said it as he changed his birth name from Cassius Clay to Cassius X to Muhammad Ali. He said it as he joined the Nation of Islam, turned to religion while running through numerous wives and mistresses, but when it came to the Vietnam War, he was a conscientious objector, forever in the news.

There was so much to Ali, the words spoken with Howard Cosell and the famous exchanges they had; the trilogy of battles with Joe Frazier; the Rumble in the Jungle, maybe his greatest fight as a professional; the Olympic gold medal before that. He was the story that never ended.

There is no one like him today. There may never be anyone like him again. Muhammad Ali passed away on Friday. He will never be forgotten.

WE WERE SCREAMING from the seats at Maple Leaf Gardens in 1974, watching on the big screen, confused, confounded. What was Muhammad Ali doing?

"He's getting killed."

This was how we watched big fights back then. Closed-circuit television. There were no radio broadcasts. There was no live home TV. There was a projector and a huge screen and a lot of smoke.

That night, we didn't understand what we were seeing until it was over. That was the beauty of the Rumble in the Jungle. It came out of nowhere. It was stunning and shocking. There was history and there was buildup and there was so much a title fight in Africa between two Americans — the heavyweight fight between champion George Foreman and the smaller, sassier, seemingly diminished Ali — that there seemed no path for Ali.

And at the end of almost every round, we looked at each incredulously and wondered: "Why is he doing this? Why isn't he fighting back?"

Ali stood in the ring in Zaire, arms crossed, barely punching, mostly against the ropes. And then it happened. He discovered the time in which Foreman punched himself out.

And then he went to work.

His invention of rope-a-dope.

His own trainer, Angelo Dundee, didn't know what he was planning. Ali waited, absorbed punches, blocked many, and then in the eighth round, he pounced on Foreman. Punch. Punch. Punch. We're now screaming wildly as is almost everyone at the Gardens. We screamed when Foreman was knocked down and knocked out and screamed all the way back to the subway and most of the way home.

Muhammad Ali was again heavyweight champion of the world. That was his greatest victory. A victory that branched out over time.

Twenty years later, I covered a heavyweight title fight in Las Vegas between champion Michael Moorer and old contender George Foreman. For nine rounds, Foreman just stood there, blocking punches, peekaboo style, throwing few. In the 10th round, he hit Moorer once, hard, on the button. The fight was over: Foreman was again champion. He had taken his lesson from Ali.

HAVE YOU EVER LOVED someone you didn't really know? I fell in love with Muhammad Ali on his way to his first fight with Joe Frazier in 1971. I fell in love with the man and his story, with *Wide World of Sports*, with his style and substance, with his comedy and drama, with his athletic brilliance and artistry.

So did many of my friends growing up. We were disciples of sorts. We watched him, talked about him endlessly, collected whatever we could. Before our televisions switched from black-and-white to colour, Ali was already in colour. When he spoke to Cosell, or whomever it was he was talking to on television, it was like he was talking to us. Each of us individually. And we were nodding along with him.

We would repeat the quotes, the one-liners, the trash talk, the poems at school: They stuck with us then, still stick with us now. No one else had that kind of footprint. No one else made so large an impression at the time and so lasting of one.

It has followed me around my whole life, from high school student, to journalist, to boxing reporter, to one fortunate enough to be around Ali three or four times in my life, but not at a time he was talking much anymore. He would still smile. He would still shadowbox with his fists to try and get you to smile, if he could. He would whisper a word or two. And how you wished to hear him in all his eloquence. He never stopped being a showman, in the ring, out of the ring, anytime he went anywhere. Even in the dramatic Opening Ceremony of the 1996 Olympic Games in Atlanta, when his hands shook violently as he lit the Olympic Torch in stadium silence.

We followed him from beginning to end, and even if we knew the stories, we told them over and over again. We laughed at the same places, cried at the same places, were forever engaged in whatever place Ali found himself. The framed posters are still on the wall of my office and my children's bedrooms. Ali vs. Frazier. Ali vs. Foreman. Ali vs. Norton. And on the bookshelf adjacent to the posters, there is a row of books on Ali.

He wrote, or was part of writing, more books than he ever read.

My favourite of the books about him being: *Muhammad Ali, His Life and Times* by Thomas Hauser; *Sound and Fury: Two Powerful Lives, One Fateful Friendship* by Dave Kindred; *Facing Ali* by Stephen Brunt; *King of the World* by David Remnick. All of them different. All of them highly recommended.

BELINDA ALI ANSWERED THE DOOR at her Sutton Place suite in 1973 and stared down at a young'n carrying a scrapbook, a reel-to-reel tape recorder and a mischievous smile.

Muhammad Ali was in Toronto to do television commentary on the Clyde Gray–Jose Napoles world welterweight title fight and my lifelong friend, Michael Pomer, knew he had to meet him. He just had to.

Pomer had read in the newspaper that promoter Don King was staying at Sutton Place, so he figured that's where Ali must be staying as well. Pomer was 15 years old, looked maybe 12, dressed up in his best clothing and carrying a suitcase with scrapbooks and biographies — enough to hopefully convince Ali he was serious. He walked the hotel, floor by floor, asking maids and room-service men if they knew which room Ali was staying in. On the 10th floor, he found a hotel worker who barely spoke English. He showed him a picture of Ali — and the worker smiled and pointed down the hallway.

"I gave the guy five bucks," said Pomer. "Do you have any idea how much money five bucks was for a kid in those days?" He knocked on the door and Belinda answered. She was charmed by the little guy. She invited him into the suite. And for the next two hours, he and Ali went through the books and the scrapbooks, clowned around a little, and Ali allowed the young man to interview him.

Pomer was so consumed by being with Ali he'd forgotten he left his friends in the lobby. About an hour in, he asked if he could bring them up. He went and fetched his buddies.

When they went back to the suite, Ali answered, this time wearing a Richard Nixon mask.

He pulled Pomer in to the suite and slammed the door on the other two kids before going back into the hallway, grabbing them, and saying in Nixon tone: "I am not a crook."

On the tape, Ali playfully demanded to know: "Are you the local Howard Cosell? Who are you anyway, coming up to my hotel suite and asking all these questions?" Their meeting didn't end at Sutton Place. That's where it began. Ali invited Pomer and his pals to join him that afternoon in the limousine ride to Maple Leaf Gardens and to be his guest at the welterweight title fight.

A few years later, with Ali in Toronto again, they met up again, sat down for another reel-to-reel interview. Said Ali on his tape: "I like your interview and I like your style, but fella, your pay is so cheap, I don't want to see you for a while."

And Pomer asked: "Can you say something to my brother, Henry?" "Henry, be cool," said Ali. "Don't be a fool, stay in school."

Michael Pomer is 59 years old now and texted me early Saturday morning, not long after midnight. "He's gone," he wrote. He didn't have to say anything more than that. I knew.

WITH WHAT WERE ONCE the quickest hands in the world, Muhammad Ali was seated at a table beside me at a Rochester ballroom, and tried desperately to remove cellophane from a piece of yellow candy.

His eyes were rather glazed, his expression of frustration was apparent as his head and hands both shook as he fumbled around with the hard candy.

It was enough to make anyone with a memory weep, watching this man of dance and beauty, the quickest hands heavyweight boxing has ever known, slumped in his chair at the Strathallan Hotel wearing a look that was part barren and rather lifeless.

That was 22 summers ago.

And suddenly, he dropped the candy and looked up. and the face without expression began to quasi-smile. He rose slowly to his feet, embraced the Canadian heavyweight George Chuvalo as best he could, with a pseudo hug and emphatic kiss. He tried to smile but his face wouldn't co-operate.

"He came here in a moment's notice," Chuvalo told me afterwards, at an event to honour the former Canadian champion and his troubled life. "He didn't have to. When you've had the kind of troubles in your life like I've had, it's easy to get cynical, it's easy to get depressed. But it's also a time when people can show you how beautiful they are.

"We hadn't talked in a few years. It's hard for him to speak now. The last time I spoke to him we had a good talk. He had just come back from a meeting with Saddam Hussein. We talked about that. He doesn't talk much anymore.

"But you know, I was always impressed with his inner strength. He always had the courage to stand up for his beliefs. He showed tremendous courage when he refused to go to Vietnam and lost the prime years of his career. He continues to show that inner strength. He doesn't whine about his problems or how difficult things are for him. When he talks, it's only about positive things. He still has a great attitude about life."

With trembling hands and a voice that belied his past, Ali was there because Chuvalo needed him. Because he was asked. He waived his $60,000 appearance fee that night. A few seats away from Ali sat Joe Frazier, who never got over how Ali treated him. But he too was there for Chuvalo.

"You look at George's life and Muhammad's life and it's so hard to understand," said Frazier. "Both men have had so much pain. George took all those punches, but they didn't seem to hurt him. Muhammad? I look at him and think: 'How did this happen? Did boxing do this to him?' You look at these two strong men and I just thank God. I thank God, because God's been good to me."

Joe Frazier never stopped disliking Muhammad Ali. They fought three times — the greatest heavyweight trilogy in boxing history — Ali winning twice, Frazier winning the initial fight, the Fight of the Century. The battles were fierce, brilliant and damaging. It was the before and the after that Frazier so detested.

If there is anything on Ali's plate that is disgraceful — perhaps other than his long run of wives and girlfriends — it was the denigrating way in which Ali presented Frazier.

"Me and him, we came from different places," Frazier told me back then. "We never understood each other. We came from different backgrounds with different religious beliefs.

"I was born in the South. We knew about animosity and bigotry and hatred better than most. If anyone had a reason to hate the White man, it was me. But I didn't have no feud with the White man, he did."

Ali called him an "Uncle Tom" and a "gorilla" and other less flattering names. When they first fought in 1971, it was Frazier who was the populist champion and Ali the rebellious contender.

Times changed, and over the years, Ali became the world's most popular athlete. Maybe the world's most popular man. Frazier became just another champion.

"I don't like what he did to me," said Frazier, a table away. "Twenty years from now, I'm going to be 70.

"Everywhere I go, people want to talk about me and Muhammad Ali. I wonder how long this will go on." Joe Frazier never made it to the age of 70. He died five years ago. He was 67.

I HAVE BEEN MOST FORTUNATE in my career. I got to spend a lot of time with Milt Dunnell, the late, great columnist of the *Toronto Star*, who just happened to be one of the select few writers in Ali's inner circle. Back when there were all kinds of fights in Atlantic City, after Ali retired, we would often fly to

Philadelphia together and then rent a car and drive the hour or so it took to what-ever casino we were staying in.

These were the hours I cherished: I would listen. Dunnell would tell stories, mostly about being around Ali and the training camps that included Bundini Brown and Dr. Ferdie Pacheco and trainer Angelo Dundee. The access was close and personal, so unlike today. So many interviews were conducted in Ali's hotel suite, often with him in bed and a bevy of reporters surrounding him.

One time, we were in Las Vegas together and we were late for a large ball-room press conference that had already begun when the speaker on the podium, Dundee, stopped talking. He pointed out to the crowd, where Dunnell and I were taking to our seats. "That's Milt Dunnell," he said. "I'll wait till he gets his seat."

New Jersey columnist Jerry Izenberg was also in the Ali inner circle, maybe more so than most.

The two were friends.

When no one in the United States would licence Ali to fight during his antiwar years, Ali came to Toronto, apparently to fight Chuvalo. Izenberg wrote about this in his Saturday *New Jersey Star Ledger* column on Ali's passing:

I went to see Muhammad in his last days of training at a place called Sully's A.C. Gym. I walked into a desultory room, dominated by a sagging ring and windows that looked as though they hadn't been washed since John L. Sullivan was champ. The only occupant was a teenaged kid whaling away on a heavy bag.

I heard faint sounds coming from a back room, so I walked past the "Gym Dues" and "No Spitting" signs until I saw Ali, facedown on a rubbing table while his masseur Luis Saria worked him over Ali propped himself up on an elbow.

"Hey, what are you doing here?"

"Somebody said there's going to be a fight," I replied.

"Aw, you know this ain't no fight (doubting Chuvalo's skills)."

Then I hit him with the question I came to ask. Was he planning to join the swelling ranks of war objectors in Canada?

I knew his answer before I asked the question, but I was stunned by the vehemence with which he expressed it.

He jumped off the table.

"I thought you knew me better than that. America is my home. Do you think I would let somebody chase me out of my home? Nobody is going to

chase me out of my birthplace. If they say I have to go to jail, then I will.
But I'm not gonna run away, and you should know it."

He stayed and fought and was vindicated by the courts.

IN A CLASSIC ROUTINE, the late comedian George Carlin made fun of the incongruity of Ali's battle with the U.S. government over his unwillingness to fight in Vietnam. Said Carlin in 1971: "It's good that he's being allowed to work again. He couldn't work for three years. Of course he had a strange job, beating people up ...

"Government wanted him to change jobs. Government wanted him to kill people.

"He thought it over and he said, 'No, that's where I draw the line. I'll beat 'em up, but I don't want to kill 'em.'

"And the government said, 'If you won't kill 'em, we won't let you beat 'em up.'"

That was funny. Ali's three-year fight with the government was not. And it divided America in many ways. Ali lost three of his best boxing years because of his unwillingness to go to war. It made him loved or loathed at the time. The popularity he became so famous for came after June 1971, after the Supreme Court cleared him of any difficulty. But to understand Ali's objection of going to war, you are best to hear it in his own words.

He speaks them clearly.

"Why should they ask me to put on a uniform and go 10,000 miles from home and drop bombs and bullets on brown people in Vietnam when so called Negro people in Louisville are treated like dogs and denied simple human rights?

"No, I'm not going 10,000 miles from home to help murder and burn another poor nation simply to continue the domination of white slave masters of the darker people the world over. This is the day when such evils must come to an end.

"I have said it once and I will say it again: The real enemy of my people is here. I will not disgrace my religion, my people or myself by becoming a tool to enslave those who are fighting for their own justice, freedom and equality.

"If I thought going to war was going to bring freedom and equality to 22 million of my people, they wouldn't have to draft me. I'd join tomorrow. I have nothing to lose by standing up for my beliefs. So I'll go to jail. So what? We've been in jail for 400 years."

Muhammad Ali won the heavyweight title two more times after being forced to relinquish it when he was banned from boxing. He lost five fights as a professional in all, and came back to avenge three of those defeats. He lost his last two fights against Larry Holmes and Canadian Trevor Berbick: Unlike anything else in his life and his career, those were fights he never should have taken. Muhammad Ali has answers for almost everything he managed in his remarkable career. Those last two fights he had no answer for.

Some wonder if that's where Parkinson's came from. A question that we'll never know the answer to. Muhammad Ali was surrounded by family at a Phoenix hospital when he passed away on Friday.

Dead End

March 20, 1989

On a morning ride on a Jersey bus Terrance Alli thumbed through a sports section and found out he had killed someone. It was right there in the paper.

Momentarily, he froze, stared at the words, then turned the page.

"I refuse to let it bother me," the fighter said on the telephone, two weeks after his bout, two days after learning his opponent had died in hospital.

"We choose this way to live. It's our choice. It's our job. We know about the possibilities.

"You know, it could have been me."

It was two Saturdays back in a sold-out arena in Paris that David Thio boxed for the final time. He was young, French, unbeaten, on his way up, until a right uppercut ended the fight and, 10 days later, his life. A cerebral contusion, the men of medicine called it.

Admittedly, Terrance Alli had thrown better punches. Admittedly, he stood in the ring waiting for David Thio to get up.

"They kept yelling at me, 'You've got to take this guy out. You're not going to get a decision here. You've got to knock him out,'" Alli recalled yesterday. "I knew what I had to do. I hit him pretty good in the eighth round. He staggered back to his corner. I thought it could have been stopped then ... I don't know ... There was so much pressure, everyone wanted him to win."

The bout ended in the ninth in a blur of confusion, commissioners, doctors and panic.

Alli never thought about the knockout or any other knockout in life-or-death terms. After the fight, he raised his own arm and waited for David Thio to get up. "I wanted to talk to him. To tell him how tough he was. You knock a guy down, you expect him to get up at the end, to shake hands. But he never moved."

Later that night, while in his hotel room, Alli was told his opponent was in a coma. "Even then I didn't think I hit him that hard. It never crossed my mind I could do this to somebody."

Hurting people never mattered to Terrance Alli. Winning was all-important. He is what he calls a professional fighter. A sweet scientist. And that is what he has been for his entire life — from the time he left Guyana for Toronto seven years ago.

He was Terrance Halley then. Young, promising, on the way up himself when he trained in Tony Unitas' gym and thought it would be neat to change his last name to Alli, with an extra *L*. He fought three times in Toronto but left the gym on Augusta and Queen after losing a bout with Canadian immigration. Once, four years ago, in an Atlantic City casino, he fought for — and almost won — the world lightweight boxing title. With that opportunity lost, he fights now because it's his profession, it's his job.

"No fighter I know thinks about death," said Alli. "A countryman of mine, Cleveland Denny, died in a fight in Canada. I felt that. But then you forget about it. You hear about it. You know it happens. It's in the paper. You just don't think it'll ever happen to you."

David Thio has become the latest statistic, another pointed argument for those who advocate the banishing of boxing. His was the 14th ring-related death of the 1980s, the 362nd since 1945. Thio's name will soon be forgotten like the Brian Baronets and the Victor Romeros before him, past victims who lapsed from canvas to coma to death.

Thio had a wife and a four-month-old baby girl and Terrance Alli is well aware of the scars he left behind in France. "I've gone over this fight so many times in my mind," he whispers. "Why did it happen? Could it have been different?

"I'm sorry. I feel sorry, but I don't really know what I'm sorry about.

"I can't sit here and hope. I can't cry. If I cry and mope my career is over. I'm a professional fighter. This is what I do. I've got to keep going."

On a morning ride on a Jersey bus, the 28-year-old Alli learned of the damage he had done and kept going. He folded the newspaper to another page, left it on the bus, went back to the gym to train.

"It's the game," he said without apology. "It's what I am."

Smokin' Joe Gone

November 7, 2011

"Some day, me and Joe are going to sit on a back porch in our rocking chairs, making peace and talking about the good old days."

— Muhammad Ali, 1990

In life, and now in death, their names and lives are inextricably linked together.

You could never say "Joe Frazier" without another voice bringing up Muhammad Ali. And if you began to talk Ali, you would inevitably talk Frazier.

One made the other, they defeated each other, they played off each other as much outside the ring as in, and in the greatest era of heavyweight boxing when both Ali and Frazier weren't simply fighters or athletes, but were cultural figures of another generation, their boxing trilogy and intertwined relationship have been measured in both athletic and sociological terms.

They never did have, as Ali wanted, the opportunity to sit back in their rocking chairs and make peace.

Maybe they should have.

They were never close, the way some opponents become close in boxing. Over time, Ali lost his ability to communicate verbally, besieged with Parkinson's syndrome, and Frazier passed away Monday night from liver cancer at the age of 67, never quite getting over the public denigration that Ali had imposed on him, all in the name of self-promotion, hype and ticket sales.

I was fortunate to have spent significant time with Frazier over the years covering boxing — specifically, once in the Poconos at the training camp of Sugar Ray Leonard, and another time in Rochester, before a dinner that honoured George Chuvalo. He talked, we listened, sometimes we understood, sometimes we didn't — but we listened no matter what.

He was, after all, Joe Frazier.

And what was clear through the conversations, that no matter how much success he had enjoyed in life, as Olympic champion, heavyweight champion and one of the great fighters of all time, he and Ali had grown old like the Sunshine Boys of boxing, with Frazier not able to forgive or completely comprehend what he believed Ali had done to him.

Ali had set Frazier up as the enemy of the Black man in America, a position Joe deeply resented. He had played him in a cultural way: He was pretty; Frazier ugly. He was smart; Frazier not. He was a dancer; Frazier a crude brawler. That was the sell.

At the time, the image stuck and hurt, and some of the hurt never went away.

"Muhammad and I had our differences and I guess we still do," Frazier told me back in 1994. "Me and him, we came from different places. We never understood each other. We came from different backgrounds with different religious beliefs.

"I was born and raised in the South. We knew about animosity and bigotry and hatred better than most. If anyone had a reason to hate the White man, it was me. But I didn't have feud with the White man, he did."

Ali had painted Frazier as a villain, calling him an "Uncle Tom" referring to him as "ugly" or as a "gorilla," and at times Howard Cosell, the famed ABC television announcer, was party to all the antics.

"I don't like what he did to me," said Frazier.

But there was always a pragmatic side to Frazier.

"It's time for us to think like businessmen," he said. "You can't grow old carrying this around. Twenty years from now, I'm going to be 70. Everywhere I go people want to talk about me and Muhammad Ali, Muhammad Ali and me, and I wonder how long this will go on."

He never did reach 70, but the talk never ended.

He and Ali. Ali and him.

They fought three times, and two of them are all-time classics. The first fight came after Ali returned to boxing having been banished for his failure to enter the U.S. Army.

The buildup was immense, with Frazier as heavyweight champion, Ali as populist No. 1 contender: It was billed as the Fight of the Century and the billing wasn't usual hyperbole. The 15 rounds weren't just memorable. They were a freeze frame of boxing history.

Their third fight, the 14 rounds better known as the Thrilla in Manila, came more than four years later. Again, the title wasn't just appropriate, it was telling.

A LUCKY LIFE

At the end of the final round, with Frazier ready to come out and fight through one blinded eye, trainer Eddie Futch put a stop to the bout.

"The closest you can be to death," Ali later described the fight.

Thirty-six years later, the death of Frazier became official.

The cause, not boxing, was liver cancer.

The memories will live longer than both.

The Myth of Mike Tyson

June 14, 2005

In a rare and revealing moment, the kind from which Mike Tyson historically has hidden, the once-meteoric heavyweight capsulized his career with brutal honesty.

"I feel like Rip Van Winkle," Tyson confessed early Sunday morning. "My career has been over since 1990."

It is 15 years, two jail sentences, five comebacks, one ear bite and 20 fights after Buster Douglas, and still we debate. The curtain is closed, the freak show is over and all that is left to sort through are the remnants of what might have been.

The great myth of Tyson, the historical misconception that so many cling to, is that he was a fighter for the ages. The stark reality is, Tyson was more attraction than boxer, initially for his ferocity, later in his career for his savage unpredictability.

The truth is — and nobody ever really wanted to hear it because it wouldn't sell — that Tyson the fighter was of remarkably weak character: a champion bully, a champion quitter, and in the words of his former trainer, Teddy Atlas, "a coward."

"Like everything in his life, it will be misread," Atlas said. "They'll say he was a savage. They'll say he was an animal ... once again, he'll hide from the truth because it's convenient for him to hide."

And convenient for a marginal sport that lived off his reputation and not his performance for almost two decades.

On Saturday night, in what likely was his last fight, Tyson did not come out for the seventh round. He was not taking a beating. He was not behind on the scorecards. He just didn't want to do this anymore. He didn't want to perpetuate the myth any longer.

"If you give him the choice between fighting and quitting, usually he'll quit. Just look at his career," Atlas said.

Just look at his career. The highlight reels of knockouts — convincing as they are — all but end after his demolition of Michael Spinks in 1988. Not surprisingly, that was the last time he fought with Kevin Rooney as his trainer. That was 17 years, a sporting lifetime, ago.

Three fights later, the image of Tyson crawling around the canvas in Japan, searching for his mouthpiece in his shocking defeat against Douglas, remains fresh. Douglas was the first skilled heavyweight to fight back against Tyson, to not cower upon entering the ring, to not defeat himself amidst all the hysterical noise.

That defeat sadly would foreshadow Tyson's future as a legitimate champion heavyweight. Douglas fought back. Tyson lost. Over time, almost everyone who fought back beat Tyson.

Evander Holyfield fought back and dominated him twice. Lennox Lewis — larger, faster, more skilled — fought back and obliterated Tyson.

Even Danny Williams and, most recently, Kevin McBride, fought back. They too were victors.

Five times Tyson fought what could be considered legitimate challengers, fighters of somewhat equal ability. Four times he lost.

The one time he won a fight when there actually was doubt was one of the 13 times I was fortunate enough to see Tyson up close from a ringside seat. I can still see the fear in Michael Spinks' eyes as he was all but shoved into a New Jersey ring in 1988. You don't forget something like that.

"Look at him," the late boxing writer Rick Fraser said, pointing to Spinks in his corner. "He has lost already."

Ninety-one seconds later it was over.

After Douglas — Tyson's 1990 point of reference — the aura of invincibility was gone forever. All that was left was a growing public fascination, and if Tyson was champion of anything, he was champion of his ability to generate revenue and dispense with it.

Which leaves him where, historically, other than $34 million U.S. in debt after $400 million in career earnings?

Muhammad Ali defeated Joe Frazier after losing to him and Ken Norton after losing to him and Leon Spinks after losing to him. The best do that, and in Ali's case, that's without mentioning his signature victories over Sonny Liston and George Foreman.

Foreman has wins on his résumé that include Frazier and Norton and Michael Moorer and Ron Lyle. Frazier defeated Ali. Larry Holmes beat everyone in his time. Lewis lost only to Hasim Rahman and Oliver McCall, both of whom he easily knocked out in rematches.

But what about Tyson?

He has all those quick knockouts against nobodies, all those bang-bang victories, but who did he ever beat? Who really?

Holmes was finished when they fought. Spinks was undersized and deathly afraid. Razor Ruddock was strong and unskilled and awkward.

Where was Tyson's signature conquest?

His career record of 50 wins, 6 defeats and 2 no-contests is eerily similar in numbers to greats of the past. Holmes lost six fights, including the kind of mismatch with Tyson that Holmes himself won against Ali. Ali and Foreman lost only five fights. Sonny Liston and Frazier lost four. Joe Louis lost three times and Lennox Lewis twice.

All of them, along with the legendary Jack Johnson, Jack Dempsey, maybe even Rocky Marciano, out-point Tyson's career for everything except earnings and headlines.

The public fascination never seemed to end with Iron Mike, no matter how bizarre his life became. He could go to jail for rape, bite off Holyfield's ear, marry and divorce actress Robin Givens, assault an old man at the scene of a car accident, and still he was a commodity. Right up until Saturday night, long after what remained of his boxing skills had gone.

Say this much for him: He was the youngest heavyweight champion in history. That may be his boxing calling card. The youngest to win, the youngest and most destructive to throw it all away.

Lennox Lewis,
the Convenient Canadian

November 6, 2008

If there is discomfort with Lennox Lewis being inducted into Canada's Sports Hall of Fame, it is our discomfort, not his.

He doesn't think he did anything wrong. He says, just like Wayne Gretzky, that he had to go somewhere else to make it big. But he never forgot who he was, or where he was from, or how he got there.

That's his story.

"To me, I blamed it on the reporters," Lewis said yesterday, before last night's induction ceremony. "They are feeding people information which is untrue ... It's not like I'd forgotten Canada in any sense."

There is no doubting Lewis' accomplishments as an athlete. There is doubting his long-term connection to Canada, at least from a public sense.

He won Olympic gold for Canada at Seoul in 1988, in boxing, in the most prestigious of all divisions. He was the dominant heavyweight boxer of his era, taking apart Riddick Bowe as an amateur and Evander Holyfield and Mike Tyson in his most memorable bouts. He was, without question, the greatest fighter this country has ever produced.

And the country did produce him. It just never warmed to him. The feeling, quite likely, was mutual, although it is not something Lewis necessarily is comfortable conversing about. Lewis fought twice in the Olympics for Canada. But when he fought in England or Las Vegas or at Madison Square Garden as a professional, when the biggest and the brightest lights shone on him, he was British or Jamaican or both, just never the kid who grew up playing high school sports in Kitchener, whom the late Arnie Boehm taught to fight. Never the kid who bought his home in Brampton and lived there more than he let anybody know.

In retrospect, it might have been easy to balance three countries and stay true to all of them. But when the decision was made, economic pragmatism reigned supreme: Lewis, for the most part, would pretend this wasn't home. It created some resentment in Canada, some resentment in England — two countries crying for a heavyweight champion of the world weren't sure what to think of theirs.

Back then, he would bristle when asked about his Canadian roots. He never wanted to talk about it when the British or American press were around. If he was proud of where he learned to fight, it was a pride he carried on mostly with silence.

The flags that accompanied him to the ring, in every fight of significance, were never Canadian. He rarely was announced as being from Canada, or being an Olympic champion who represented Canada. It was easier and better business to be British.

"I did," Lewis said, "have three flags on my trunks. One of them was Canadian."

But still, his place in the Sports Hall of Fame isn't dubious but it is debatable.

Why should we care about someone who seemingly never cared about us? Why don't we love Lewis the way we adore George Chuvalo? And no, this isn't a question of colour. Chuvalo always seemed part of the culture, part of the sporting fabric of Canada.

Lewis lived his entire career post-Seoul detached from Canada, so different from the Donovan Baileys and Steve Yzermans who also were honoured last night. No matter where they were, who they played for, what event they were part of, they never stopped wearing the red and white, never stopped carrying the flag.

For Lewis, some of the distance is understandable. He moved here at age 12 and was mostly gone by his early 20s. And a part of him — something he still has trouble coming to grips with — never got over the '88 Olympics.

It was the greatest moment of his athletic life, lost in a week in which Canada was consumed by the disqualification of Ben Johnson.

Lewis was superb in Seoul. His timing, none of it his own doing, could not have been worse. He won his gold medal on the last day of the Olympics. By that time, the hand-wringing over Johnson had become a national sport.

"It was a difficult situation for a lot of the medallists," Lewis said. "We took off our Canadian uniforms. We didn't want to be known as Canadians. We didn't want to be identified. We didn't want to be approached and asked about (Ben).

"If you weren't there, you can't understand what it is was like."

The Shattered Dream of Billy Irwin

May 5, 1997

Billy Irwin bit his lip, closed his eyes, stood trembling and it was then he began to cry.

As he walked down the steps, out of the ring, into his new reality, he walked past his wife of three months, past his manager, past his trainer, past his promoter, slowly away from the ring.

"Don't worry Billy," a well-wisher shouted out.

"We're still with you, Billy," a former fighter screamed.

"We love you, Billy," a woman in a slinky dress yelled.

Billy Irwin didn't look up, stuck his hand out slowly, shook a few hands and kept on walking.

It has been five years since he has known this kind of pain. It has been five years since the Olympics of Barcelona, the last night he had lost a boxing match, the last time he had felt so lost.

"I forgot the feeling," he whispered afterwards, and then he began to cry again.

He had forgotten what it is to lose.

The championship train that was Billy "the Kid" Irwin skidded to an unfortunate halt last night in a smoky ballroom at the Toronto Airport Hilton Hotel. Where once he had big dreams and bigger hopes, it all came crashing down when he was taken apart for the second time by a lightweight from Ghana named David Tetteh.

The first time, the judges awarded a gift victory to Irwin. This time, not even the judges could take away a result that was so dominant, so one-sided, so absolute.

Billy Irwin had blood on his back, blood on his forehead, blood on his nose, a welt beneath his right eye and a nasty sliced eyelid above his left eye; the look and the feel matched. Once, he talked about the future with a gleam in his eye and a bounce in his step. He talked about Oscar De La Hoya. He talked about championship fights and the steps he would take along the way. He would talk about all that.

Last night, it just became idle talk, another fighter with another dream, and words that can't necessarily be taken seriously.

"It's a big setback," said Mickey Duff, the British boxing promoter who represented both fighters in last night's main event but cheered openly for the investment he had in Irwin. Several times through the fight, Duff left his ringside seat and loudly shouted instructions to Irwin's corner. They didn't help. On this night, nothing would.

Tetteh seemed quicker, smarter, busier, more skilled. He scored with jabs and power punches, and so often Irwin seemed more spectator than fighter. Sometimes this happens to fighters when they try to run faster than they are able. They stand and watch, and they freeze.

"I felt like a robot," Billy Irwin said late last night. He felt stiff and wooden and beaten up.

"And where does he go from here?" Mickey Duff was asked.

"I don't know. I honestly don't."

The same question was asked to Pat Connaughton, Irwin's trainer. "I don't have any answers," Connaughton said. "I don't know what happened. I don't know what we do now."

Connaughton was so frustrated in the final round that he stood in his corner and actually pounded on Irwin's back in the hopes of egging his fighter on. "I was trying to bring him to life," Connaughton said.

It was the only life Irwin showed in 12 rounds of allowing Tetteh to have his way.

As he stood in his corner afterwards, answering questions he really couldn't answer, trying hard to explain what he couldn't understand, his wife, Maria, stood beside him, running her hand up and down his back, slowly wiping the blood away. This is the first time since they were married that she has seen him fight professionally. Every time Billy tried to look over to her, she would lean towards him and begin an embrace. Every time he looked to her, she would stand strongly and would work hard to hold back the tears.

"What can I say on a night like this?" Maria said. "What can anybody say?"

We have seen this night before, the night of unfortunate Canadian boxing truths. We saw what Bert Cooper did to Willie deWit and how Simon Brown took apart Shawn O'Sullivan. This wasn't so stunning or final, but it was just as certain.

Not even Billy the Kid, who used to dream of championship nights, could speculate on where he goes from here. In the final round, with his back to his corner, he threw wild, frantic, desperate, hurried punches, trying to get back in three minutes what he had lost in the previous 33.

He went out showing the heart of a champion but not the skills, and because of it Billy Irwin is a champion no more.

The Night Evander Holyfield
Exposed Iron Mike

November 11, 1996

LAS VEGAS — Mike Tyson walked slowly towards Evander Holyfield, bowed respectfully and then spoke softly.

"I just want to shake your hand, man," Tyson said, with his head down, his eyes looking to the ground. "I just want to touch you."

And in that startling moment of post-fight humility, the message was abundantly clear. The Tyson era had ended in the desert shock of Saturday night and Sunday morning, and with it, the Tyson aura also died.

The popular myth of invincibility took no less of a beating than Tyson did at the MGM Grand Garden Arena. He is no longer the great intimidator. He is no longer the baddest man on the planet earth.

He is no longer heavyweight champion of the world.

His face was swollen, his memory was uncertain, he couldn't stop the whistling sounds that trumpeted uncomfortably in his ears. There was one cut just above his left eye, another not far away.

"My eyes," he said afterwards. "My eyes hurt."

The images of the post-fight press conference were as startling and revealing as those of the 11 rounds of boxing. There was Mike Tyson, polite, humble, soft-spoken, respectful, completely out of character and thoroughly beaten by Evander Holyfield.

There was Mike Tyson, the grade school bully, beaten up for the first time when it really mattered, and the only thing he didn't do was cry.

He came out for the opening round against Holyfield the way he always comes out for the opening round. He was wildly aggressive. He was lunging. He was throwing hooks with both hands. He was trying to end the matter early.

And then it didn't happen.

And then he didn't know what else to do.

In the third round, the fight changed. Holyfield began hitting Tyson, really hitting Tyson. There was a left hook and a right uppercut that left Tyson stunned.

"From the third round on I just blacked out," Tyson said. "I don't remember going down (in the sixth). From then on, I don't remember the fight.

"I didn't know where I was. I didn't know anything. I was in the corner and I couldn't hear a thing."

Afterwards, he made no excuses. There were no arguments, no controversies, no rationalizations, none of the usual boxing silliness.

In the ring, Tyson had been stripped naked by Holyfield, exposed as a flawed, one-dimensional, unoriginal, unimaginative boxer who simply didn't know how to respond when his opponent fought back, when his opponent's will was greater than his own.

"You could see it when he got a little blood on him," said Don Turner, Holyfield's trainer. "He was all upset. He was acting like a baby who gets cut for the first time, always touching it. You could tell how much it bothered him."

And that was only part of the vanishing mystique. The undeniable truth was this: Only twice in Tyson's career has his opponent fought well, was not intimidated and fought intelligently.

And both times Tyson lost. Both times he was knocked down. Both times he was frustrated. Both times he either refused to change in the fight or was incapable of change. And both times, after being hurt, he didn't protect himself, he didn't try to hold his opponent: he either panicked or simply froze.

"Tyson didn't know what to do," said Lou Duva, Holyfield's former manager. "It was simple movements, nothing fancy. But it was like a professional against an amateur. And it was amateur night in their corner. They didn't help him a bit."

This has long been an issue with those who follow Tyson, but normally it hasn't mattered. Early knockouts against inferior opponents have masked the lack of competence of those with whom he surrounds himself.

The questions won't go away after Saturday night, so many questions now.

There are questions about himself, about his place in history, about those he employs as trainers and managers, about his future, about his talent.

And after the Holyfield fight, will anyone fall prey to Mike Tyson's game of street intimidation again and be beaten before the opening bell even rings? Will anyone be afraid of Tyson?

"People lose," Tyson said. "Everyone loses. We lose in fights. We lose in life. It's how we come back that counts."

He didn't come back against Buster Douglas and he didn't come back against Evander Holyfield.

"I've always said he was weak of character," said Teddy Atlas, Tyson's former trainer. "But until now, until tonight, nobody ever believed me."

CHAPTER 8

From Here, There and Everywhere

Nearing the Finish Line

July 31, 2002

There comes a time, Boris Becker was saying not long ago, when you don't have an answer anymore. "Some people say it's an easy decision," said Becker, speaking of retirement, speaking of his own career, but mostly speaking of Pete Sampras.

"They do not know. They do not know how hard it is. They have not been athletes."

Nobody in our lifetime — maybe nobody ever — has played tennis better than Pete Sampras.

The numbers tell us that much.

The 13 Grand Slam championships, two more than Rod Laver and Bjorn Borg. The record-breaking six-year reign as the world's top-ranked player.

He was the Tiger Woods of his game before there was a Tiger Woods, without similar endorsements and without such a public story to tell. Everybody else played for No. 2.

But not anymore.

Not like we want to remember it.

Sampras arrived at the Canadian Open last night, and from the tension in the crowd early on at the National Tennis Centre, there was a feeling that this could be the last we see of Sampras.

The last of him here.

And that's what it's like to be Sampras on centre court anywhere these days. You arrive with a certain trepidation. Nothing comes easily, nothing is taken for granted.

Those watching must wonder, "Will we ever see you again?" These days, when Sampras plays tennis, he isn't only playing against Wayne Ferreira, the way he was last night. He is playing against his own past, against what he once was and against what he can't be anymore.

He still can win matches, as he did last night in 2 hours and 15 minutes of excitement and discomfort. He won 7-6 (6), 5-7, 6-4 on his serve and guile and just by being Sampras, but it's clear by watching him he is not a likely champion anymore. Maybe he's the favourite of the fans, just not the morning line favourite.

Watching Sampras play now is not at all reminiscent of what it was like to watch Willie Mays stumble in his last days in baseball.

The fall isn't that far, that apparent, that upsetting.

It isn't like watching Muhammad Ali being beaten up by Trevor Berbick, with your stomach aching from the pain he was feeling.

It's more like watching Wayne Gretzky at the Winter Olympics in 1998. There still is some game, still some smarts, still an aptitude for the sport. A moment here. A big serve there.

But the dominance, that's gone. This was life and death with Ferreira, who has won the Canadian Open, something Sampras, in all his mastery, has not.

A bounce here, a bounce there, and it's Ferreira winning and Sampras heading home. It was that close, that indecisive.

And there is no sadness in this case. There are only great memories of what once was.

Even Sampras, at 30, married now and with a child on the way and too many asking about retirement, understands this all too well. He has altered the way he looks at each week on the tennis tour. Once upon a time, it meant everything for him to be the best in the world.

Last night, when he walked off the court, he said, "It feels good to win a match. It was a good one to get through.

"It has been a struggle this year."

That's how he speaks now, in different tones. He once said, "I play for history, that's my motivation ... The more I have won, the more I want to win."

Now fast-forward to this tournament and a tennis year in which Sampras has won only a few more matches than he has lost.

But hear his words and listen to the difference.

"I really have no interest in getting back to No. 1," he said here a few days ago. "I know what it takes to get there. I don't have it in me like I used to ... Being No. 1, you have to live, eat and breathe tennis."

And you have to have an answer, the kind of answer Sampras had on centre court last night, the kind of answer he doesn't have too often anymore.

Tiger Woods' First Day on the Tour

August 30, 1996

MILWAUKEE — An hour after the round began, a course marshal was still standing on the first fairway by the place where Tiger Woods landed his first professional drive.

"It was right there," he kept saying over and over to anyone who would listen, pointing it out to the passing gallery, displaying his piece of personal history. "That's where he hit it. Right by me. Got to be 340 yards minimum. Can you believe it?"

It was all part of a long, spectacular and very believable day at the Greater Milwaukee Open, the first professional round for a golf legend in the making named Eldrick "Tiger" Woods.

He took the gallery's breath away. He teased. He taunted. He entertained. He did everything he was expected to do, and at times he did more than even that.

And on the sixth hole, a 556-yard par five, he hit a drive and a 5-iron to leave himself close enough to the pin for his first professional eagle.

"This guy's unbelievable," John Elliott, a little-known pro who played with him, turned to the gallery and said. "I can't believe he just did that."

The sentiment lasted all day long. The round of 67 Tiger Woods scored at the Brown Deer Park Golf Course yesterday doesn't begin to tell of the excitement he created for a tournament that rarely creates any.

It wasn't his score as much as it was his shot making. He averaged 333 yards per drive. He routinely hit fairway irons 200 yards–plus. He turned par fives into child's play.

"And if he had made his putts today, he would have shot 62," said Elliott.

Woods was just happy to have the day. He'll take the 67. "That's an ideal start under the circumstances," he said.

The circumstances have been the emotion and the trauma of the past few days. Winning the U.S. Amateur title for the third straight time. Deciding to turn professional. Mapping out his schedule. Signing a multimillion-dollar contract with Nike while negotiating another such arrangement with Titleist. Doing photo shoots for *People* and *Newsweek*. And that's all in the past two days.

"It has been awfully hard," said Woods, 20. "I didn't realize it was going to be this hard. I expected it to be crazy, but I didn't expect it would be as draining as it was.

"But getting out on the course, there I'm in my element. The fiasco of yesterday and the day before ... just trying to get some practice in was impossible.

"Finally I got to play. I'm laughing and joking. I'm back in my element. I'm back playing golf."

Few remember the first professional round Arnold Palmer or Jack Nicklaus or Sam Snead ever played. When was it? Where was it? But this was one of those special moments in the modern world of controlled sporting media events.

It was one that actually lived up to the hype and expectations. The television cameras followed Woods as did a huge crowd for his entire round.

The gallery got so large that on one par three the crowd outlined the entire hole. It was a most remarkable sight.

And it has only just begun.

"When you see what he's doing on the course, you can understand what all the fuss is about," said Jeff Hart, who played in the threesome with Woods. "There were times I felt like applauding."

The four-under-par 67, while impressive for a first time out, wasn't good enough to get Woods' name on the leaderboard. Nolan Henke shot a tournament-record 62 but played second fiddle to Woods. Bob Estes, at 64, was a sidebar. Even a round of 66 for a disappearing act named Dave Barr, from Richmond, B.C., hardly was worth a mention on this day.

On this day, it was all about Woods. Every shot he took seemed to take on some kind of historic significance as the gallery wanted to be part of the first birdie, the first bogey, the first eagle, so one day they can tell somebody they saw him when.

"It was an experience," said Woods, who already is learning about the business of golf. He soon will move his home from California to Florida because "of the state income tax" laws. But the number he was most concerned about yesterday was 67.

"That's a good number for me," he said. "I'm right in the tournament. That was a perfect start."

It was a perfect start for everyone but his mother, Kultida. She missed her son's drive on the opening hole and was one of those who was given the play-by-play by a court marshal.

As it turns out, Kultida had arrived at the course at 2:30 PM, anticipating her son's tee-off. She had read the times in *USA Today*, not knowing they were Eastern times. This is the Central time zone. She was an hour late.

"Rookie mistake," said Tiger Woods. Hers, not his.

Laughter Helps
Ease the Pain

May 6, 1986

ST. LOUIS — In his quiet moments, when the one-liners have been put away and the audience has gone, Charles Bourgeois opens his wallet and leaves his sense of humour behind.

He pulls out the wallet-sized photo that never leaves him and stares at it. He doesn't cry, although sometimes he feels like it.

The picture is of his father, Aurele Bourgeois, who was the most important man in his life.

Corporal Aurele Bourgeois of the RCMP was shot in the head and buried in a grave he was forced to dig for himself. His body was discovered in Moncton, New Brunswick, on December 15, 1974, the victim of one of the most bizarre murder cases in Canadian history.

His oldest son, Charles, now a National Hockey League defenceman with the St. Louis Blues, was 13 years old at the time. He was alone, skating on the small, choppy ice rink his father had made for him, when he learned of his father's death.

"I saw my brother-in-law walking towards me," Bourgeois remembered on Wednesday. "He didn't have to say a word. He just looked at me and I knew.

"For three days they searched for him. We didn't know if he was dead or alive. That was the hardest part. It was tough not knowing, then so tough finding out."

Aurele Bourgeois was one of two RCMP officers buried in tiny graves after being shot while investigating a Moncton kidnapping. The boy who was kidnapped was returned to his family after a $15,000 ransom was paid.

The two kidnappers were convicted of murder.

More than 11 years later, Charles is telling his story for the first time in public. He is sitting in the dressing room of the St. Louis Blues and wanted to talk about his dad in between days of a Stanley Cup playoff series. Bourgeois is not your typical NHL player. He wasn't drafted and isn't a particularly gifted athlete. But he managed to make it to his fifth NHL season. This has been his best year, as a Campbell Conference finalist with the Blues. This may be the closest he will ever get to the Stanley Cup.

"At times like this, I wish he was here," said Bourgeois, the former Calgary Flames defenceman, who was signed as a free agent out of the University of Moncton. "My father's dream was that I'd be a pro player. He would have loved this. He wanted me to play hockey. He did all the things dads do to make that happen.

"I learned to skate on the outdoor rink he made for me. He was an amazing man, really. A lot tougher than I am. But he helped me, he made me into a better person. I carry this picture of him everywhere. It's always with me."

A death in the family often causes children to take so many different directions in their lives. Bourgeois turned his energies to hockey as a young man. His younger brother wasn't as fortunate. He had problems with the law and with the bottle.

"Nothing was ever the same after the death," Bourgeois said. "The entire family structure was upset. Sometimes I think I didn't take enough responsibility. You don't know what you should have done for the family. But you know it wasn't enough."

He couldn't replace his father. He knows that. He knows he tried.

"He was a quiet, strong man," said Bourgeois. "People in the city looked up to him. He was such a giving person. Instead of locking up the drunks, taking them to the station, sometimes he brought them home, tried to clean them up, give them a hot meal. He was always doing things for people.

"When they (two RCMP officers) died, the people of Moncton were incredible. They raised about $400,000 for the families. And that was in a poor town. Some of the people donating money were the drunks and bums my father tried to help."

Charles Bourgeois returns to Moncton every summer to speak at banquets, to do work for Big Brothers, to be a part of his community and a part of his own family. His mother, usually too nervous to watch him play, still lives in Moncton, as does most of his family.

Now he is here in the heat of St. Louis, playing hockey every other night, trading one-liners with the media on off-days, something Bourgeois is better known for than his ordinary skill as a sixth defenceman.

A new Bourgeois dressing room line is welcomed like the opening of a Broadway show. It's cultivated, then reviewed, then repeated, until the next one-liner. He has become something of a cult figure with the media for his original sense of humour, which is certainly unique among those who are paid to play.

"I always thought I had two choices," said Bourgeois. "I could laugh or I could cry. I chose laughter. I've always felt my sense of humour was my salvation. It's kept me sane."

The Interrogation
of Ross Rebagliati

February 13, 1998

NAKANO, JAPAN — The cellular phone rang sometime into the fifth hour of the police interrogation. Ross Rebagliati smiled for a brief instant, ran his fingers over the gold medal that was hidden in his pocket — the medal that was again his — and then went back to the questions.

Questions about his drug use. Questions about his life.

He was sitting in an interrogation room on the second floor of the Nakano Police Department when he heard the news. There were six different officers asking him questions, asking the same questions differently, over and over again. He couldn't take a moment to celebrate, to whoop, to pump his fist, to say how stoked he felt. He was again the gold medal champion.

And no one around seemed to care.

Imagine what these 96 hours were like for Ross Rebagliati, who a week before was just another pretty face in the hidden world of snowboarding. Then he won a gold medal. Then he got disqualified. Then he spoke on his own behalf in the appeals process. Then he was asked to turn himself in to the Nagano police.

"The only thing I wanted to do was go home," an exhausted Rebagliati said in an exclusive interview when he finally emerged from almost seven hours of police questioning. He was pale when he left the police station late Thursday night. He was almost beaten-looking. Too much had happened in too short a time.

"You can't begin to comprehend what this has been like," said Brian Wakelin, the Canadian chef de mission. "I don't know how this young man can stand up right now. I'm just amazed by his composure."

The police investigation began the instant Rebagliati's positive test for traces of marijuana became public. "They had no choice but to open an investigation," said Pierre-Paul Periard, the RCMP officer who doubles here as the security chief for Team Canada. "The drug issue is very sensitive in Japan. This is how their custom works. They had to do something or what would the press have said?"

They asked Rebagliati and other members of the Canadian delegation to come in for questioning. Rebagliati was interrogated in one room. Wakelin was interrogated in another. Even Periard, the police officer, was interrogated also.

But that wasn't all.

The Japanese police obtained a warrant to search the hotel room in which Rebagliati was staying. This was part of the long, drawn-out process. The search warrant was fine. But when the police arrived, Rebagliati had been moved to another place, his bags taken with him.

This delayed the process further. Eventually, the Canadian delegation produced the suitcases. By then, it was already early evening.

"You have to understand how it works in Japan," Periard said. "Illegal drugs come with very high penalties here. This is an issue they are very sensitive about here. We told our athletes that before we came.

"The whole (police) process is very different than what we're used to. First of all, you do not appear with a lawyer. If you appear with a lawyer, there is an assumption you're guilty. So he was in the room only with the translator from the embassy.

"There were six different officers rotating questioning him. But everything was handled properly and professionally. I had prepared Ross for what would occur. I told him it's going to be a whole day, just be patient. They take their time. Part of the problem was the language barrier. Every question and answer took about 10 minutes when translated back and forth. But he handled it well, he handled it very well."

Ross Rebagliati isn't asking for any kind of apology, nor is he offering one. He probably made a mistake. The IOC probably made a mistake. The matter has been dealt with properly.

He has won a medal, lost a medal, tested positive for marijuana and spent more time in a police station than any man should. All in the span of too few hours. Last night, he was tired and ready to go home. But with the investigation over and his medal back around his neck instead of hidden in a pocket, he instead spent last night watching Team Canada play its first Olympic hockey game. He is, for the time being, staying at the Games.

"I'm so proud of this young man," Wakelin said. "He finished up at the police station and he thanked them. Can you imagine that? He wanted to close this case with dignity. He thanked them."

"It has been an experience I'll never forget," said Ross Rebagliati, once again a gold medallist of some controversy, his fingers sliding happily over the prize around his neck. Finally smiling. Finally relaxed. Finally cleared.

The Olympics from Hell

February 25, 1992

ALBERTVILLE, FRANCE — No ending to the lousy Albertville Olympic Games could have been more appropriate.

The 1:40 bus to Geneva never showed up.

So there we were, from Canada, from Germany, from Norway, from Italy, from all over the globe, all with luggage, all with travel arrangements, all holding our fancy Olympic bus reservations.

Waiting for a bus that never came.

"Amazing," said the man from Germany. "The only bus we want to take all month and it's not here."

The man in the Olympic transport office shrugged his shoulders. Every time he was asked a question, he shrugged his shoulders.

"I am doing all I can," said the man.

"What exactly are you doing?" I asked.

"All I can," he said.

It is little wonder these were the Olympic Games at which most of the athletes left early. Somehow, in this picture postcard of a region, in the dreams of Jean-Claude Killy, nothing ever felt right.

The Olympic spirit always seemed missing.

The Calgary Olympics were *alive*. You could feel it anywhere you went. The pride. The hospitality. The pure enjoyment of the sporting entertainment.

Here none of that was evident. The locals always seemed inconvenienced, bothered by the people who had infiltrated their region, crowded their roads, altered their lifestyle, spoke other languages. If there was Olympic joy in the Savoie region, I never saw it. I never felt it. No one I know experienced it.

The winners, the athletes, in their moments of excellence, showed life and exuberance and everything that is supposed to be Olympian. And they always spoke of their dream, their Olympic dream. It sometimes sounded cliched. But it, more than anything else here, was genuine.

This was a difficult Olympics to compete in. It was difficult to feel part of so chopped-up an event. Ken Read, who recites the Olympic oath before he goes to bed most nights, said there was a feeling of displacement here.

The athletes felt it. Everyone felt it.

The hockey players lived in one village. The male skiers in another. The female skiers elsewhere. Kevin Martin, who curled not that well for Canada, said he never saw an Olympic athlete or another event in his time in the region. "I could be anywhere," he said.

Perhaps this feeling of displacement, the coming together that didn't happen, meant that this was an Olympics of smaller stories and fewer stars. Kurt Browning slipped. So did Midori Ito. Alberto Tomba won one gold medal, not two. The Swedish hockey team went home disgraced.

In Calgary, there were clowns and there was comedy. The athletes or freak athletes didn't make those Games special. People did. Here it seemed there were only long bus rides and jambon baguettes. And if you wanted variety, you could have jambon baguettes and long bus rides instead.

Even Juan Antonio Samaranch, who upon conclusion of every Olympic Games, always declares the latest Games the "best ever," didn't say that here. He called these Olympics "among the best ever."

He was stretching it.

My favourite moments were the sporting moments. Franck Piccard of France almost winning the downhill on his home course. Team Canada playing hockey. Any short-track speed skating race. Kerrin Lee-Gartner watching the clock and waiting.

But there were too few moments, and today we leave with too few memories and too much clothing that will have to be disinfected to remove the stench of cigarette smoke. These were the smoke-free Olympics where everyone smoked.

After the exhilaration of the Calgary Olympics, Alberto Tomba had the good sense to turn the rest of his skiing season into one long party, living up to both his vast reputation and his expanding waistline.

His plan this time? "I start tomorrow," said Tomba.

That is, assuming his airport bus arrives.

Ours never did.

Pinball, One of a Kind

November 21, 2004

For once and maybe for the only time in his life, Michael "Pinball" Clemons paused, tried to find the right words and found himself uncharacteristically silent.

"What does this Grey Cup mean to you?" he was asked, standing on the turf at the stadium named for Frank Clair.

"I'm not often at a loss for words," said Pinball, the Argos head coach, and several seconds passed before he collected his thoughts. "(Today) is as special to me as any day I've ever been on the football field."

For all the wide smiles, the handshakes and the hugs, this has not been an easy ride for Pinball Clemons. One day he was a great player, and then he was a desperate publicity stunt as coach, and then he was team president and suddenly he has grown into the coach no one thought he could ever be.

A coach like no other. The only kind of coach he can be. A coach who defines his own methods, who disregards conventional thinking, who cares more about people than wins, and wins because he cares more about people.

"He approaches things differently than any other coach I've played for," said Sandy Annunziata, the Argos offensive lineman, who played for six other coaches before Clemons.

"His style is so personal. If something is going on in your life, he wants to know about it. He wants to find a way to help you. First and foremost, he's about the person. Football is a secondary thing for him. He wants to find a way to make you better."

But today, it is everything to him. This isn't just a championship game for Michael Clemons. This is professional and personal validation. Not that he needs it. He can't be any more beloved than he is by a Canadian public and by his own players, but from where he began — plucked by Sherwood Schwarz to stop the bleeding — the coaching ring may mean more than any he put on as a player.

"I am who I am," Clemons said. "That hasn't changed. I just happen to coach.

"I never said this is what a head coach is supposed to do and this is the way he's supposed to act. I can't be what the textbooks say I'm supposed to be. I have just been myself and incorporate that into what I do."

Just being himself has taken this unlikely Argos team to today's Grey Cup. A team that was supposed to be built around the running of John Avery, the control of Damon Allen, the receiving of Tony Miles. But one by one, that didn't happen. Avery never got going. Allen and Miles spent a great deal of the season injured. Pinball had to adjust on the run.

"A lot of coaches would have given up on guys Pinball has patience for," Annunziata said. "He's a unique man in the truest sense of the word. He sees something in everybody, then he wants to pull it out of him.

"He was unique as a player, unique as a man in the community and now he's unique as a coach."

During a team meeting earlier in the week, Clemons took the time to single out every player on the Argos roster, almost playing his own game of word association. He would name a player and then describe his greatest attributes.

"It made us feel amazing," Arland Bruce said. "When he did that, it's like, you'd do anything for the guy."

Some coaches barely talk to their players. Some experience them from arm's length. Michael Clemons never stops talking, selling, encouraging, believing.

And now there is a game to play. And he can't think about today without recalling the strange beginning of four years ago. On that confusing day when he took off his uniform and suddenly was head coach, he was asked a question he recalled yesterday: "How do you know you can do this?"

"I don't," Pinball Clemons said.

That was then. This is Grey Cup Sunday. It isn't a question he gets asked anymore.

Looking Back at Ben

February 6, 2018

Mark McKoy can still hear the banging on the hotel room door and the words that immediately followed, just like it was yesterday.

"Ben, get dressed. You'll have to come with us."

That was almost 30 years and one Olympics in South Korea ago. The morning Olympic-sized drug chaos began to expose McKoy's close friend Ben Johnson and apparently change the world of sport. "From that point on, it all got kind of crazy," the Canadian hurdler remembers.

"I was visiting Ben at his hotel. He had run his race. I hadn't run mine yet. Suddenly, the chef (de mission, the late Carol Anne Letheren) was at the door. And she was kind of frantic. Nobody knew exactly what was going on."

The last time the Olympics were in South Korea the story and the scandal were all about drugs and the historic news of Johnson testing positive after breaking the world record in the men's 100 metres. And now as the Olympic Games of Pyeongchang are about to begin, this time Winter Games, the overwhelming story surrounding the event is the state of systemic drug cheating in sports, so much of it involving Russian organizers and athletes.

And McKoy, now 56 years old, still involved in training and developing athletes, wonders how much has really changed in all the years since Seoul.

"What's really changed?" he asked.

"We were a small group of athletes. A few athletes that nobody really knew about and it wasn't state-run or anything like that. Now you're seeing entire countries (like Russia) and it's like the government is behind it. I have no evidence, because I'm not involved, on whether there is more than there used to be or less, but you know it's more sophisticated. And remember when everyone was saying (Seoul) was going to change sport forever? Well, things haven't really changed, have they?

"Ben Johnson took drugs. Big effing deal. But Ben Johnson paid a price for his mistake that no one has ever paid. He became the poster boy, the victim for everything that was wrong with sports. We all know what we did was wrong, but he was overly crucified for it, especially when you see what's happened since then.

"Normally, you'd think your country would treat you better than any other country because it's your country. But in Ben's case, he was persecuted more by Canada than he was by the rest of the world. We were the hardest on him. The rest of the world forgot quickly about Ben, but I don't think Canada ever forgot. And the way Ben was treated made some of us want to leave Canada, and I think some of that played a part in Lennox (Lewis) leaving (the country)."

McKoy was considered a medal contender in Seoul in the 110-metre hurdles. He ended up finishing seventh and then abruptly leaving the Games. He said he left early because of an injured Achilles tendon. He also said he needed to escape the continuing chaos after Johnson's positive test. Some still believe McKoy left and tanked his race to avoid drug testing, a scenario he vehemently denies.

"I was having my own issues at the time with my Achilles, and everything else just made it so hard to focus," said McKoy. "After the (positive test) story broke in the Village, it was a nightmare, really. It seemed the press was everywhere we went. We couldn't leave our rooms. We were part of Ben's team. We were part of his family. I'd known him since high school. Anyone involved with Ben was swarmed."

McKoy, who won his gold medal in the 110-metre hurdles in Barcelona four years later, was like a lot of athletes who wound up leaving Seoul with a certain bitterness that took years to come to grips with. Boxers Lennox Lewis and Egerton Marcus couldn't go home early. Their gold medal matches were on the final days of the Games. Lewis beat Riddick Bowe in a classic super heavyweight fight, winning gold. Marcus ended up with a silver. Those were two of Canada's five medals from Seoul.

But the gold for Lewis, which normally would have brought with it national celebration, generated little acclaim. "I don't know if he ever got over that," said McKoy. "I've talked to him a few times about it. In a way, I think that drove Lennox out of Canada if he ever had a chance of staying."

Lewis went on to a Hall of Fame boxing career and two terrific runs as heavy-weight champion of the world.

McKoy left Canada for a time but still considers himself Canadian and spends some of his time now speaking about his Olympic experiences.

"The first question the kids ask is, 'Do you regret your involvement in drugs?' It was one of the worst times of my life, and yet I call it the best thing that ever happened to me. That sent me in the right direction. I can talk about being young and driven and you get persuaded to do things you shouldn't do. There was money involved. It's in every sport. I tried everything legally and I was just off the podium. And you're thinking as a kid, 'How do I get to the podium?'"

McKoy got to the top of the podium in 1992, after living through the intensity of the Dubin Inquiry in Canada and the craziness of Seoul. And far removed from the Summer Olympics, he will tune in this week to do what he always does: watch the Olympic Games on television.

"My TV will be on 24/7," he said. "That's the way it is when it comes to the Olympics. I always watch the Olympics, summer and winter. I'm not much of a winter person. But I'll be watching the luge, the downhill skiing, some obscure sports. Why? Because it's the Olympics."

The Golden Goal

March 1, 2010

VANCOUVER — There is a new hockey game, a new moment, a new national memory to cherish forever.

A brand-new footprint for a generation of Canadians was born Sunday when Team Canada ended our greatest Winter Olympics with a record-setting 14th gold medal, earning a frantic, frenetic, emotionally charged 3-2 hockey overtime win over an impressive, resilient Team USA.

There was one game with everything to lose and everything to win for Team Canada and everyone watching. And in the best of Canadian traditions it could have gone either way, but just as Paul Henderson managed 38 years ago in Moscow, Sidney Crosby made history all his own here in Vancouver.

History he will be known for forever.

A new trivia question for the future: It is no longer "Where were you in 1972?" The new Henderson is now Crosby and the shot he didn't see go in, like so many famous goals before him. It came 7 minutes and 40 seconds into overtime of an unforgettable gold medal game.

For those too young to remember Henderson, this is the moment of all Canadian sporting moments — more electric than the Ben Johnson win before the disqualification, more exciting than the Donovan Bailey victories in Atlanta, more amazing for the country than the Joe Carter home run or the Mike Timlin toss to Carter at first base in 1992.

This is the new team. The new standard. The greatest of all gold medals in the sport we so cherish at our very own Olympic Games.

"Words can't even describe this," said Eric Staal, who like so many of the young Canadians has won the Stanley Cup but had never felt anything like this before.

"For us to come here in this environment, with this crowd, and deliver, it's pretty awesome. I'm proud to be a Canadian.

"This is a once-in-a-lifetime opportunity. A chance to win an Olympic gold in your home country. People are going to remember this for a long, long time. And people are going to remember Sid's goal for a long, long time. It was huge for him, huge for us."

Huge for Canadian sport.

After the medals were presented, after the first bout of crazed celebrations on the ice, the Canadians stood together, arm in arm, with gold medals around their necks, swaying back and forth, screaming and singing.

"I don't care that I have the worst voice in the world," said Jonathan Toews, voted on to the tournament All-Star team. "I was belting it out as loud as I can."

And everyone at GM Place, maybe everyone across the nation, was belting out the national anthem along with them.

Crosby just shot the puck and heard the noise. His explanation was reminiscent of Carter's World Series home run explanation. He shot and didn't know he had scored until he heard the screaming.

And then everything exploded in celebration for the Canadians. A building already loud grew to deafening heights. And a country spilled out onto the streets. The absolute perfect ending for an Olympics that was so much about celebration on the streets.

"I can't explain what this feels like," said Mike Richards, who played such an impressive role for Team Canada. "I can't put it into words. I've never played in a game like this, never played in a building like this, never felt anything like this before."

Like Crosby, he didn't see the winning goal either.

"I just heard the noise," Richards said. "Our bench was shaking. People were jumping onto the ice. I just followed them."

That's what the best teams do.

"This is unbelievable," shouted Ryan Getzlaf. "It's nothing like I've ever felt before. I've won two world juniors. I've won the Stanley Cup."

And then he paused for a second to find the right words.

"This is for Canada," he said. "This is amazing."

The Uncomfortable Mixture of Sports and Politics

August 16, 2004

ATHENS — Arash Miresmaeili carried the flag of his country proudly in the Olympic opening ceremony.

He marched with the athletes, listened to the lyrical speeches about uniting the athletes of the world, heard the oaths and understood the expectations of being a gold medal favourite.

And then he took the money and ran — because really he had no choice.

The statistics will say that Miresmaeili did not make his weight and therefore did not participate in the Olympic Games. The statistics lie.

The real story is about Middle Eastern politics and a conflict that never seems to end, and all that should have little to do with either sport or these Games. But the real story is that Iranian authorities will pay Miresmaeili a significant sum of money — hundreds of thousands of dollars, in fact — for his apparent refusal to fight an Israeli opponent in judo yesterday at the Ano Liosia Olympic Hall.

This is the second scandal of a Games that are only two days old, an athletic disgrace of politics that has no place on this stage. "I feel sorry for him," said Ehud Vaks, the Israeli judoka who was awarded a win over his Iranian non-opponent and then wound up being eliminated from the Games one bout later.

"No athlete I know would do this," he told the *Toronto Sun*. "I feel for him as an athlete. An athlete would want to go to the mat. He would want to compete.

"They put him up to this. They make him do this."

Miresmaeili was *Sports Illustrated*'s choice to win gold in the event. Vaks was nobody's choice to win much of anything. The Iranian was supposed to be a hero here. At home, where hatred seems the national pastime, perhaps he will be.

"This is a brutal violation of the Olympic values," said Ephraim Zinger, head of the Israeli Olympic delegation. "This is not why we are here. We want to believe we are all united under the Olympic flag. For this athlete, this is a dark day, and a dark day for the Olympic Games.

"But you must also understand, he has to follow the rules (of his country). He has to return home after the Games and live there."

Give the Iranians some credit for how they managed this mess. Once the draw came out, it was expected that Miresmaeili would withdraw rather than fight an Israeli. He even told an Iranian news agency that he was taking this stance in view of his support of Palestine.

But had he simply withdrawn, he would have been sanctioned by the International Judo Federation. Because he didn't make weight — although no one knew exactly what he weighed — the IJF had no recourse but to penalize him.

"I hope the judo federation realizes what happened here and reacts appropriately," said Zinger. "I hope they reach the right conclusion.

"We were certain when we saw the draw that he would not show up. The only question mark we had was: What would be the excuse? Illness? Overweight? Headache? We didn't know ... This is not the first time this has happened in an international arena."

IJF spokesman Michel Brousse said he was surprised by Miresmaeili's failure to make weight. And if he was, he was the only one in the building surprised.

At the World Table Tennis Championships in 2003, competitors from Yemen and Saudi Arabia refused to play against Israeli opponents. One athlete was suspended for a year by his sport and returned home to a national hero's welcome.

The government of Iran had promised one million rial to any gold medal athletes; no Iranian has ever won gold before. Some government officials have already gone on the record as saying Miresmaeili should be paid gold medal money for pulling out.

For the Israeli delegation, this is yet another setback. At some point, they would hope that sport could be sport and political sentiments could be removed from the playing fields. The athletes themselves want to believe that.

"We have to be optimistic. What choice do we have?" said Zinger. "We have to hope one day this will end. We don't know when. We continue to hope."

Kerrin Lee-Gartner:
Then and Now

February 21, 2018

PYEONGCHANG, SOUTH KOREA — In the starting gate of the race of her life, Kerrin Lee-Gartner began to melt down. She wasn't nervous early in the day, and she wasn't nervous for the most menacing downhill course in Olympic history, and then it all hit her at once.

"Carl," she said to her trainer, Carl Peterson. "I'm nervous, I'm really nervous."

And he just made a silly face and started laughing out loud.

"Of course you are," he said. "It's the biggest race of your life. Now go."

And she started laughing too, beginning on her way to history as the only Canadian ever to win an Olympic downhill race. That was 26 years ago at the Albertville Olympics, and in some ways it seems like yesterday for Lee-Gartner — and in other ways it feels like a lifetime ago.

"Wow, I think the one thing that really stands out as I age and more time passes, the more surreal this whole thing becomes, the more I'm almost in awe of the little-girl dream I had and realized how bold of me it was.

"I didn't know the history," said Lee-Gartner, working another Olympic Games for CBC. "I assumed the Crazy Canucks had won everything. I assumed Nancy Greene had won everything. I didn't pay attention to history. I'm surprised another Canadian hasn't won since. Edi Podivinsky came close in the next Olympics. I thought Erik Guay would win. You realize, looking back, how aligned the stars were. I needed to be at my very, very best. I needed to have a course that was awesome for me. So many things went my way."

The course at Meribel was considered dangerous at the time, so dangerous it has never been run again. "Racers were vomiting in the starting gate," Lee-Gartner said. "There were a lot of reasons to be scared. People had broken backs, broken legs, torn knees on that course. For some reason, I was fully prepared to embrace that.

"I was a long shot. I wasn't a favourite. But I was so in the bubble of my little-girl dream of winning. I was in my deepest place of belief. My greatest strength as a skier was my mind."

She drew bib No. 12 for the downhill that Saturday morning in France. The top two racers in the world drew No. 11 and No. 13. "I remember saying to Max (her husband and sometimes coach), 'If they can win with 11 and 13, I can win with 12.'" And when she reached the bottom of the mountain, even with a full slate of skiers to go, Lee-Gartner celebrated as though gold was hers.

"It was brazen of me to do that," she said. "But honestly, I didn't think someone was going to beat it. At the moment I thought, 'This is my dream coming true.' This was the birthday cake. I had willed myself to ski that awesome that day. And when you grow up as a shy, timid little girl who didn't make the provincial team, you have all these thoughts inside of you. I believed so much in that childhood dream, and when I saw No. 1 on the scoreboard, I did this dance and let go with these squeals of joy."

She won gold by six one-hundredths of a second.

She became the Winter Olympics version of Donovan Bailey without the relay race.

And the older she gets — she's 51 now — the more meaning she finds from her golden race.

"You realize how much the little things matter," she said. "When you realize how little you win by six one-hundredths of a second, you realize the critical role of everything that's around you."

She and Max decided to rent their own place in Meribel for the Games, to avoid village life and the difficulties of travel.

"We paid for it ourselves," she said. "We had this little attic in a French cabin. That allowed me to be happy. We watched a lot of hockey at night. It's funny now seeing Sean Burke with Team Canada. He was the goalie. (Eric) Lindros was there. We would watch two periods of the games and I would go to sleep."

And now she works the Olympics, as she has for most Games, as a television commentator.

And she will be watching on Wednesday as the women race the same event she won eight Winter Games ago. Almost every Games bring with them a certain memory of the past, something that changes or enhances her view of her Albertville triumph.

"When I interviewed Lindsey Vonn after her win in Vancouver, my teenaged girls said, 'Oh my god, Mom, you did that. You won that race.' That was an 'aha' moment for me as a mom. It's one thing for me to understand what happened. But for your kids? The more time that passes, the more things seem to add to (the legacy)."

Her memory seems crisp on the events of 26 years ago. Just not every day. And not all the time. Lee-Gartner suffered a serious neck and brain injury from a car accident in California 16 months ago. Her brain, she said, works a little differently now. Every day is a challenge of some kind. She wears tape on her glasses to cut down the brightness. She has vision issues.

"My processing is a bit slow," she said. "I guess you could say I'm a work in progress.

"You can't just determine your way through this. The brain doesn't work that way."

So she fights with the same tenacity she took to the downhill course at Meribel, not knowing what the eventual outcome will be.

Until Further Notice, This Is Our Life

April 2, 2020

Yesterday morning I turned to my kids — who are now adults — and asked a simple question.

"Do you know what's in 16 hours?"

Nobody answered.

"Bedtime," I said. We laughed for a moment — and why not, considering the circumstances? It's healthy to have a laugh or two or more when you're locked in your house with nowhere else to go. In a way, this reminds me of rainy days at our tiny summer cottage when I was a kid. You weren't allowed outside. You didn't have much inside. You stayed in and watched the rain. There were no televisions or computers or phones to play with, but somehow the time passed, and usually quite pleasantly.

Now this isn't a rainy day or two or three. This is months. This is a global pandemic. This could be our summer. Right now, this is our lives and our city and our world, all of it changing and shrinking daily.

We do have television and Internet and phones and video games and ways of communicating online to either amuse us, anger us or exhaust us, depending on the circumstances, but in a way that's probably to our detriment.

Information overload gives me a headache among other things. But a drink with friends can be nice online, even if you're not together. A visit with the grand-kids online is great, but after a while that could almost get worse rather than better.

We have 15 hours or more to fill each day, depending on when you go to bed, when you wake up and if you're like me, when you sleep.

It became April on Wednesday. Normally this is when March Madness ends and baseball begins. There's not much I like better than a March Madness pool sheet and tomorrow's probable pitchers. Normally, this is the best sports month on the calendar, with those frenzied, wondrous first two weeks of the Stanley Cup playoffs and the opening round of the NBA playoffs. And, oh yes, that golf tournament at Augusta that we can't take our eyes off annually. All of it now on pause.

April is the sporting month of dreams: So much to watch, so much to take in, so much to digest. It's our kind of information overload. And for the few of us who do what I do for a living, it means a plane ride and a Marriott booked and another plane ride and another hotel. And waking up some days not knowing what city you're in. A lot of us have done that over the years.

Now we're home. For the month. For next month. For who knows how long. Some of us are working. Some of us are trying to work. Some are hoping to invent some kind of work. All of us are worried — and with good reason. And too many of us are alone.

We don't know what tomorrow is. We don't know if we'll have jobs in a few months, if our companies will survive, if we can see our parents, what the economy is going to look like, where the stock market goes, how long we can go without paying rent. Never mind the small picture, when Hyun-Jin Ryu will throw his first pitch for the Blue Jays.

There isn't anything we really know, except how to be smart and safe and indoors, which can make us anxious and nervous — and for those of us who live every day kind of anxious and nervous, the walls can close in on you. I understand that. I have lived that on occasion. I wouldn't wish it on anyone.

But sometimes I go back to being that kid on that rainy day at the cottage, remembering how disappointing the day began but somehow human spirit and thought and playfulness and creativity made the days memorable over time.

We found things to do. We played cards and records and Monopoly and Rummoli and backgammon and Scrabble and Boggle, depending on what age we were. We danced. We sang. We made up songs. We invented games. We read books — remember when people read books? We did push-ups and sit-ups. We did crossword puzzles. We played charades. We did jigsaw puzzles. Everything was some kind of competition. And we ate lots of snacks.

My father began to teach me how to cook on one of those rainy summer days. Onions and eggs, if I remember. It's now one of my favourite things to do, cooking. If you get a day, and you don't have anything to do, teach your kids to cook or your spouse to cook or yourself to cook. Show them some simple things around the kitchen. They may not be happy doing it today; they'll be happy tomorrow.

It's easy to get lost on Netflix or Amazon Prime — there is so much quality out there. But how much can you consume in a day? How much binging can you do before you have to submit? When I would travel to places such as Australia or China, being a nervous flier, I would plot out my time on the airplane. This much time for watching movies; this much time for reading; this much time for sleeping. I find myself doing that now with my days.

The difference is, we do that today, we have to do it again tomorrow and the day after that. This is our *Groundhog Day* without Bill Murray. It's not a movie.

Until further notice, this is our life.

Magic Johnson, a Ray of Hope Amidst Sadness

November 9, 1991

He cried when he heard the news, and afterwards there was a feeling of elation.

The man is 40 years old, paper-thin skinny, droopy-eyed, living on assistance, and dying of AIDS.

The man is also a Magic Johnson fan.

A fan yesterday. A huge fan today.

"God couldn't have picked a more perfect spokesman for AIDS," he said. "What a figure he can be. I know that's what so many of us are hoping for.

"I know this sounds terrible, but most people I talked to today are thrilled Magic Johnson is HIV-positive. I mean, really thrilled. They think it's fantastic.

"I loved what he did yesterday. Magic showed a maturity and an innocence. To do what he did showed so much guts and character. I would have broken down. I don't know anyone who wouldn't have.

"You don't know how hard it is. Admitting it. Saying you're HIV-positive. Going public. Everyone I know went through a period of denial. I had three tests before I admitted it, and I still didn't believe it until I got sick.

"But he stood up and said he was going to do something about it. He said he was going to keep on living. No one has ever done that before. It's not like Rock Hudson getting AIDS. Who really cared about Rock Hudson, anyway?"

The man walked along the streets of Toronto yesterday, took a subway ride, drifted past Casey House and felt unique for the first time in months. He felt up, encouraged, enlightened by the courage of Earvin Johnson Jr.

"There were 10 people outside on the porch at Casey House on a cold day and they all seemed to be smiling," he said. "On a cold day, you never see hardly anyone outside. It was, almost, like magic. They were all smiling. It was like a signal."

A signal that it's OK to have AIDS. A signal that those suffering, more than the rest of us can ever know, are cheering today with Earvin Johnson, and for him.

"You don't understand what it's like," the man said. "It's like having leprosy. You're treated like you're a leper. I don't think there are many people being more mistreated than AIDS victims. People won't even look you in the face. It's like you don't exist.

"I kept thinking, 'Magic can make this acceptable.' What a gift that would be. I've talked to a lot of others (AIDS victims) and they're thinking the same thing. That's what we're hoping for. I hope this will cause the lessening of the discrimination."

We see it differently, those of us who distance ourselves from this deadly disease. We can't possible comprehend the horror and the pain. We cry for Magic Johnson, mostly out of ignorance. We cry for basketball. We cry for what has become of our society.

Those suffering from the HIV virus have similar emotions, only more understanding. They live AIDS; they speak AIDS.

"It's a tragedy for him. But for AIDS, I can't think of anything better that could happen. Imagine the kind of money he should be able to generate for AIDS. I can't think of anyone else who could generate this kind of money. As I understand it, they're getting much better drugs but they're still in the development stages. You need a lot of money to make a difference.

"But even more important, Magic will get people talking about AIDS. The more people talk about a problem, the better things will get. You could even see how different it was today. I saw more people wearing Lakers clothes. It was like it was a tribute to Magic. People were showing their support. That was uplifting."

The world, unfortunately, is full of ignorant people. People who hear about AIDS and assume it cannot happen to them. The man with AIDS sees it today. In the gay bathhouses. People not using condoms. People taking risks with their lives. "It's insane," he said. "It's completely insane."

Magic Johnson made a difference every time he stepped on a basketball court and every time he smiled at a kid. Sadly, through illness now, he can begin to make the greatest contribution of his life.

The man written about in this piece was my brother, Jody Simmons. He passed away of AIDS on February 16, 1995. Magic Johnson, miraculously, lives on.

And Don't Forget the Snacks

September 14, 2002

There were about two minutes to play in the playoff game and I was pacing behind the bench anxiously, barking out whatever instructions seemed important at that very moment. You watch the game and you watch the clock in those final seconds, often at the very same time.

Our team was up by a goal, poised to advance to the next round of the playoffs, when I felt a tug on my jacket.

"Ah, Coach," one of my little players said from the bench.

"Yeah," I answered, concentrating more on the game and the clock than on him.

"Are there snacks today?"

"Whaaaat?" I barked, somewhat exasperated.

"Did anyone bring snacks today?"

"Huh?" I said as I looked back towards the game.

"I hope they didn't bring apple juice," the young boy continued. "I don't like apple juice."

The moment froze me in all the playoff excitement, the way all special and meaningful moments should. If, somehow, I could have captured that brief conversation on tape, I would have had one of those telling sporting moments for parents everywhere, the kind you need to play for coaches and executives and trainers and managers and all of us who take youth hockey way too seriously.

It isn't life-or-death, as we like to think it is. It isn't do-or-die, as often as we pretend it to be. In one tiny moment in one elimination game, kids' hockey was reduced to what it really is about: apple juice. OK, so it's not really apple juice, but what apple juice happens to represent in all of this.

The snack. The routine. The end-of-game ritual.

Kids can win and lose and not give a second's thought about either at a certain age, but don't forget the post-game drinks. If anything will spoil a good time, that will.

You see, this is all part of the culture of hockey. Not who wins, not who scores goals, not which team accomplished what on any given afternoon, but whether Mom and Dad were there, whether their grandparents were in the stands watching, whether their best friend was on their team and yes, about what they ate post-game.

When you get involved in hockey as I have, when you truly put your heart into the game and into the environment and into all that surrounds it, that's when it's at its best. The game is only part of the package. The sense of belonging, the post-game snack, matters also.

Minor hockey can become a social outing for parents. It is a social outing for children. It should never be about who is going for extra power skating and who is going straight from mites to the Maple Leafs, but about building that kind of environment, building memories for kids and parents and families that they'll have forever.

Sometimes, when I stand around the arenas, I can't believe the tone of the conversations I hear. The visions are so short-sighted. The conversations are almost always about today and who won and who lost and too much about who scored. Not enough people use the word *fun* and not enough sell it that way, either.

And hard as we try to think like kids, we're not kids. Hard as we try to remember what we were like when we were young, our vision is clouded by adult perspective and logic, something not necessarily evident with youngsters.

Ask any parent whether they would rather win or lose, and without a doubt they would say win. But ask most children what they would prefer, playing a regular shift, with power play time and penalty killing time on a losing team, rather than playing sparingly on a winning team, and the answer has already come out in two different national studies. Overwhelmingly, kids would rather play a lot and lose than win a lot while playing little.

Ask a parent the score of a certain game a week later and he or she will know the answer. The child won't necessarily know. Like I said, it is about the apple juice. It is, after all, about the experience.

Often, you can't know what's in a kid's mind. I was coaching a team a few years ago when I got a call from the goaltender's father. It was the day before the house league championship game. The father called to tell me his eight-year-old son didn't want to play anymore.

"Anymore after tomorrow?" I asked.

"No," the father said. "He just doesn't want to play anymore."

"Did something happen?" I asked.

"He won't tell me," the father said.

I hung up the phone and began to wonder how this happened, and who would play goal the next day, when I decided to call back.

"Can I talk to him?" I asked the father.

The young goalie came on the phone.

"I don't want to play anymore," the young boy told me.

"But you know what tomorrow is, don't you? Are you nervous?"

"No."

"Then what? You can tell me."

"I don't like it," he said.

"Don't like playing goal?"

There was a pause on the phone.

"They hurt me," he said.

"Who hurt you?"

"The guys," he said.

"What guys?"

"Our guys. They jump on me after the game. It hurts me and scares me."

"Is that it?"

"Yeah."

"Do you trust me?" I asked.

"Yeah."

"What if I told you they won't jump on you and hurt you anymore? What if I promised you that? Would you play then?"

"Are you sure?"

"I'm sure."

"Then I'll play."

And that was the end of our goalie crisis.

The kid was scared and wouldn't tell his parents. The kid loved playing but didn't love being smothered by bodies after victories.

You can't anticipate anything like that as a coach. You can't anticipate what's in their minds.

It's their game.

We have to remember that.

They don't think like we do or look at the sport like we do.

They don't have to adjust to us; we have to adjust to them.

We have to make certain we're not in any way spoiling their experience.

Our experience is important, but the game is for the children. We can say that over and over again, but the message seems to get lost every year.

Lost on too many coaches who lose perspective and who think nothing of blaming and yelling and bullying.

Lost by parents who think their son or daughter is the *next this* or the *next that* and are already spending in their minds the millions their little one will be earning by the time they finish hockey in the winter, three-on-three in the summer, power skating over school break, special lessons over March break, pre-tryout camp before the tryouts in May and a couple weeks of hockey school, just to make certain they don't go rusty.

Over the years, I have asked many NHL players how they grew up in the game. My favourite answer came from Trevor Linden, who captained more than one team in his day. He said he played hockey until April and then put his skates away.

He played baseball all summer until the last week of August. No summer hockey. No special schools. No skating 12 months a year.

"I didn't even see my skates for about five months a year," he said.

"I think the kids today are playing way too much hockey, and all you have to do is look at the development to see it really isn't producing any better players. We have to let the kids be kids."

I asked Gary Roberts when he thought he had a future in hockey.

"When I got a call from an agent before the OHL draft," he said. "Before that, it was just a game we played."

Do me a favour: Until the agent comes knocking on your door, and even after that, let's keep it that way. A game for kids.

And one reminder — I don't care what the age: Don't forget the snacks.

Of all the columns I've written over the years, none hit a nerve in a positive way the way this one did. And I didn't see that coming. It has been printed and reprinted and then printed some more. It is still used by minor hockey and minor sporting organizations all over the globe. And for that, I am forever grateful.

Acknowledgments

All the pieces in this book first appeared in either the *Toronto Sun*, the *Calgary Sun*, or the *Calgary Herald* ... I am thankful to Kevin Hann of Postmedia for granting permission for them to appear in this forum ... I am thankful, as always, to my bosses at *Toronto Sun*, sports editor Bill Pierce, assistant sports editor Jon McCarthy and copy editors Joel Colomby, Paul Ferguson, Dave Hilson, Dan Bilicki, Donald Duench and others of the past for making this happen ... Also thanks to previous sports editors: Wayne Parrish, for first hiring me in 1987 in Toronto; to Scott Morrison, who put up with me; to Mike Simpson and Pat Grier, who got the most out of me; to the late George Bilych in Calgary, who hired me twice at the *Herald*; and to Bev Wake, maybe the best editor I ever got to work with, although it wasn't for nearly long enough...

Thanks to Doug Gilmour, the Hall of Famer, who followed me to Calgary and then Toronto and was willing to write the foreword for the book ... Thanks to my *Toronto Sun* writing colleagues over the years, in particular to those who have so inspired me and occasionally challenged me: Steve Buffery, Bob Elliott, Rob Longley, Terry Koshan, Mike Ganter, John Kryk, Mike Rutsey, Ken Fidlin, Mike Zeisberger, Lance Hornby, Ryan Wolstat, Perry Lefko, Mike Koreen, Mike Traikos, Scott Stinson, Frank Zicarelli for their work and always for their opinions ... And thanks to my companions on the road, where I've spent more than 3,000 days away from home over the past five decades: the late Jim Hunt, Buffery, Longley, David Shoalts, Terry Jones, Cathal Kelly, Bruce Arthur, Doug Smith, Pierre LeBrun, Scott Burnside, Zeisberger, Cam Cole, David Naylor, Mark Spector, Ed Willes, Ted Wyman, Steve Milton, Scott MacArthur, the late Rick Fraser, Bruce Garrioch, Rosie DiManno, the late Christie Blatchford, Gary Lawless, Michael Farber, Richard Griffin. The next Diet Coke is on me ...

And a big thanks to all those in management — coaches and general managers, team presidents and players, agents too, all of whom are too many to name — that could be a book by itself. You all put up with me over the years, answering my queries, my texts, putting up with my curiosities, arguing with me, arguing for me, and against all odds you rarely stopped taking my calls ...

And thanks, as always, to my wife, Sheila, and the kids who aren't kids anymore, Jeffrey and Michael, for putting up with too much of my self-indulgence. Writing can do that to people.

A project such as this doesn't come together without the help of many: Thanks in particular to those at Triumph Books who championed this project, beginning with managing editor Jesse Jordan, dogged book editor Katy Sprinkel Morreau and my agent, Brian Wood.

I have written more than 9,000 columns for Canadian newspapers. This book represents less than 1% of that work. It was difficult to determine which columns would appear. The list is personal. I hope, with some help from others, I chose a healthy variety of subjects here.